Domestic V
Both Sides of the Coin

By
Cheryle E. Dawes

DOMESTIC VIOLENCE: BOTH SIDES OF THE COIN

© Copyright 2004, Cheryle E. Dawes.
All rights reserved.

No part of this publication may be reproduced, stored in a retrieval system, or transmitted, in any form or by any means, electronic, mechanical, photocopying, recording, or otherwise, without the written prior permission of the author.

Note for Librarians: a cataloguing record for this book that includes Dewey Decimal Classification and US Library of Congress numbers is available from the National Library of Canada. The complete cataloguing record can be obtained from the National Library's online database at:
www.nlc-bnc.ca/amicus/index-e.html
ISBN 1-4120-2380-7

DISCLAIMER

The author has made every effort possible in the preparation of this book to ensure the accuracy of the information provided. However, the content of this book is sold without warranty, either expressed or implied. Neither the author nor publisher will be liable for any damages caused or alleged to be caused directly, indirectly, or consequentially by the information in this book.

The opinions expressed in this book are solely those of the author.

Book Cover Design By: Jimmie Banks

Unless otherwise indicated, all scripture quotations are taken from the King James, Living Bible and New International Version's of the Bible.

TRAFFORD

Offices in Canada, USA, Ireland, UK and Spain
This book was published on-demand in cooperation with Trafford Publishing. On-demand publishing is a unique process and service of making a book available for retail sale to the public taking advantage of on-demand manufacturing and Internet marketing. On-demand publishing includes promotions, retail sales, manufacturing, order fulfilment, accounting and collecting
royalties on behalf of the author.
Books sales in Europe:
Trafford Publishing (UK) Ltd., Enterprise House, Wistaston Road Business Centre, Wistaston Road, Crewe CW2 7RP UNITED KINGDOM
phone 01270 251 396 (local rate 0845 230 9601)
facsimile 01270 254 983; info.uk@trafford.com
Book sales for North America and international:
Trafford Publishing, 6E–2333 Government St.,
Victoria, BC V8T 4P4 CANADA
phone 250 383 6864 (toll-free 1 888 232 4444)
fax 250 383 6804; email to bookstore@trafford.com

www.trafford.com/robots/04-0208.html

10 9 8 7 6 5 4 3 2

FOREWORD

Cheryle has a powerful mandate on her life. She **must** share her incredible life journey. Her story is filled with unbelievable circumstances and unimaginable pain. However, to a victim of these horrific crimes, her story is neither unbelievable nor unimaginable. It is this nightmare that is a reality for so many men and women of domestic violence. It is the **root** of so much of the violence that is ravaging our families, our neighborhoods and our country. Can someone experience the horror that Cheryle has had to live through and not have a divine purpose? Her journey has propelled her to another level mentally, emotionally and spiritually. Her passion and commitment to help heal the hurts of others is born of her pain. Pain that flows through her veins like the blood that sustains her life. Pain that was as much a part of her as the beating of her heart. Cheryle is not a survivor. She is a Thriver! Her healing has been continuous and her drive unstoppable. She has accepted her calling with grace and dignity. And with each and every endeavor…continues to soar! This book is unique. As an Advocate for Domestic Violence, I highly recommend.

Jackie Goodwyn, Executive Director
Families Living Violence-Free
Granville County Domestic Violence and Rape Crisis Center

ACKNOWLEDGEMENTS

I always acknowledge God for giving me the compassion for hurting people and the heart to write this book. I thank Him for being my guide, strength and source and for making provision for this vision. To my son Kevin, your encouragement and support has been invaluable, precious and shall be forever embedded in my heart. I send heartfelt special thanks to Dean Young, Jackie Goodwyn and Dr. Mike Murdock. Your uniqueness of providing me with wisdom, knowledge, insight and support has allowed me to take my passion for *Domestic Violence* to a new level. Dean, this should be your book. The countless hours you have spent on this project with me is reflected in the final product. When I asked you to stand in agreement with me that God would send me a mentor for this project, you told me that maybe God was calling me to be a trail blazer in this particular arena. Thank you for being a positive friend, teacher and role model for me. Your warm heart and tender spirit is so greatly received and appreciated my friend.

To Kelly, I send to you special love and appreciation for your support, your tender heart and for filling in the gaps in our household as you have stood by me and encouraged me to pursue my dreams. Special thanks to my contributors Delphine Riley, Catherine Harris and Trafford Publishing. Thanks to Families Living Violence Free and other agencies for the educational resources that were provided for the book. Special thanks to Mr. and Mrs. Harris, Little E and "J" for allowing me to share their domestic experience in this book. Thanks to my family and friends for always praying and encouraging me. A very special *Thank You* to the readers, without you, I would not have a reason to write.

Love, Cheryle

PREFACE

What is Domestic Violence? It is a pattern of abuse and control exercised by one person in a relationship over another. When the word "abuse" is used here, it refers to situations and actions in which people experience coercion or fear for their safety or for their very lives. It consists of physical assaults, physical threats and assaults, isolation, verbal attacks, attacks against property and pets.

There is a myth that the abuser assaults their partner when they becomes angry and loses control, when really just the opposite is true. Abusers use calculated tactics to control the other person to get something they want.

Battering is not a mental illness that can be diagnosed, but a learned behavioral choice. Because battering is learned, it can be changed. However, the goal of nonviolence cannot be achieved through traditional marital couples counseling. When couples counseling takes place, the victim, under the control of the batterer, may put himself or herself in danger by telling the truth, and the batterer often avoids the truth through minimization, denial, and blame. Batterer's will not change unless someone holds them accountable.

North Carolina Coalition Against Domestic Violence

Domestic Violence Statistics

Domestic Violence is the second leading cause of death to women between the ages of fifteen and forty-four in America.

Domestic Violence is the leading cause of injury to women in the U.S.

Seventy-five percent of all homicides of women are *Domestic Violence* related.

One in every four members of the faith community are victims or survivors of abuse.

National Coalition Against Domestic Violence
US Department of Justice
FBI Crime Report

TABLE OF CONTENTS

FOREWORD

ACKNOWLEDGEMENTS

PREFACE
    Domestic Violence
    Domestic Violence Statistics

INTRODUCTION ....Page 2

MY STORY ....Page 10

CHAPTER 1
    IN THE BEGINNING ....Page 19
        Definition of Love
        The Impacts of Lack of Love: What Causes It?
- Alcohol and Drug Abuse
- Promiscuity
- Early Pregnancy
- Suicide

CHAPTER 2
    THE CYCLE BEGINS ....Page 43
        Domestic Violence: Generational Behavior
- Dating and Marriage
- Here Comes the Kids: The Pressures On

CHAPTER 3
    THE ABUSE: POWER AND CONTROL ..Page 79
- The Warning Signs
- Who is the Victim?
- Angry Outbursts
- The Batterer
  - Why?
  - The Angry Man
  - The Angry Woman

CHAPTER 4
    TRANSITION ....…...**PAGE 146**
- Getting Out
- Your Safety Plan
- The Stalker
- The Protection Order

CHAPTER 5
    BREAKING THE CYCLE: THE HEALING PROCESS ....……**PAGE 175**
- Mourning the Loss
- The Mentor
- Spending Quality Time With Yourself
- Rebuilding Your Self-Esteem
- Substituting Wrong Behavior for Right Behavior

CONCLUSION ....…...**Page 237**

RESOURCE SECTION................................…..**Page 243**
- The Rights of Battered Men and Women
- Fact vs. Fiction
- Sex and Trust
- Five Steps to Safer Sex
- Abstinence
- I Care About You
- Types of Abuse
- Characteristics of Relationship Addiction: Men and Women Who Love Too Much
- High Risk Indicators for Serious Injury or Death from Domestic Violence
- Warning Signs While Dating
- Reinforced Positive Habits
- What Churches Can Do
- Suggestions for Clergy Dealing with Abusive Men

- How to Appropriately Assist Victims of Domestic Violence in Your Congregation
- What About Forgiveness?
- Warning Signs in a Potential or Failed Marriage
- Red Flags to Look for in an Abusive Personality
- What is Codependency?
- How to Talk With Someone Who is Being Abused
- How Will I know if He or She has Changed?
- Why Do Men or Women Stay in Abusive Relationships?
- Why Women Leave Men?
- What to Expect if He/She Leaves a Violent Partner
- The Journey Through Grief
- Stalkers
- Common Traits of Stalkers
- Top Mistakes that Stalking Victims Make
- Myths About Lesbian and Gay Domestic Violence
- A Brief Safety Plan
- Personalized Safety Plan
- The Protective Order
- Domestic Violence and the Affects on Children
- Emotional Reactions of Children to Domestic Violence
- Ways to Help Children Cope with Domestic Violence
- Warning Signs of Youth Suicide
- Youth Suicide: Tips for Parents
- Youth Suicide: Tips of Teachers
- Tips for Parent and or Friends of a Battered Man and Woman
- Domestic Violence Guide for Physicians
- What is Advocacy?
- The Love Bank

- Quick Tips to Give Your Attitude an Extra Boost
- Unloading Baggage
- Redefining Your Image: Who Do You See When You Look in the Mirror?
- Are You Mastering Money or Is Money Mastering You?
- Love Is
- You Are Special

REFERENCES ....**Page 356**

ABOUT THE AUTHOR ....**Page 358**

Any story sounds true until someone tells the other side and sets the record straight.
                    Proverbs 17:17

   New International Version

"INTRODUCTION"

It was December 18, 2002 when the call came in from a church member, wife, mother and friend. She was a beautiful Arabic decent woman with a warm and captivating smile. The fear and trembling that gripped her voice through the telephone gripped me as well. A few months prior, I had just handed her a copy of my book that I had written on the domestic violence and my business card. She could have called the church for help her or some other local organization. Why was she calling me and what made me an authority to help her?

While developing another book, something very dramatic happened to that nice Christian couple, the Harris'. At church, the clapping of hands, the powerful prayers being petitioned to God from the couple, especially the husband appeared genuine. Everything was not what it appeared. This appearing loving family whom I have grown to love and respect was in deep trouble. I would have never imagined that they were in a domestic violence crisis. After all, they loved God and were in the church where family values were strongly taught. The husband had the appearance of be very attentive, charming and pleasant in the presence of his wife, son (Little E) and others. But, at home there was different picture playing. When I got the frantic phone call, she told me that she needed to get out of her home with their son who was a year old at the time. As speedily as I could talk, I inquired about what was happening in the household. With little time to spare, she told me that her husband had hit her. It was apparent from her voice that this was not the first time. That same day (Sunday) at church, the couple arrived and the husband approached me and wanted me to go and speak with his wife. I asked what was wrong, he replied, "I' don't know". This was the same night of the call. My heart ached with pain from the news. But I knew at that moment that mom and Little E needed to get to safety. I was glad that in her moment of chaos, she remembered she had my business card. More importantly, I was home to get her call. I picked mom and baby up at an agreed upon location and took them into my home until we could get some clarity and direction on the situation. I began to have flashbacks of my own abuse and my first instinct was to male-bash her husband, the batterer. I thought to myself, how could he call himself a Christian and beat his wife and traumatize his son? Immediately, I put my personal feelings on the back burner, realizing that no matter what the situation, both were my brother and sister in Christ. I wanted both of them to get the help they needed (victim and batterer). This would be crucial even if they decided not reconcile their marriage. I was willing to avail myself and resources to them. I knew first hand that if **all** participants of the domestic abuse cycle did not get experienced, wise, compassionate counseling, mentors and support, the cycle of domestic violence would repeat itself (Generational Behavior). More importantly, Little E was caught right smack dab in the middle and this needed immediate attention.

While assisting the couple, I developed this unusual pain in my heart. It wasn't a heart attack like symptom, but heartache like that of losing a loved one. It was and emotional feeling that I didn't quite understand. All of my previous associations with domestic violence victims had been with women outside of the church walls. But, I couldn't shake this feeling. Then, after talking with one of my mentors, Dean Young, the answer came to me why I was feeling this way. I now had empathy for the husband (batterer). Although the wife was temporarily out of the home, when she got ready to go back with him out of the home (it was in her name), who would offer him a place to stay? I began to wonder who was going to feel sorry for him or come to his rescue. Who would comfort and help him understand what was happening to him? Why was he battering someone he had vowed to love, support and protect? Was he enjoying breaking down his wife physically and emotionally? Then, I was led back to ask my mentor and friend, Dean to help. Dean is a well-respected man who counsels and mentors men and boys about controlling their anger and emotions. Dean has a heart for guiding them in the right direction by helping them to eradicate – wipe out their bad behavior. He gives 150% of himself in this area. So, I placed the call and informed Dean of the situation and he immediately went to see Mr. Harris. Later, when Dean and I met to discuss the situation, the discrimination of domestic violence emerged. The husband-batterer was treated differently by some church folks and so-called friends than his wife. The husband got criticized, tagged and labeled as a wife beater. Statements from other individuals like, "How could he do such a thing"? They depicted him as that expression, "A low-down dirty dog." What does that expression mean anyway? The frowns on their faces infuriated me. How upsetting it was to hear Christians say such harsh things. After all, Jesus was always moved with compassion. If they didn't know how to respond they should have just embraced him and not condemned. This is a question that we will address in (Chapter 3). But, do we look for an answer or punishment with regards to the behavior of the battterer? The truth of the matter is that domestic violence happens more often in churches than we want to admit. Mr. Harris went to those individuals looking for spiritual advice and help. Some advised him that he needed to pray to ask God to forgive him for beating his wife. Others told him that he needed get a job and that everything would be okay because typically they don't hold a job for any significant length of time. Others didn't know what to say, so they just said the cop out thing, "We are praying for you." Someone even told him that although he was no longer in the home, that his wife still had an obligation to have sex with him. This was absolutely ludicrous. He was hurting and the advice he was receiving was only putting a Band-Aide on his open wound. The wife, on the other hand, got all the sympathy (because society portrays it that way). Women in the church who knew her situation embraced Mrs. Harris. Why not? After all, she was a victim. But, it became clearer to me that the victim did not want to be beaten and the batterer did not want to batter. Furthermore, their son, Little E, without early intervention, would have serious emotional scaring.

Hosea 4:6 – "My people are destroyed from lack of knowledge."
New International Version

Education is vital to obtaining healing, wholeness and breaking the cycle of domestic violence. Now, the same drive and passion that I have for female victims of domestic violence, I now have for the male victims of domestic violence. Even more to my surprise, I have acquired a deeper passion for the batterer. I want them to try and understand why they batter and try to help them to break abusive cycle from off their life. From this sudden twist of events, this book, **"Domestic Violence: Both Sides of the Coin"** was written.

What makes me an authority? I survived domestic violence after being beaten brutally in my walk-in closet. I am a survivor of rape and a mother who has survived the suicide of her oldest son. I wanted to die when Chucky, at age 23 took his life and some almost five years later, it still feels like yesterday. All these horrific tragedies happened to me within seven years. I am the author of, "Abused, Battered, Broken-hearted, and Restored". It is a book of hope written to encourage people to never to give up on themselves regardless of their circumstances. With all of these misfortunes, I continually purpose to be a warm, compassionate and loving individual to all who want my knowledge on how to break the cycle of abuse. I am strong and I have committed myself to helping mend the hearts of broken people, especially domestic violence. I've turned my personal pain into passion for others. I recognized that few people are weeping or fighting for the pains and cries of hurting people anymore. We live in a society that says, "It's all about me." I've decided to be a person of action and not just talk – I dare to be different. I want to shed light into a place where there is fear, darkness and despair. But, most of all, I care about you and your pain this makes me an authority.

I grew up in an environment that I thought was normal. But, when I became an adult and got set free from the abuse, I learned that my normal environment was not so normal after all. My "Family –Tree" or "Family History" was not a big strong oak tree with strong roots and beautiful branches. A family tree is how your family began. I inherited domestic violence from my mother who inherited from her mother, three generations of domestic violence. Most of us know some things about our grandparents. But, we have little knowledge of our great-grandparents. In essence, we know very little about our family history or heritage. This lack of information could greatly affect our lives individually and collectively. Unknowingly, we could end up marrying our brother or sister thus, generating a rippling effect of genetic defects in our offspring. You could have a particular habit and don't quite understand why you do certain things. Or, you could have a particular talent and wondered where it came from. No one else in the family that you know has a unique talent like yours. However, if you were able to trace your family history, you probably would learn that your talent could be traced back two, three, or four generations.

Most individuals tend to look at domestic violence from a victim's point of view because of what society and the media portrays. It is anticipated that this book will enable you to have a clearer perspective about domestic violence with regards to gender and explore the imbalances and prejudices presented to the individuals. More importantly, I hope to wake-up any biases that may have been formed in your mind about the batterer. As I continue to pursue and find ways to promote prevention of domestic violence rather than intervention, this book, I believe, will attempt to shed some insight and help victim and batterer to work through their trauma. Hopefully, the batterer will learn of the traumatic impact they have on their victim and understand that their actions may not totally be their fault. Unknowingly, the victim and batterer could be a product of generational behavior. Domestic Violence, for the most part, is an acquired learned behavior. **Education** is the key.

When you glanced at the cover of this book, you may have had the perception that this book depicted men and women who are victims of domestic violence. On the contrary; while the cover represents the outward scars of both male and female victims of domestic violence, it also represents the scars and pain that you don't see inside the batterer that causes them to go into a rage of violence. Most of us have empathy (understanding, being sensitive to others feelings or emotions) for victims. However, it takes a tremendous amount of energy for the batterer to victimize. While the batterer's main objective is to have power and control, the metamorphosis (change of physical form, character or circumstances) that takes place puts them in a state of instability both mentally and physically. While battering, they do not realize that when they are battering their victims, they are battering themselves as well. This is why looking at both sides of the coin is vitally important to help break the cycle of abuse.

It is my belief, that if individuals, whether victim or batterer can create a problem or situation (consciously or unconsciously) by choosing to stay in an unhealthy relationship (domestic violence), then they can create a solution or make healthy choices to resolve that problem or situation. In the world of domestic violence, there will be many detours. The pain of those detours is sometimes high on the pain tolerance scale. Physicians use this scale to rate the pain of their patients. On a scale of 1 to 10, 10 being the highest, I would rate domestic violence a 10+ depending on the contributing factors. But, no matter what the severity, pain is pain. Research for this book has made me re-examine my own prejudices about the batterer. As I daily continue to heal from being victim to victor, I am constantly thinking about how other women of domestic violence feel. Now, I can relate to her pain, fears, anxiety and alienation of family members and friends. So, as I began to educate myself about domestic violence, I attended support groups, seminars, lectures, volunteer-training sessions and read numerous books. Never again did I want to be caught up in the web of domestic violence again. For many others and me, domestic violence is like an addiction or terminal disease and feels that it is a choice. However, I choose to treat my domestic violence as though it is an addiction. Thus, allowing me to choice to continue in the cycle or break it. I feel that I am no different from the alcoholic or the drug addict. I wanted to fix me and be clean from the violence forever. This would be the best prescription medication I could ever take. Because of my choice to go through the detoxification from the abuse, I am now an advocate for domestic violence and I am very selective about the environment and people that I associate with. Remember that we are products of our environment.

This book, I believe, will be a valuable resource tool to educate victims, batterers, schools, civic organizations, ministries, law enforcement, medical institutions, youth groups and personal enrichment. Furthermore, it is my desire that this book will enable you to understand the many facets of domestic violence. As everyone involved in this cycle begins to make the transition from abuse to healing, I encourage individuals to attend one-on-one counseling sessions, read other resource materials and attend support groups. As you read the various chapters, take a moment to discuss and answer the questions at the end of some of the chapters. These questions and discussion are intended to get your wheels turning on how you would respond to that particular situation.

In closing, domestic violence is not just a "woman thing". Men get battered and abused too. It's a society thing. Men and women who batter are hurting too. These individuals need lots of love, support and education to heal. There will be a time of mourning the loss of the relationship for victim and batterer. They **MUST** mourn and let go of the baggage that has oppressed them. This process can sometimes be very painful especially if the person they are mourning is still alive. So, they will have to learn how to mourn knowing in the back of their mind that person is still on the street and maybe victimizing someone else. I expect this book to bring some controversy. Women may think that I am a traitor. I assure you I am not. I just want to awaken your awareness just as I was awakened to look at both sides of the coin in the world of domestic violence. Hopefully, this awakening will prevent our sons and daughters from becoming a victim or batterer. If we don't understand both sides of the coin – the cycle of abuse will continue. Finally, this book will go places that I can't go and touch lives that I can't reach. Organizations far and wide may never invite me to speak or do a workshop, but if they use this book as an educational resource tool to reach just one person and help them break the cycle of abuse, then my mission has been accomplished.

Enjoy the Book and Let's Get Started !

"MY STORY"

"But He was pierced for our transgressions, He was crushed for our iniquities; the punishment that bought us peace was upon Him, and by His wounds we are healed".

Isaiah 53:5 – New International Version

There I was trapped inside a building that was supposed to be called home. In this desolate place, every good quality that I had ever thought I had acquired within me was now being stripped like old wallpaper. I was an educated woman with family, a good job and good friends. But, somewhere in the cycle of the abuse, I lost those too. My abuse lasted longer that I ever want to remember. When you are a victim, there are lapses of memory and time frames.

I met him during a very vulnerable time in my life. I had just gone through a horrific rape where I was brutally assaulted. After the rape, I went to one rape support group meeting and decided that I did not want to be there. So, I thought I could get through the rape on my own. I was mistaken. Because of my lack of counseling, I found myself drawn to a man who appeared to be good who later turned out to be bad for me. I guess you can't always judge a book by its cover – except this one (Smile). There I was in the clutches of domestic violence – just like my mom.

He was smooth, charming and good looking. He made me feel like I was the most important person on the face of the earth. He cooked, took me to nice restaurants and appeared to be a good housekeeper. He sent me flowers on the job. And when I was with him nothing else seemed to matter. Even the pain from being raped didn't hurt so much. Although I had materialistic qualities, I depended on him to make me feel better. He had a job and that was important. More importantly, he was a great lover in the bed and I thought that was important, was I wrong. After the rape, I wanted to prove to myself that I was still sexy. So, I used sex to camouflage my pain. I enjoyed his company as he did mine. But, now I could see that we both had different reasons and this scenario went on for a while. Well, the honeymoon period lasted for a short time and the abuse began. Then, my prince charming was no longer charming. He became a Dr. Jekyll and Mr. Hyde (split personalities). He began to question me about what time I would get back from my various locations. He would call all day long on my job and would show up unannounced just to make sure that I was there. When he couldn't reach me, he became furious and accused me of being out with another man. This behavior began to affect my job performance. Still, I thought nothing of it and found it rather flattering that he cared. He would tell me that he was just concerned about me and wanted to make sure I was okay. After all, I did share with him about my rape. I thought that was a noble and sweet thing. The next turn of events was the isolation from my family and friends. He said that he wanted my undivided attention and that I was the most important thing to him. He would tell me that my family and friends didn't care anything about me, only he did. I believed him because my relationship with my family was not sturdy. He has isolated me from them. Although I had witnessed domestic violence in my home as a child, I thought his behavior was normal, as was my custom.

There was an incident during the abuse in the grocery store that is still very vivid. Before leaving, he asked, "How long will you be in returning from the store?" He always wanted an exact time of arrival. While standing in the checkout line, I turned and there he was - out of nowhere. The fiery and rage that was in his eyes frightened me. He began to loudly cuss me out in that checkout line and accused me of sleeping with the checkout boy who appeared to be about seventeen years old. When we got to the parking lot, he hauled off and hit me knocking the bags of groceries out of my hand and made me pick them all up. What was even more disturbing, the people who were on the parking lot didn't stop to help me. He got in his car and followed me back home. When we got into the house he began to call me names like, "b_ _ _ , whore, slut", and began to slap me around. I inherited a black eye and a bloody lip that day. Later, he became very apologetic and began to caress me. Out of ignorance, I forgave him. My mom did with my dad. That same night he wanted to have sex with me. I told him that I didn't want to, but he forced himself on me. He held me down, ripped off my panties and began to thrust his penis inside of me. There I was being reminded of my raped all over again and this time not from a stranger, but someone who said they loved me. That Sunday morning I went to church with sunglasses on my face on a cloudy day hoping that I could feel a touch from Gold to help me. He didn't like to go to church. He said that all preachers were pimps and crooks. When service was over I went to the front of the church to speak with the pastor and his wife and I turned around there he was standing at the back of the church. Once again, he made a scene on the church parking lot. And once again no one helped me. I thought the church was a place where I could feel safe. However, I felt unprotected. When we got home I got beaten once again and he destroyed all of my biblical literature and music. He knew those items were precious to me. He resented the fact that reading the bible and listening to music took time away from him. But, this gave me a sense of peace from my personal pain.

    There were numerous incidences that triggered his temper and I had the beatings and bruises, physically and emotionally to show for it. All of this drama, because of some fixation he had in his mind of having power and control. There was never an opportunity for me to explain or give my point of view. He was always right and I was always wrong. I would forgive him hoping that he wouldn't beat me again. Or, I would forgive him based on his promises that he would seek help for his anger. He would say all the things that I wanted to hear and the honeymoon stage began all over again. I thought that if I didn't do anything to antagonize him that things would be fine. I no longer had a mind of my own. His words controlled my thoughts and actions, as I slowly became a victim of his brainwashing. He even convinced me that he would go to church with me and ask God to help him be better. What I didn't realize was I was trying to fix him when I was the one who needed fixing. But, he never said he would go to get help to stop abusing me and the abuse continued. Because of my love for God, I continued to forgive him over and over again. My forgiveness reminded me of being on a merry-go-round. As a child, that ride made me sick and so did his abuse. Isn't that what the bible teaches, to forgive and love our enemies? He was definitely my enemy. Plus, I did not want to be a failure in another relationship. I've learned that those who do not love God will take advantage of your forgiving spirit. I was weak. He was controlling and possessive. Because of his temper and lack of respect for those in authority, he lost many jobs. The paycheck that I got every two weeks became his paycheck. I no longer had any say into how the money would be spent (economic abuse). As he attempted to get new jobs, they didn't last long either. After the bills were paid, the rest of the money was spent on his alcohol, drugs and partying. I had to beg for money for personal items, even down to buying soap, deodorant, stocking and panties.

    I left many times during the abuse and always returned in hopes that things would be better. During the returns it was like being on a honeymoon. In marriage, I never got carried over the threshold; however, I got knocked over the threshold many times. This is when he tried to right his wrong. So, he rolls out the red carpet to win me back. And, like a bride walking down the isle of the runner, I was walking back to him. However, the time came when I knew I had to find a way to get out. The beatings were coming more frequently especially when he was drinking or smoking marijuana. By this time, I had no family or friends to depend on and no money. I allowed him to isolate me from everyone that cared about me. I was like the little girl in a fairy tale book that cried wolf. When I was finally ready get out of the abuse, no one believed me. So, I was out there, alone in my wilderness trying to figure out how I was going to survive. It was at this point that I began to relate to how the Negro slaves must have felt trying to plot their freedom. Or, how the children of Israel felt trying to leave Egypt from the evil rule of Pharaoh. Whenever he was out of the house, I was always happy. There were no threats, put-downs and rape. There was nothing but total peace and tranquillity. This reminded me of a being on a beautiful tropical island. There were times when I wanted to leave when he was gone, but I had no car keys and no place to go. The fear and intimidation of what I had become gripped me. I was a hostage in my own home. Amidst all the physical and mental beatings, it was not enough to make me gain the courage and strength needed to get out. No one on my job talked about my bruises or offered me a place to stay. No one ever shared with me about shelters for abused women. I was too embarrassed to ask for help and I wasn't sure whether people wanted to get involved or just didn't know what to do.

The night of my **FINAL** tragic beating, a bright light bulb went off in my head. When that light switch came on, it let me see that this would be the night that I would take my last beating from him. No more abuse, even if it cost me my life. He had gone out earlier to the club with his friends and come home intoxicated and high, as was his custom on the weekends. It was around 3 a.m. I heard a noise. As I was awakened out of my sleep, the noise appeared to be coming from the living room. I opened the bedroom door to investigate, to my astonishment; he was having sex with a lady in our living room. His eyes connected with mine as to dare me to say anything. Again, fear gripped me from his look and I immediately tried to block out what I saw. But, little did he know that I didn't give a damn. I closed the bedroom door and thought to myself, he's not bothering me and better her having his nasty penis (that I once liked) in her than me. I closed the door and snickered at what was transpiring. I guess it was from the shock. As I lay in the bed pretending to be asleep, he entered the room and wanted me to have sex with him. The nerve of that _____ (you fill-in the blank). Now that really infuriated me. I had already made up my mind that I no longer was going to have bottles inserted into my vagina to appease his erotic sexual fantasies. I had gone through that mutilation when I was raped. Sex was supposed to be something pleasurable enjoyed by two people. Many times I felt like Ms. Cecily in the movie the Color Purple, when she said, "I feel like mister is doing his business on me." Now, every good quality within me was awakened from the deep sleep of denial. Saying NO to him was a word I tried not to use in my vocabulary. Whenever I said NO, it got me a beating as if I was some little child disobeying their parents. For him it was all about power and control and wanting what he wanted. However, I was no longer afraid of him. I had taken control of me and it felt damn good. If having control of my life meant dying, I was willing to die to be set free that night.

    He got into the bed with me and began to fondle me. I pushed his hands away from me and told him NO. I refused to have sex with him now or any other time. Suddenly, everything in that room became like a hurricane that had shown up out of nowhere. Before I knew it I had been knocked out of the bed and dragged into the walk-in closet. It seemed like the 4th of July. Fireworks were going off in that closet and the blows and hard punches were coming furiously. I tried blocking the blows, but I was trapped. I could feel his feet continually kicking me in my ribs. My head was being knocked from side to side like a boxer working out on a punching bag in the gym. My hair was being pulled like I was a cave woman from the prehistoric days. He dragged me from one end of the house to the other. Lamps, vases, plates and any other objects in the way of the beating were being broken. He punched holes in the walls; the phones were ripped out of the wall jacks. I begged him to stop. The more I begged for my life, the harder he beat me. It was though he was getting a rush, from beating me, like a junking taking in their fix. I tried to fight back, but I was not strong enough to resist. He reeked of alcohol and who knows what else he had ingested. I tried to make it to the door. He blocked me. I tried screaming loud enough that someone would hear me. No one came to my rescue. I had blood dripping from areas of my body that I couldn't pinpoint. I was stumbling around in a daze.

Although I had already made up in my mind that I would be willing to die, I began to pray silently, "God please don't let me die in here." I thought to myself, I can't' die in this house, because he would probably bury me in the back yard. However, whatever way it went, I was prepared. Even in my beating that night, he still controlled me. There was a time when the beatings first began that I would beg him to stop. During the night of my final beating, as I was kicked, slapped, beaten, cursed and dragged, I didn't say a word. I didn't care. I knew from past experience with him that he would get tired of beating me and would eventually pass out. Then, just maybe, I could attempt to get some help. When I went to look in my purse, he had taken my car keys and the little money that I did have while I was asleep. I knew that when he awakened that he would not remember much, but would attempt to apologize and beg for my forgiveness. I could hardly move and everything on my body was hurting. I knew that I had to get immediate medical attention. I knew that he would not take me because he would have to answer too many questions. So, I sat up in the living room chair until the sun peeped through the mini blinds praying that when he awakened he would let me go to the hospital since I was the excruciating pain. I waited in my private jail cell in my living room of my own home for him to unlock the door. He awakened and I begged for my keys so that I could drive myself to the hospital. As I dragged myself up from the chair to the door, I began to crawl like a baby. My pain was so intense. As I gazed at myself in the mirror, I was black and blue in my face. I was petrified. With fear of uncertainty of what I might do on his face, he handed me my keys not saying a word as he looked upon damage that he had done. As I drove off, in his mind, I believed he thought I would return to him, as was my custom in the past. I had no money, only the clothes on my back and for some odd reason, three pair of panties in my car (thinking perhaps one day I might need them if I ever left). I was leaving my home and all my possessions and I was never going to look back.

When I arrived at the hospital emergency room, a special team of trained nurses for domestic violence attended to me. They were very compassionate. As I looked around the room, there was a lady police officer and another woman dressed in a suit. The nurse asked me if she should call anyone and I told her to call my family. No one ever came to see about me. The nurse, after getting my x-rays, showed me my face in the mirror. I couldn't believe what was staring back at me in the mirror. My face was unrecognizable. It looked like a piece of raw liver as the tears began to roll down my face. I sustained numerous injuries during my beating that night. I had cracked ribs, dislocated vertebrates to my neck, broken nose, chipped teeth and permanent nerve damage to the left side of my hip. Although in pain, I considered my beating that night "My Medals of Honor". My batterer may have won the battle that night, but I won the war. That moment in the hospital, confirmed what I had already known, I would never go back to the abuse again with him or anyone else. From the hospital I went to live in a shelter for battered women. It was a beautiful, peaceful place where I would now learn how to begin a new and healthy life. During a very critical time during my transition at the shelter, a counselor named Ms. Della got inside the shower with me to help bath me because I was so badly bruised that I couldn't move some of my limbs.

Eventually, I transitioned from the shelter, months later into my own home. It was difficult. Now, I had to learn how to be deprogrammed. Later, my batterer began to stalk me on my job and he located my new residence. Even with my "Court Protective Order" in place, that didn't ease my fear nor stop him. By the time I called the police, he would be gone. This drama persisted for a while. Then one day he tampered with my mail. I called my domestic violence advocate who suggested that I press charges for mail tampering which was a federal offense. I had been sleeping with the enemy long enough – my batterer. Even living in my own home he tormented me in my sleep. From the court process, my batterer, stalker, rapist, left me alone once and for all. He knew that he had lost power and control over me and now he would move onto another target. There were so many warning signs at the beginning of the relationship that I ignored. Signs like jealousy, questioning, stalking, isolation, intimidation and disrespect. He was always right and everyone else wrong. Ultimately, it almost cost me my life.

Something To Think About !

Discussion: How would you have handled this abusive relationship?

What would you have done when he knocked the bags out of Cheryle's hands at the grocery store?

What would you have done if you witnessed the sex scene in the living room?

Discuss the medical attention Cheryle received at the emergency room that day.

CHAPTER 1

"IN THE BEGINNING"

"You must realize what is actually going on before you can effectively deal with it"

Ralpha

Over the years, life experience has taught us that there is a great price to pay for having a lack of love, support and attention from our parents or guardians. Let's look at how Webster defines love.

Definition of Love

"A strong affection for another arising out of kinship or personal ties; to hold dear or cherish, an admiration."

Studies have shown that the number one cause of domestic violence can be attributed to learned-behavior. More specifically, experience of abuse in the home where they were raised. Eight-five percent (85%) of batterer's learn their behavior at home. Children have either witnessed the abuse or have been beaten by the batterer. In most cases, somewhere in the scheme of things, there was a missing element from their lives. For example, father's being absent from the home (work, death, divorce, etc.), single female head-of-household which can lead to promiscuity, early pregnancy, substance abuse and suicide.

In a newspaper editorial written by the HERALD SUN, Durham, NC entitled, **"Two-parent family remains the ideal"**, suggests that the two-parent family with children have healthier, more intellectually and emotionally satisfying lives. On the other hand, children in a single female head-of-household are twice as likely to develop psychiatric illnesses and addictions as they reach adulthood. In another study, done by a group of researchers in London, they suggest that the kind of people who end up as single parents might not have done well by their children even if they were not single parents. They could have transferred this mind set to their children unless their spouse had a strong enough personality to over shadow their shortcomings and create a more balanced environment. This can be a real challenge because they have learned to be very independent. These single parents tend to be more critical in relationships and derogatory towards other people. They believe that it is harder to be a warm, non-critical parent when they are bringing up a child alone.

Due to these missing links, daughters seek affection from boys and men at an early age to replace that missing father affection that was unavailable in their home. In an article published in the Duke Dialogue in 2003 entitled, **"Dad's Absence Affect Daughter's Behavior"**, researchers at Duke, Indiana, Auburn universities and New Zealand have identified that lack of a father in the home put daughters at risk for early sexual activity. Duke Sanford Research Institute researchers believed that having dad absent during the first five years was a unique risk factor. Their findings suggested that the longer dad is out of the equation, the more the daughters are exposed to their mother's dating and future relationship behavior. Then, daughter tends to believe that if mom can do it so can I. With regards to sons, they tend to look for affection, nurturing and guidance from older girls or women mainly due to single female head-of-households.

Because women are nurturers by nature, they are more likely to try and **FIX** things for their sons rather than being patient and showing them how. This can sometimes lead to a lack of responsibility and accountability. Sons raised under single female head-of-households are accustom to their moms bailing them out of trouble. This learned behavior is sometimes carried over into relationships where they may expect their significant other to do the same. When a problem arises, his significant other expects him to get involved, but he procrastinates. He is not use to having to make responsible decisions thus, causing strife, which can lead to conflict, anger and violence. All of these variables push boys, girls, men and women into relationships that are unhealthy. This chapter begins to set the stage on how and why domestic violence resides in victim and batterer (male and female) in dating, marriage, children and how the pressure builds which leads to abuse. It perpetuates into what is discussed in Chapter 2, "The Cycle Begins."

Let's Get Started !

"The Neighborhood"

I grew up on Shirley Avenue, in a neighborhood called Park Heights in Baltimore, Maryland. It was a neighborhood where we had block parties and from time to time community festivals. During those hot summers months, the neighborhood fire department would come and take the cap off the fire hydrants and the neighborhood kids would have their own private pool party that didn't cost a dime. It was a lot of fun. Single moms or grandmas raised the majority of the kids on the block. There were few households where the dads were present. My home had an absent dad. What I remember when my dad periodically showed up was that he would bring all the children a few presents. It felt more like a bribe or peace offering because he didn't want us to hate him for not being around. What would he bring our mom? He would bring her more heartache, pain and at times horrible beatings. I compare some of those beatings to how the master would beat the slaves, whipping them on their backs over and over in the same spot. My mom was a little woman and my dad was huge. Whenever he showed up, you could see the fear in her eyes. I remember him beating her when she was pregnant with my younger sister. Being a little child, I could not understand why he would beat her. On television I would see moms and dads hugging and kissing. Our household was definitely not a Ward and June Cleaver on the television show, "Leave it to Beaver". It terrified my oldest brother and me to watch the abuse and couldn't do anything; we were powerless. My mom would motion us not to get involved. Isn't that just like a mother? She wanted to protect her little chicks from the blows, knocks and at times bullets.

I looked for love. Where was I going to learn of it or even find it? My childhood memories are vague. I can't remember many good times. I guess this is why I sometimes act like a big kid in my adult life. I enjoy dancing, laughing and cutting-up. When I was a little girl, I played with dolls, jumped rope, played hopscotch and hide and go seek. I had some neighborhood friends and got into a few fights. Fights were a common occurrence in our neighborhood. I enjoyed playing with the other girl's dolls because I had none of my own. There were times when I would get mad at my friends because they wouldn't let me play with their Barbie dolls. These dolls were very popular, but we couldn't afford them. I never would have thought that something as minor as not having a Barbie Doll would impact my adulthood. How ironic that a simple thing like a doll would give me an appetite for seeking after material things in my adult life to bring me happiness.

"The Party"

There was another incident that I remember very clearly. Now, some thirty-five years later it still touches my heart as I write. One day my mom and godmother (who was godmother to all of us) gave my younger sister a birthday party. I remember going wild and throwing a terrible temper tantrum. A rage came over me that I couldn't stop or understand. I went from sweet to ugly and out of control in a matter of minutes. I felt like the animated character, Incredible Hulk. I terrorized that party like hurricane Isabel did in North Carolina in September 2003. Why did I act this way? You see, I had never had a birthday party.

I was about eight or nine years old. The party was at our godmother's house that lived across the street. They rolled out the red carpet. My sister had all the trimmings. There were balloons (lots of them), party hats, horns, food, music, dancing, cake (with her name on it) and ice cream. There were lots of kids there. I couldn't understand why my mom and godmother would do so much for her. I was the oldest girl. Why was my sister being treated so special? I wanted to know if I had done something wrong that no one had told me. I felt like they loved my sister more than me. They must have. They were throwing her a party. I was crushed.

At the party, I began to cry and taunt the other children. My Incredible Hulk personality came alive. I could feel the transformation happening, but I couldn't stop it. I was out of control. Before I knew it, I had smashed my sister's birthday cake. I kept screaming, "This should be my party." My mom became furious with me. My sister was crying because I had just ruined her beautiful precious party. I was snatched up like a tornado by my mom. She whisked me home. I knew I was in big trouble. I was yelling, kicking and screaming all the way.

The neighborhood kids were staring and laughing as they watched me make a fool of myself.

    Needless to say, not only did I not get to stay at the precious party; I got the worst whipping ever. My mom had broken a switch from off a tree in the back yard, peeled off the twigs until the green showed. Then she had me drop my clothes (my mom didn't believe in beating clothes), turned me over her knee and whipped my butt until I couldn't sit. I wasn't allowed to come out of my room for the rest of the day. I should have been a good girl. But, I just didn't feel loved.

    Let's See Who This Unloved Child Was!

Cheryle, the party wrecker and her mom.

"The Clubhouse"

As I got older, I began to hang out with the boys in the neighborhood clubhouse. There I felt accepted. This was something I never felt with my parents or siblings. The clubhouse provided a place for me to escape from my family and the pain I felt for a little while. It was in that place that I could play with the boys, ride their bikes and wear their skates. I could climb the trees for apples and cherries. I could be wild and adventurous. At the clubhouse I would let some of the boys pat me on my butt or my little breasts that were starting to bud. I would tell them to stop, but I kind of liked their touch. Once again, I was seeking attention and they gave it to me. I was now the center of their attention. With my siblings, at times, I felt like an outcast – a misfit. I felt like the animated character Babe. You see Babe was a pig trying to fit in an environment that was not natural. Because he was a misfit, there was envy, jealousy and strife among the other animals because the owner of the farm treated Babe like a dog. He allowed Babe inside of the house and the other animals were not. When the owner's dog could not compete in the upcoming fair competition, Babe was asked to take the dog's place. Like Babe, where did I fit in the family structure? In the clubhouse, I fit in. I looked for love. Where was I to find it? Who was going to teach me what was acceptable behavior and what is not? I wasn't even "Daddy's Little Girl."

"Born to Lust or Love"?

The lack of love has a great impact on children when they are little. This lack can play a major role in how they will turn out in life. When I was in my thirties, I learned that my dad wasn't my dad (the batterer). This news was easy for me to accept since my dad wasn't around much. You know that saying; "You can't miss something that you've never had." I found out accidentally at a family gathering about my biological father. The newer generation of women would call him, "The sperm donor" or "My baby's daddy." Here's how I came into the knowledge of who my biological dad was:

> *There was this good-looking older man sitting in the living room at my grandma's and mom's house (they lived together). My grandma was in the kitchen cooking when I asked her, was that her new boyfriend sitting in the living room. She replied, "No, that's your father." Isn't that a hell of a way to find out who your daddy is? I went out to the front porch and asked my mom to come in the house with me. We went upstairs to her bedroom. I asked her who that man was downstairs in the living room. My mom got quiet and looked at me strangely. I let her know that we weren't leaving the room until she told me the truth. She gave in and told me that the man in the living was my father, Mr. Smith.*

Now, I began to understand why I looked different from my siblings. I proceeded to ask my mom to introduce us, she did. Mr. Smith informed me that he had known about me since the day I was born. Those words gave me the creeps. I felt like I had been raped or stalked again by a complete stranger. I told my mom that she could leave us alone. I sensed that she was feeling uncomfortable. Mr. Smith asked if he could hug me. I gave in. My other dad never hugged me so, I had nothing to compare Mr. Smith's hug with. As we hugged, looking at him was like looking in a mirror. I had his skin color, wavy hair texture and nose. He proceeded to tell me that he loved me. I couldn't receive that because I didn't know what love was. I had no one to teach me. Mr. Smith told me that he and my mom had an affair while she was married to my other dad. He said that the affair happened because my dad (who I thought was my dad) was abusive to my mom. I knew the abuse part was true. This unveiling information was like the *Lifetime Channel* series. I could now understand from those movies why the women who were abused, would fall into the arms of another man especially, if that man were warm, sensitive and not beating her. Or, why the men who are abused would confide and lay with another woman even if he didn't love her. Sex would just be a comfort to get them through the hard times. Mr. Smith proceeded to tell me that he knew the exact moment I was conceived. I felt no comfort in that piece of information. Was I to be impressed that a man would remember such an intimate moment? I think not. He said that it was a cold snowy night in December 1958. As I did the math, which was about right and on September 4, 1959, I was born. Now I had two fathers and still no dad to nurture, guide, teach and love me. How was I to learn how a man should treat a woman? Was it to come out of books or television? Since learning about Mr. Smith, I've tried to have a relationship with him, but the result of this effort seemed artificial. I was trying to create something that wasn't. I had these two big cups (2 dads) that were empty when all I wanted in my cup was love. I wanted to put my straw in my love cup and sip slowly just so that I could say, "Good to the last drop." Today, my dad is just Mr. Smith.

"ALCOHOL AND DRUG ABUSE"

During my high school years, I went to live with my great uncle and his children. The high school I wanted to attend was close to their house. My uncle was a widower. His wife's aunt (Aunt Ann), came to live with them to help take care of the house and children. He had converted his basement into a one-bedroom apartment for Aunt Ann. When she went to sleep, we kids got wild. I began to drink wine. Back in those days it was Thunderbird, Richards Wild Irish Rose and Boone's Farm. I smoked marijuana and even popped a few pills. I was hanging out with the crowd. I was accepted. I wasn't having sex yet, however, the drugs made me think about it. I would go to house parties with my cousins. The music was either jumping to the tune of Jungle Boogie or Disco Inferno. Or, it was that smooth 70's music. We were grooving to such greats as The Isley Brothers, The Temptations, The Ojay's, Smokey Robinson and the Miracles, Earth, Wind and Fire, Patti LaBelle, Elvis Presley and Tom Jones (I loved to shake my skinny body to the tunes of Elvis and Tom). With tunes like that who wouldn't get aroused. I learned this behavior when I was little. My mom and her friends threw their parties to the tunes of Sam Cooke, Isaac Hayes, Brooke Benton, Lou Rawls, Nat King Cole, Aretha Franklin and many more. My peers and I had the blue lights and strobe lights down in the basement. This atmosphere made for good slow dancing, dipping and grinding with the guys. That gave me a good feeling and the guys too. I could feel their penis getting erect and I would back-up from them while dancing. Alcohol and drugs moved me into another arena. Let's travel there.

THE IMPACTS OF LOVE: WHAT CAUSES IT?

"PROMISCUITY"

Even in the clubhouse with the boys I was frisky. At age fifteen I started high school. I lived in a community where there was not a trade school. Even while living in the ghetto, I had dreams. I wanted to be somebody and make something out of my life. I wanted to be a secretary like I had seen on television. Secretaries were working in offices, courtrooms, wore nice clothes and looked important. I wanted to feel like that. I wanted to make my dream come true. For this to happen, I had to get into trade school. My mom got permission from my great uncle to let me live at his house during the week so that I could attend Carver Vocational-Technical High School, which was in walking distance. I got accepted in their Business Curriculum. Living at my uncles with my girl cousin who was a year older than me was like living in a mansion. I thought they were rich. They had a nice home and all of his children had their own bedroom. They wore fine clothes, not hand-me-downs. They had a variety of foods to eat. No more spam, rice, and welfare peanut butter with that thick oil on the top for me. No more cutting that block of welfare cheese to make grilled cheese sandwiches. Now, I had Kraft singles slices that I could peel and eat. Boy, I felt rich. Most of all, I had freedom from my mom, brothers and sisters. I was footloose and fancy-free. Although I had freedom, I wasn't really free. This newfound freedom would cost me plenty in the end. **Warning**, everything that looks good isn't good and the grass really isn't always greener on the other side. My uncle worked third shift. My freedom would now allow me to take my experience with boys to higher level. I could now talk to boys on the phone and in public. There were a few boys in high school that I hung out with at their homes. Although we would kiss, give each other "passion marks – hickies", touch and fondle, I wouldn't have sex. I was a cute, petite girl and used these characteristics to become popular with the boys. My mom and dad never told me that

I should be like actor Kevin Costner who played Elliott Nest in "The Untouchables." I wasn't taught to be tough enough to say no and fight back. Remember that I was suffering from a **lack of love**. All I saw in my environment was, "Give men what they want – you get what you want." So, I became promiscuous.

      I was a good student and popular among my peers. I was in the Future Business Leaders of America Club (FBLA) and the Modern Dance Troupe and enjoyed being the center of attention. Why? I didn't get any at home. I love my mom and she was giving me the best she could. She was probably repeating the cycle that was handed down to her with regards to raising children. I dated a few boys in high school. I allowed them to kiss me and even touch me in areas where they shouldn't have. You see, I was familiar with that from my *Clubhouse* days. It was about a *Lack of Love*. One morning while walking to school, this shiny black 1973 Volkswagen Super Beetle pulled up beside me. The guy in the car proceeded to talk to me and as I walked, he drove. He was a cute dark black man and he had a car too. You see, a car was something most guys in high school didn't own. Again, maybe it was the Barbie doll fetish that leads me to the materialistic world. They either walked or had a bus pass. Wow, that impressed me. He was five years older, but that didn't stop us from exchanging phone numbers. He worked third shift so that was convenient for both of us. I could see him when I got out of school and we could get to know each other better. I seized the moments with him. I had a man paying attention to me. My new friend listened to me and bought me clothes and took me out to dinner and the movies. I was definitely moved by the material things. My mom finally got an opportunity to meet him. She had no concerns about the age difference or him dating her daughter. Her only comment to him was, "Don't you hurt my daughter". In her mind, I believe, she was talking about physical abuse because of what my dad had done to her. Little did she know that by allowing me to date an older man without supervision and guidance had already set me up for some unexpected and unprepared problems. I must interject here to let you know that *I LOVE MY MOM VERY VERY VERY MUCH*! She is my best friend. Eventually, the door of opportunity for sex was wide open. Sexual intercourse felt good to me. Or did it? How was it supposed to feel? No one told me about it. On television when people were having sex it always accompanied the words, "I Love You." So, I thought sex meant love --- and I was getting plenty of sex.

"EARLY PREGNANCY"

There have been numerous studies linking single parent families and domestic violence can lead to early teenage pregnancy as we read earlier. Now days you can't even say teenage pregnancy because children are getting pregnant as early as age 12. I was promiscuous and a little hot box as a teenager. Previously, you read about me dating the older guy with the 1973 Black Volkswagen Super Beetle and how I had sex because I associated it with love. On November 6, 1976, the cutest little baby boy was born to me at age 16. We named him Charles, after his dad. But, we affectionately called him "Chucky. "

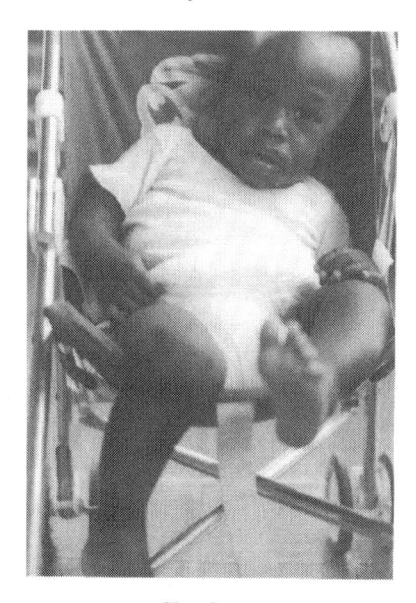

Chucky

I was struggling to be a mom, get through high school and have a boyfriend. When I got pregnant, I was no longer popular among my peers. I could no longer participate in the activities that I enjoyed the most and I had to move back home from the mansion (great uncle's house). My life was now all rearranged. I was not ready to be a mom, but abortion was out of the question. So, between my family and his family, we worked out a schedule. Chucky's dad would pick him up in the morning when he got off work and they would take me to school. At the close of school, they both would be waiting for me so that dad could go home to get some sleep to get ready for the night shift. At my home, my mother helped me while I did my homework and after that, she no longer would baby sit. But, she would look after her grandson if I needed her too. She was crazy about him. There was no such thing of her baby sitting while I went out to have fun. So, the three of us (dad, mom and child) spent wonderful family time together. This was something I didn't have.

In June 1977, with the love and support of my family, I graduated high school with my Business Diploma. My dream of becoming a secretary had come true. However, a baby was not a part of the dream. I wanted to go to college. I would have been the first from my mom's family. I tried juggling college and a baby, but it was too difficult. I was fortunate; however, to obtain a high school diploma and was able to get a State job. I was making $6,000/yr. That was a lot of money back then. I could now do things for my son and my mom. I purposed to have a birthday party for my son every year. There would be no **Lack of Love** for him.

"SUICIDE"

It is astonishing to think that your child that you carried in your womb for 9 months would want to commit suicide. We bring them into the world to have a full, happy and productive life. However, the reality is that it is happening more frequently than we may want to admit. In a National Institute of Mental Health Suicide Facts Report of 2001, suicide was the 11th leading cause of death in the United States. It was the 3rd leading cause of death among young people 15 to 24 years of age. The suicide rate among adolescents ages 15-19 was about 11% and the suicide rate among children ages 10-14 was even higher.

In another report by The Funeral Directory, data from Statistics Canada indicated that during the period 1993-1997, 229 Canadian children ages 5-14 years of age who actually completed suicide. Two of these suicides were by boys under the age of 10. Of the remaining 227 children, 155 were male and 72 were female. Although suicide is also very rare among Americans under age 14, studies have shown high rates of nonfatal suicidal behaviors and ideation among children. In another report by the National Center for Children Exposed to Violence, children who witnessed violence at home tend to display emotional and behavioral disturbances as diverse as withdrawal, low self-esteem, nightmares and aggression against peers, family members and property. Over 3 million children are at risk of exposure to parental violence each year. More astonishing is that children who are successful in committing suicide have witnessed domestic violence and are homosexual. These individuals do no attempt suicide – they complete it. If you find this hard to believe, keep reading.

As you can see, suicide is no longer confined to adults or older teens. Children as young as six years old think about killing themselves. In an article featured in the Reader's Digest, "Why Children Commit Suicide," Dr. Sharda Prasad, Director, National Crime Records Bureau, New Delhi says, "That the incidence among child suicide continues to increase over the years." The figures are probably much higher as so many of these cases do not get reported. Why are our children thinking about this? As stated in Chapter 1, absenteeism from the home (dad absent, single female head-of household), school work, pressure to perform well, sometimes chronic illness and lack of love makes children and teens feel that the only way out is suicide. Some may find it hard to believe, but children as young as age 6, even if they do not commit suicide, they will be thinking about it as they move into adolescents or teenage hood depending on their environment. During that time they are more likely to following through with the suicide. Take a journey with me as I share with you a small portion about the suicide of my son, Chucky.

"Chucky Gets His Peace"

Three years later after Chucky was born, I married Chucky's dad. On July 7, 1981, our second son, Kevin was born and in 1993 our divorce was final. As a parent, I attempted to give our sons the love and affection that I didn't receive as a child. But, even with all you try to do sometimes it's not enough to stop the pain of our children. While sitting here writing this section, it has occurred to me that there is a five-year age difference with our sons just like with their dad and I. Although Chucky and Kevin shared the same set of parents, their personalities were like night and day. The qualities that made Chucky unique were his leadership abilities in school and church among his peers. He had a special love for senior citizens and attempted sports. He was an excellent cook and a good student. What made him extraordinary was how warm, tender and big of a heart he had. Kevin, however, was every dad's dream child. He was exceptionally smart in school, very athletic and very low-keyed. Did not like being seen, just heard from the background. In my first book, **"Abused, Battered, Broken-hearted and Restored"** I go into depth about some of the variables which tormented Chucky. While divorced, Chucky could not understand why his dad and I could not stay together, yet we were communicating better than when we were married. In middle school, this affected Chucky's ability to stay focused in school. His grades began to suffer and subjects that once were once easy for him became a challenge and suffered with low self-esteem. There were numerous instances where he became withdrawn. When Chucky was about thirteen years old, he tried to cut his wrist. Later, he attempted to run away from home. He ran away to my moms and she sent him back home. These were all warning signs for help. For Kevin, the drama of the divorce did not affect him. He was getting attention from his parents and had school and sports to build his confidence and as an outlet.

And on Father's Day 1999, my loving son, Chucky, my first born committed suicide. He set himself on fire. Oh, the pain I feel at this very moment as I write. I want to stop right here and move onto the next topic, but I can't. **PAUSE BREAK** ---------- My tears are emerging. If you would like to cry right now it's okay. There's a lump in my throat and a funny feeling in my stomach right now. Oh, how I miss him so very much in the physical. However, in my heart he is always with me. Over the years I have learned that a mom's greatest pleasure is to know that her children are okay. No pain, no hurt, no sorrow. Chucky now has that peace he was longing for. Recently, while having a major bout with menopause, I found myself slipping into a state of depression. It took everything I had within me spiritually and physically to fight the depression. What I had an opportunity to experience, for a brief moment, was that I understood how Chucky could love God, slip into depression and take his life. Now I could experience a mother's hurt and a sons hurt. My comfort comes in knowing that whatever mental torment he was feeling, is over now. A portion of his suicide note, from what I remember, was this brief excerpt:

"Dear Mom: I love you and I am sorry for what has happened. I am tired of living. You have been a good mother and friend. Please forgive me. You are special to me. Love, Chucky"

What's the point I'm trying to make here? When there is a lack of love in an individual's life, it can cause all types of emotional things to happen. As a young child Chucky witnessed domestic violence. For several years I tormented myself about whether I had done something wrong as a mom to contribute to his death. I had to ask myself if he was angry with me. When he died a piece of me went with him. However, I had Kevin to live for. He was going into his first year of college a week after his brother's burial. I have learned how to forgive myself for what I may not have given Chucky. Whatever my shortcomings, God does not hold me accountable for not knowing how to love, nurture and raise my sons or out of ignorance. Because of the death of Chucky, not only am I a better mother to Kevin, but a stronger person to myself. So, Chucky's suicide was not in vain. Even in his absence, his spirit is very much alive. I think that singer Tina Turner says it best when she sings her hit song, "What's Love Got to Do With It", I say everything.

Kevin (Front) and Chucky (Back)
My Blessings – Younger Years

As we close out Chapter 1, I know you may find all of this hard to believe, but it's all true. I hope that it gave you some insight through my personal experiences on how your beginning can determine how your future or the future of your children will turn out. I believe that there is a strong correlation with absent fathers, single female-head-of-household and learned behavior. As previously stated:

"You must realize what is actually going on before you can effectively deal with it".

Ralpha

As we begin to build the foundation for domestic violence, let's journey further to see what happens when, ***The Cycle Begins.***

Let's Get Started !

CHAPTER 2

"THE CYCLE BEGINS"

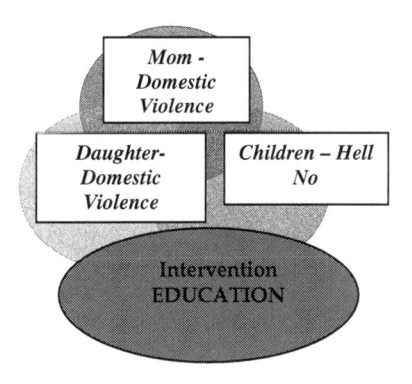

```
         Mom -
         Domestic
         Violence

  Daughter-        Children – Hell
  Domestic              No
  Violence

         Intervention
          EDUCATION
```

There have been many debates, research studies and forums over whether domestic violence is caused by learned, generational, disease or a matter of choice. Many psychologists believe that there is a direct link with this behavior – no matter what the contributing factors, the individual chooses. But, if positive choices are not made, it can lead to destruction. Those links are like building blocks that many of us may have played with when we were little children. If we were to replace those building blocks to fit our modern day terms, we would have such variables as: dating, marriage, children and financial pressures. Just like those building blocks, if you stack them up too high and then apply that one block that adds that additional weight, the blocks will begin to tumble down. If this behavior is generational, then let's look at how Webster defines generational:

"The action or process of producing offspring; a body of living beings constituting a single step in the line of descent from an ancestor (family tree)".

When these variables are not properly taught at an early age, failure in relationships, are inevitable. In some instances, there has been a lack of teachers, counselors and role models to teach individuals what to expect as they begin to date or marry (broken family structures). The dating process is supposed to be fun, sweet and romantic. There should be a time of learning about one another in good and stressful situations. He or she has found their soul mate. Someone they can confide in and who they want to spend the rest of their life with. They get engaged, set a wedding date and get married. Oh Happy Day! Now, the two individuals must learn to adjust to what they think marriage should be. The meshing of two fleshes will be a difficult process at times. Will they have good role models to pattern their marriage after? Will they learn it from television? Or, will they just learn as they go along.

It is crucial that positive role models are present or marriage counselors available to help their marriage avoid major pitfalls that they are surely to encounter. The couple strives for a happy and fulfilling marriage. But, if the couple is not careful, due to the lack of role models or counseling, they will find themselves arguing about small things. The building blocks begin to stack up. There is no communication and to keep down conflict one of the individuals begin to shut down. Another building block is stacked. The sex department is drying up. Now we have two building blocks on that stack. The couple is unable to manage their finances (never took the opportunity during the dating or engagement phase to discuss a budget). Another block stacked. Now, an unplanned baby is on the way. Another block stacked. The blocks are stacked so high now that they just fall down and so does the relationship. The bad thing about this turn of events is the baby is caught in the middle. The anger and resentment builds. These are all external factors that increase stress, but they don't necessarily cause domestic violence. The internal factor, "learned behavior", is one of the causes of domestic violence. Women who are raised by a single female head-of-household are more inclined to be independent and have a take charge attitude. This causes strife with their partner who was raised in a two-parent household. If the other partner has been raised to take charge (*Two Chiefs*), this can cause problems as well. The male who is raised in a single female head-of-household is inclined to be dependent on the female. This causes strife if their mate was raised in a two-parent household. The other partner expects them to take charge (*No Chiefs*). Although you think this could not happen to you, it could if your eyes are not open to the possibility that building blocks can and will happen in the relationship. This chapter will help you realize how important it is to take time to know each other while dating, before marriage and the importance of getting counseling. If you are not aware of these variables and warning signs, you will definitely find yourself caught in a cycle of abuse and looking for a way to get out.

Something To Think About !

Discussion: What are the building blocks in your relationship? List them:

1.
2.
3.
4.
5.

Do you think the dating process is an important part of the relationship? How long should it last? What would you look for during this process?

Would you seek counseling before marriage?

If married, how does your household monitor the finances. If considering marriage, how would you handle the finances?

Are children important to discuss before marriage? What would you discuss?

"GENERATIONAL BEHAVIOR"

So often we hear people say such things as:

- **You are just like your daddy.**

- **You are a product of your environment.**

- **Watch the company you keep.**

Once again, domestic violence researchers, advocates, psychologists, counselors and I pretty much agree, for the most part, is learned behavior that may begin in the home. When I talk to men and women who are in a domestic violence situation, one of the major questions I ask is, "Tell me about your family history." Physicians do this when they are trying to assess their patients for diagnosis and treatment. I do this so that I may not judge the victim or batterer harshly thus, allowing myself to stay objective. I try to explain to the victim and batterer that domestic violence is a bad seed that has been planted into their life. Like a good farmer who plants for a good harvest, when that harvest comes in bad, the farmer will usually dig up the entire field from the root and replant all over again. Or, like wild grass that continues to choke out your beautiful flower-bed, domestic violence works the same way. You have to get to the root of the problem. We need to understand that we can no longer put a Band-Aid on the situation. By this I mean:

- Anger management programs for 12-weeks ordered by the court system. *Is this enough time to get rid of years of anger?*

- Incarceration. *Do we help them or hinder them?*

- Churches providing counseling sessions. *Do they (batterer) show remorse or just want reconciliation of the marriage or the facts about the abuse?*

- Reading books. *Will they put into practice what they have read?*

- Attending healing, deliverance, men and women conferences. *What do they do when they return back to the abuse?*

I consider all the above Band-Aids. I believe that, domestic violence should be treated like any other disease, addiction or terminal illness that could lead to death. I will share my view on this in the section entitled, "**Substituting Wrong Behavior for Good Behavior**". We don't give cancer patients two doses of radiation and send them home. They would die. Instead, there is a protocol that is used to treat the disease. This may include medications, physicians and nurses, support groups as well as holistic medicines (mental, physical, and spiritual) to help them get through the healing process. We don't tell patients with high blood pressure to keep eating pork or foods that have high salt content. Or, we don't tell patients with chronic obstructive pulmonary disease to continue to smoke. This same concept should apply to domestic violence. If the victim or batterer is serious about changing the cycle of abuse, they will need to begin a treatment plan for their healing as well. This process may take a while and you may have to start with one a day at a time. Then a week, a month and even year(s) until they begin to see the final results are here - no more abuse. I don't want domestic violence to be just in remission. We want it removed from their lives and the lives of their children, family and friends forever. Let's take a look at a few true stories of generational behavior and how this cycle can be passed on from generation to generation.

"My Brother - Tony"

Our father was always absent from the home. I learned lots of things about our father as I got older. I use to wonder why he was like a revolving door. Our father was a convicted felon. He had robbed banks and numerous people. I remember a story being told about how our father had robbed a church while the people were praying. It has been said that he's murdered a few individuals as well. Most of dad's adult life was spent on the running from the law. This ugly behavioral pattern got transferred (learned) to my oldest brother, Tony as a child and followed him into his adulthood (no guidance in the home to nurture and direct). In elementary school, Tony was very much out of control (no drugs back then for hyper kids). There was an incident in the fifth grade when a girl with a long ponytail was sitting in front of him. Well, he claimed he couldn't see the blackboard because her ponytail was in the way. What does he do? He gets a pair of scissors and cuts it off. Of course, he got sent home from school that day. But, that made him happy – he hated school (didn't like people telling him what to do). There was another incident in elementary school when the teacher said something about our mother. This set Tony off and he picked up a chair and hit the teacher across the back. This time he got put out of school for good and this landed him in reform school. He was always getting in trouble. The beatings my mom would give him with broom handles, frying pans, belts and whatever else that was available would have been enough to make anyone straighten up, not Tony. He got worst. He had gotten to the point where he wouldn't cry from the harsh beatings and this angered our mom and she would beat him harder. According to today's laws, my mom would have gotten arrested for child abuse. Tony didn't know that he had learned or inherited generational behavior, bad seed, just like our father. At times during his beatings, our mom would say to him, "You are just like your damn father." She was doing the best she could to raise all of us. But, somehow she knew that she didn't have what it took to control him.

In his teenage years, he began to do drugs and hang out with bad company. He did such drugs as sniffing glue from a paper bag (chemicals in the glue) and drinking Robitussin Cough Syrup (contained enough codeine to give you a buzz). It was a way of getting high at an inexpensive cost. I guess he was trying to escape his pain and frustration. When those drugs did not satisfy him, he turned to taking pills (uppers and downers) and then marijuana. Still the war between good and evil inside of him tormented him and his pain and anger persisted. As his love/hate relationship grew towards our mom, so did Tony's drug addiction. Now, he began snorting cocaine and eventually began to shoot up in his arms and wherever else there was a vein available. His addiction led him to a life of crime and violence. He began to steal, flem flam and scam people out of their money, which led him to a life of incarceration. Can you begin to see the pattern? Is he just like father, like son? Based on these events, I would say yes to learned and yes to generational behavior. What do you say? While in prison, Tony was diagnosed with kidney disease. Our father had kidney disease too. I was saddened because I did not want my brother to die. You see, out of all my siblings, my brother and I was the closet.

Although there were times when he would beat me up when I was little, in the end I still liked to cling to him. Tony developed a heart condition. So did our father. The most heart breaking news was when my brother told me he had contracted AIDS from his drug abuse. Tony frequented lots of women. So did our father. My brother's women supported him financially and sexually. Our father had women who did that for him as well. My brother was abusive to many of his female companions. But, they seemed to love him, so they said. I guess Tony and our father must have been great lovers! My brother died in 1998 – "Renal Failure and AIDS". Our father died in 1990. The cause of death was "End Stage Renal

Disease." I have shared this story with you so that you may understand that your unhealthy patterns and behaviors may not be totally your fault. However, once you recognize and accept that, you do have a choice. No one understood why Tony did the things he did, not even Tony himself. However, it is my opinion that he was definitely, "like father – like son." Tony tried to escape his pain and anger by participating in crime and drugs. These were all open wounds being covered up with Band-Aids. His issues were deep and were a reality in his daily life. Pretty bizarre, but true.

Something To Think About!

Discussion: Was there learned behavior and similarities between Tony and his father? If so, list those behaviors.

1.
2.
3.
4.
5.

Let's visit another true story.

"Aunt Louise"

Aunt Louise was my mom's sister. She was a single mom. Not long ago, she died from a long battle with cancer. What makes this story so touching is that Aunt Louise buried all three of her children before she died? They all died tragically. We are talking about generational behavior. As this story unfolds, you will begin to see a pattern of the generational behavior that ran wild in her children. In Chapter 1, we discussed how the lack of love can led to a cycle of other issues such as promiscuity, early pregnancy, alcohol, drug abuse and suicide. Aunt Louise had two sons and one daughter and all had different father's who were absent from the home. She never married and yes, she was a single female head-of-household. Although we don't know the background of the fathers, we know that they were absent from the home. This absenteeism can have a major impact on children's behavior. You have a sense of Aunt Louise's background because she is my mother's sister. And their mother, my grandmother was a single female head-of-household as well.

Aunt Louise was born to my grandmother. She had four sisters and one brother. She was a mother, worker and great cook of the family. She loved to party and play cards. She was once a casual drinker – then became an alcoholic and heavy smoker. Relatives in a small town in Virginia raised Aunt Louise. She lived in Philadelphia for a while and then moved to Baltimore. When we had family gatherings, some family members hated for her to come around. They knew once she got to drink, she became obnoxious. Aunt Louise was sweet and kind when she was sober and that's when we loved her company. She had had numerous operations on her back, which gave her no relief from her pain. When she was diagnosed with cancer, she gave up alcohol and cigarettes and gave her life to God. This was one of the best times of her life. For once God was controlling her and not substances and relationships. She became a source of strength to our family. The words that she heard from God through the bible and in her spirit, she imparted into those of us who wanted to listen. As our family pulled together to help care for her during her last few months, we saw a new Aunt Louise although diagnosed to die – she was very much alive in spirit. Before departing this life, she gave warm words to all that were gathered by her beside to say goodbye.

Something To Think About!

Discussion: Do you sense a pattern of learned or generational behavior with grandmother, mother and sister here?

Write down what you think it may be.

Let's visit the life of her oldest son!

"Michael"

From what I can remember about Michael, he was always withdrawn. I never knew or heard anyone talk about Michael's father. Most of his life he was raised by our grandmother. Michael did okay in school and was never a problem child like my brother Tony. When Michael completed high school, he joined the Marines. Something happened to him in that place. It was said that he got acquainted with drugs. During his visits home, he socialized with the family for a while and then off to himself once again. He became paranoid about certain issues like hating the white man, not eating eggs produced by a certain vendor and many other wild things. Eventually, he was discharged from the military for medical reasons. Michael became schizophrenic and was treated for depression. During this time he was living on his own and his mother and other family members became very concerned. Although he had a home, there were times when he would sleep on the street like he was homeless. Michael lived a couple of houses away from a funeral home. For days our family tried to locate him. One rainy day a phone call came from Bett's Funeral Home to tell us that Michael had died on their front steps. Cause of death, "pneumonia" three houses away from where he lived.

Something To Think About!

Discussion: What do you think may have contributed to Michael's mental illness?

Let's visit Michael's sister's story!

"Gwen"

She was the middle child of Aunt Louise's offspring and the only girl born to her. When Gwen was little she had serious medical problems. She suffered a lot with her feet and eczema. Through all of her medical challenges she was always full of energy and had a way of making you laugh. She was pretty smart in school as well. Like her brother Michael, Gwen had never had a relationship with her dad. As Gwen got older, I noticed that Aunt Louise was much harder on her than she was to Michael. Aunt Louise required more responsibility from Gwen like cleaning, cooking and obedience than she did from Michael (son – single female head-of-household). There was a different set of rules and standards. When Gwen was not with her mother, she was with Aunt Dot (my mom). Gwen said that Aunt Dot was her favorite because she spent time with her and listened to her. As Gwen got to become a young adult, her relationship with her mom became estranged. Once she graduated high school, she got a job and she moved out on her own. This cut down on the arguments and kept Gwen from being disrespectful to her mom since most of the arguments surfaced when Aunt Louise was drinking.

Gwen had lots of friends. I guess this compensated for the friendship she didn't have with her mom. During her dating process, she became acquainted with certain male company that was not good for her. Because of her relationship with Aunt Dot, Gwen was like clockwork in calling her everyday just to say hello or to get some words of encouragement. Then, that pattern changed. Three days had passed and Gwen had not called. This was so out of character for her. Our family became concerned. Not only that, but she was faithful to her employer and never missed time from work. They became worried. Finally, our family placed a missing person's call to the police department to file a report. Later, the news of her whereabouts was revealed. Gwen was found floating in a stream behind a local community college. Her body was decomposed. To make this short story even sadder, we learned that Gwen was pregnant. The police said that Gwen knew information on a particular crime and the people involved had her killed. Aunt Louise had now buried child #2 and her unborn grandchild.

Something To Think About!

Discussion: What could you conclude about Gwen's story?

How do you think this favoritism between Michael and Gwen affected Gwen?

Did Aunt Louise's relationship with Gwen's absent father play a role in how Gwen was treated?

Let's take a visit to the life of the Michael and Gwen's baby brother!

"Vance"

Vance was a little terror from the day he was born. When he was a toddler he would cuss, fight and get in all sorts of trouble. His mom would not let anyone correct him. She thought those obnoxious things were cute. No one in our family would baby sit him. When Aunt Louise would through parties at her house, she would let Vance drink beer and sometimes let him taste liquor. As Vance grew in age, he began to make drinks for his mom, dad and for himself. Vance did not do well in school and thus became a dropout in his early teens. This led him to a life of crime and association with bad company. He began to sell drugs and partake of them. Vance managed to get arrested on many occasions. It was quietly told that Vance had raped his mom while she slept. Aunt Louise would always bail him out of trouble. However, she was never there to aid and assist Gwen. She had this special attachment to her sons. Vance was rebellious and the family hated to see him coming. He had no positive role models to help him sort through his issues. His father, although in the picture, just dismissed his behavior and buried his head in the sand. There were few male role models in our family for the young boys in our family to look-up too.

I remember one day Vance calling my Aunt Louise from a phone booth to get money from her. Evidently, he owed some people on the streets money or they were going to kill him. Aunt Louise bailed him out. Can you imagine her guilt? She had already buried two children and an unborn grandchild. Every time she bailed him out of trouble, the more trouble he got into. Then finally, he was tragically gunned down on the street and Aunt Louise now has to bury child number three.

Something To Think About!

Discussion: What do you think could have prevented Vance from a life of destruction?

Is there some learned or generational behavior connection between the death of this family (mom and children)?

What type of background do you think Vance's father came from?

What lessons can we learn from these horrible experiences?

"DATING AND MARRIAGE"

I have learned from my many failed relationships (some which included domestic violence), that it is very important for individuals to take time to enjoy the atmosphere of dating. My grandmother calls it courting. This is when you get to learn about a person. What they like or dislike. What their family is like. Are they responsible with their finances? Are they able to hold down a job? What is their credit like? How do they react under pressure? What are they like in a public setting? How do they react in a social setting or around your friends? It's a lot of questions, but ones that need to be addressed to our children and adults who are ready to start new relationships (divorce or widowhood). Personally, I recommend that the dating process take at least one year or more. It is important that you not only love that individual and not be drawn by the lust (the physical attraction leading to sex), but find out where they want to go in life (dreams). If they don't have any, this could be a good indication that the relationship could be in trouble later down the road. The two should respect one another for their differences and should build up and encourage each other. Consider how you might feel about your partner when the sex department runs dry. A relationship should be built on more than sex. It's important, but not a priority. Then, what would be the glue or foundation to hold that relationship together. Trust me the lust and sex will wear off real soon. Let's recap from Chapter 1 in the "Promiscuity" section of my dating experience and how my shortcomings impacted me as I married at a young age.

"The Dating"

Previously in Chapter 1, I shared with you how I was frisky with the boys at the clubhouse and how I dated a few in high school. I allowed them to kiss me and even touch me in areas where they shouldn't have. I told you that I got pregnant at age sixteen. This caused many frustrations for me with trying to be a mom and trying to get through high school. Because of my lack of knowledge in so many areas in my life both childhood and teenage years, unknowingly I may have been a contributing factor in Chucky's suicide. Please don't let this lack of knowledge happen to you. This is why this book is available. If someone really loves you, they will wait until you are ready and not pressure you into sex. They will take time to know you and respect you for whom you are. While dating there are some things that you should be aware of. Remember, dating should be enjoyable and a time of learning.

Warning Signs While Dating:

- Do you feel nervous around him or her?

- Do you have to be careful to control your behavior to avoid his or her anger?

- Do you feel pressured by him or her when it comes to sex (**See Sex and Trust Page**)?

- Are you scared of disagreeing with him or her?

- Does he or she criticize you, or humiliate you in front of other people?

- Does he or she always check up or question you about what you do without him or her?

- Does he or she repeatedly and wrongly accuse you of seeing other guys or gals?

- Does he or she tell you that if <u>YOU</u> changed that he or she would not abuse you?

- Does his or her jealousy stop you from seeing friends and family?

- Does he or she make you feel like you are wrong, stupid, crazy, or inadequate?

- Has he or she ever scared you with violence or threatening behavior?

- Do you often do things to please him or her, rather than to please yourself?

- Does he or she prevent you from going out or doing things you want to do?

- Do you feel that, with him or her nothing you do is ever good enough?

- Does he or she say that they will kill or hurt themselves if you break up with them?

- Does he or she make excuses for their abusive behavior by saying it is the alcohol or drugs or because he or she can not control their temper, or that he or she was just joking?

- Does he or she often blame you for what goes wrong?

Something To Talk About !

Discussion: List the questions that may apply to you or someone you know.

1.
2.
3.
4.
5.
6.
7.
8.
9.
10.

If you wrote down three or more, your relationship could be in trouble.

"The Marriage"

When people say that they are going to get married, the first thing I normally ask is, "Are you sure." I ask this because marriage means commitment, denying yourself for your spouse, giving up control of your finances and your freedom to come and go as you please. That sounds like a lot of work. Guess what, it is? Marriage is two people walking in agreement. That is more work. If during the dating process you do not take ample time to learn about each other, you will be faced with many obstacles in the relationship that you were not prepared for. Here is a short list of some warning signs in a problem marriage. I wish someone had shared these warning signs with me. Maybe, I would not have had a failed marriage and numerous relationships. This list was presented in a bible study class that I attended. It was refreshing to see prevention being taught rather than intervention after something has gone wrong. You may want to highlight these and bookmark this page for future reference.

Warning Signs in a Potential or Failed Marriage

- The couple meets or married shortly after a significant loss (divorce, death, dating, etc.).

- The couple meets and marries in less than six months.

- The couple wishes to distance from one's family of origin.

- The couple has family backgrounds which are different (religion, education, social class, ethnicity, age).

- The couple comes from incompatible sibling constellations (both are babies of the family).

- The couple resides either extremely close to or a great distance from either family of origin.

- The couple marries before age 20.

- The couple marries after a relationship of less than six months or after more than three years of engagement.

- The couple's wedding occurs without family or friends present.

- The wife becomes pregnant before marriage or within the first year of marriage.

- The couple may have a poor relationship with siblings or parents.

- The couple may consider his or her childhood or adolescence an unhappy time.

- The couple's marital patterns in either extended family were unstable.

- The couple can not come to an agreement about raising the children or finances.

I must pause here ---- and say that from the above list, eight of these items applied to me. How many apply to you or someone you know? All of these pressures can fan the flame for domestic violence. Both individuals are bringing heavy baggage into the relationship neither expected. During the dating process (which is crucial), you can learn about their baggage and begin to unload it at the check-in counter before considering marriage. When baggage becomes too heavy for one of the individuals to carry, they will begin to act out that frustration in the form of abuse (verbal or physical). Come and journey with me as I share my experience of getting married before the age of 20 (#7 on the above list). It was a very frustrating marriage. I had no one to pattern what a good marriage should be like. Once again, we were not Ward and June Cleaver. Remember that our environment has a major role in whom and what we become in life. I felt like a mouse in a maze trying to find my way to the cheese (happy marriage). It would have been helpful to have the book, Who Moved My Cheese" available to me.

Something To Think About !

Discussion: How many on the list applied to you or someone you know?

Write them down.

1.
2.
3.
4.
5.

What do you think are the ingredients for a successful marriage?

1.
2.
3.
4.
5.

"My Marriage Experience"

After dating my boyfriend at age 15, getting pregnant at age 16, age 19, I got engaged and married Chucky's dad (strike one). I felt like I was somebody special. I got a diamond engagement ring and on June 30, 1979, I walked the aisle of St. Abraham Baptist Church where Chucky was the ring bearer. I was enjoying the married life because I could have sex as often as I wanted. We had our own apartment and my husband was teaching me how to cook. I didn't learn many culinary skills at home. I enjoyed being a so-called loving wife and loved being with our son. We were a family unit father, mother and child, something I never had. We both worked and did okay in the area of our finances. With all of that, I still felt a sense of loss. I could not put my hands on it. I felt empty inside. There had to be more to marriage than sex, working, cooking, cleaning and sleeping. I was only nineteen. My friends were out having fun and partying. I was home learning how to be the submissive wife, loving, mother, housekeeper and cook like the bible and the preacher said. Was I having fun? No! The best part of the marriage was spending time with our son at home, in the park or other recreational activities. During the course of the marriage my husband and I had our share of disagreements. We had some screaming battles and at times a few domestic violence (physical) episodes. Once again, I didn't know what to do. I had no role models to show me what a good stable marriage should be. My mom didn't leave me a good blueprint. My husband, at times, liked to hangout with his friends. He was five years older and I didn't like being left behind. However, I was determined in my heart that the marriage was going to work. Most of the women in my family had children by different men and plenty of failed relationships. The youngest child was born to a relative under the age 14. However, the women in our family were taught to be strong and provide for our children. In essence, we were in the single female head-of-household category (Chapter 1). I nagged and complained to my husband blaming him for not making me happy. Now, I realize that it was my own responsibility to make myself happy. Caution – never marry someone because you are lonely. You may just find out that once you are married, you will still be lonely. However, family was and still is very important to me. My husband and I were very excited about our little family. One very important element that I regretted during that marriage was not getting good marital counseling. Eventually, we ran into financial problems, sex problems and the list grew and our building blocks got stacked higher and higher. There was a communication break down, which led to other breakdowns, which led to divorce early on in the marriage. Had we taken the opportunity to grow together in mind and spirit first – lust may not have been a factor in our decision to have sex and marry early. Some twenty something years later, we are best friends with a great love and respect for one another. The most positive thing gained from our marriage was our sons and our ability to stand strong in the midst of our storms as parents, especially losing Chucky.

"HERE COMES THE KIDS: THE PRESSURES ON"

On July 7, 1981, another bundle of joy was added to our marriage before the divorce (another building block). Our second son, Kevin was born. This was every man's dream to have sons. Kevin brought great joy into our lives. He and his brother Chucky were very close from babies until the day Chucky died. As parents, we tried to give our sons the basic necessities of life (love, shelter, food, clothing, toys and vacations). While I am sitting here writing this section, it has occurred to me that there is a five-year age difference with our sons just like their father and I. Is this a coincidence? I divorced when Kevin was five years old. Wow! The divorce was a difficult process for Chucky to understand. He could not understand why his dad and I could not live together, yet he saw us communicating without arguing. The divorce affected his self-esteem, grades and at times withdrawn. What pressure for childhood to endure? This added tremendous pressure as his father and I tried to give the kids more love, more time and basic needs from separate homes and we consulted on issues regarding them. We purposed to walk in agreement. Their father was very involved and active in their lives. There was a time when Chucky was in middle school, while in his bedroom, he tried to slit his wrist from the pressure of the divorce and other unknown issues. We went to counseling, but he refused to talk about his feelings. Can you imagine the pressure he was feeling? Chucky's experiences of trying to understand what was happening around him made him confused and caused him great emotional pain. During his time here on earth, Chucky gave lots of love to many, but forgot love himself. While being a single female head-of-household, I found it difficult trying to juggle work, school, sports and other activities that the kids were involved in. But, I was determined to have the kids exposed to things that would give them good choices in life even if it meant having added pressure on me. Maybe I thought this would make-up for their dad being absent from the home.

Parents tend to think that the decisions they make or the things they do in the presence of their children don't matter. Well, it does. It's no longer about you. What about our children and who will protect and guide them because of our bad decisions and choices? I am glad you asked. That's your job as parents. I learned from my own personal childhood that a lack of love and guidance could push children into a state of sometimes no return (sex, drugs, crime and suicide). Chucky harbored resentment towards his father for not being in the home, especially when his father started dating. These symptoms interfered with his health causing him to have high blood pressure at age 15. And later, he was diagnosed with a heart murmur (was it a broken heart?). As parents, we tried our best to reach him, but he would not let us into his private world where he felt safe from pain and pressure. So often I remind parents that as much as we would like for our kids to talk to us about anything and everything, it may not happen. As parents, we saw Chucky smiling on the outside, giving to others and mentally dying on the inside. But, the wall was built and he would not let anyone in.

In June of 1999, Kevin graduated from high school and we celebrated with a big family cookout with both sides of the family and friends. During the celebration, Chucky was not being the gracious host that he always was during family gatherings. It was as though he was saying goodbye to everyone. I thought it strange and confronted him about his behavior. He said that he was just tired from all the preparation of Kevin's party and that he was okay. Yet, I sensed that there was a much deeper problem. Of course, I didn't believe him nor did I press the issue and continued to mingle. And, on Father's Day 1999, two weeks after the cookout and Chucky's final good-byes to family and friends, he committed suicide. He set himself on fire. This was painful not only for his parents, but for Kevin, because he was entering his first year of college. He now had to adjust to college and the death of his big brother and best friend. This was a tremendous amount of added pressure to everyone who knew and loved him. But, through it all, Kevin's, father and I have stood by each other in love and support until this day.

Earlier I stated that as parents what we say and do in front of our children is very important. Those visions of what they remember are played over and over in their minds like a hit song. Chucky's pain caused us great pain as we watched him lie on his hospital bed with 80% to 90% of his body with second and third degree burns. As we watched our loved one lying there wrapped in white bandages from head to toe, a piece of his dad, Kevin and I slipped away daily just as Chucky did. With his arms and feet stretched wide on the bed, he reminded me of a snow angel. So, whenever I entered the room, although he was on life support, that's how I would acknowledge him, "Hey, Chucky, mommy's snow angel." When I think about the marriage, divorce and the pressure that our kids felt, it brings tears to my eyes. During Chucky's hospitalization, one afternoon the three grandmothers and I decided to take a couple of hours break from visitation, I prepared a delicious seafood lunch and while cleaning up the dishes, the telephone rang and we all looked at each other. It was as if we knew the time of Chucky's departure had come. Chucky's father told us that we needed to come now to the hospital. By the time we had arrived, our beloved son, brother and my snow angel was at peace. He had taken his rest. Whatever pressure he felt was now gone.

Kevin is doing exceptionally well. He has gotten to the place in his life where he can talk about his brother and smile and laugh of the joy they shared as brothers. He graduated from Johns Hopkins University in May of 2003. He lives a very full and productive life that includes football, mentoring, fun and a strong spiritual life. As a family, we've turned Chucky's death into a quest to reach out and touch other lives. Although in the beginning the pressure was on with the kids, right now, **ALL IS WELL.**

Something to Think About!

Discussion: From this story, can you pick out any warning signs that could have helped his parents prevent his suicide?

Did the divorce and being a single female head-of-household or absentee dad contribute to Chucky's death?

Do you think that the pressure was on this family? Explain?

Let's journey into another part of my life. Be patient. I am laying the foundation for how all these turn of events can lead to Domestic Violence!

"The Weekend Before"

When I was married, the neighborhood my husband and I lived in was pretty safe, so I thought. The pressure was truly on. We had a break-in one night as my husband slept on the sofa in the living room. The boys and I were asleep in our separate bedrooms. The burglar came into my bedroom. I yelled out and my husband at the time jumped off the sofa. I screamed that a burglar was in the house. The burglar escaped. Needless to say, I was petrified for the safety of our children. You talk about pressure, now I had to add this to the other issues we had going on in our marriage. You never know how a sequence of events will impact your life – the kids – my household.

It was Sunday evening. My sons and I had just come home from an evening program at church. My husband greeted us. He informed me that he was going out to meet one of his friends that lived around the corner. I had asked him to stay home with us since we had a break-in the week before. He assured me that he would not be long and off he went. It was getting late and I began to prepare the boys for bed and prepare for the week. Frightened of being alone, I thought that this would be a somewhat normal routine night. I checked the house to make sure that all was secure. That Monday, we were going to have bars placed on the windows as an added security measure. The windows and doors looked normal and secured, so I thought. My sons and I said our prayers together and good night we went.

About 11:50 p.m., I was awakened from my sleep in a daze. I could feel a warm fuzziness over me. I thought it was our cat Max. Half asleep, I asked Max to get off the bed. When I looked up there he was the intruder, the rapist. The rapist asked me to get up out of the bed. I told him no because my children were in their rooms sleeping. He began to call me horrible names with a knife to my throat. At this point all I could do was pray. I began to pray Psalm 23 from the bible aloud. The rapist told me to shut-up. So, I began to pray silently. It was apparent that he had been in our home for a while. My sons had separate bedrooms and Kevin, the youngest, was now down the hall in the bedroom of Chucky. I was grateful that they were hard sleepers.

The rapist took me into Kevin's bedroom and began to rape me. I remember praying to God and the rapist telling me to shut-up again. I told him that he could do what he wanted to me, but not to hurt my sons. He told me to shut-up b_ _ _ _. I continued to pray to God to send His angels <u>NOW</u> and protect my children from hurt, harm and danger. God did what I requested. He put a hedge of protection around them and they never awakened. As the rape was taking place, I was not afraid. I guess I was in shock. He continued raping me and I continued to pray silently. My body was numb; however, my spirit was connected with God. It was as though God was saying to me, "Cheryle, fear not for I am with you". At that point it was like my spirit has separated from my body and I was looking down on what was happening to me. Medical books have said that this is sometimes how the body responds to trauma. When the rapist finished with me, he told me not to call the police. He told me that if I did that he would come back and kill my children and me. I was petrified because here I was again under more pressure. Well, the police was called. The policemen had to break the window to get in because I was in shock and couldn't move. I could hear them calling my name, but I couldn't answer. I remember the ambulance attendants talking to me and giving me oxygen. My husband had come back home just about the time the ambulance attendants had arrived and were treating my injuries. This was difficult for him to handle. As a man, husband and father, he felt like he had let his family down.

When I arrived at the emergency room I felt needles penetrating my butt and thighs. I was getting antibiotics to help prevent me from any sexual transmitted diseases. The medical team was snipping hair from my head and pubic area for evidence. I began to hyperventilate and was given more oxygen. I had received stitches in several fingers that had been cut. My mother told me that I must have been struggling with the rapist and got cut with the knife he was holding me under his power and control. I had strangulation marks on my neck and he had inserted a knife into my vagina with caused major trauma internally. I'm not sure if this was when my body and spirit got separated. Again, I don't remember. I know that God was looking after me. Sometimes being numb and fearful has its advantages when going through this kind of trauma. You don't get to feel pain. Through that experience, I had to learn how to forgive my husband for leaving that night. I thought that if he had stayed, none of this would have ever happened. The kids never knew what happened that night until much later. Today, forgiveness has taken place. He is remarried and we have a wonderful friendship.

As we close out this chapter, "The Cycle Begins", I wanted you to see how Generational Behavior, Dating and Marriage, Here Comes the Kids: The Pressures On, can greatly influence how a man or woman can end up in the domestic abuse cycle. The behavior that we observe as children can greatly impact the types of boys, girls, men and women that we attract into our lives. We need to be careful, cautious and conscience about how we tell our kids to "Do as I say and not as I do". As parents we are suppose to be instructors. Our children are not our buddies. They are a gift on loan from God. We are just managers over their lives. We should be in control of them and not the other way around. Unfortunately, the generation of kids today will not accept this double standard like we did with our parents and grandparents before us. If you are a two-parent household, the children that are entrusted to you need your nurturing, wisdom and knowledge on what to expect as they go through the different stages of life. You don't want your daughter or son to be a product of rape.

Although the principles of domestic violence would not have prevented my rape, it did lead me into a life of promiscuity. For this reason, I attracted the wrong type of men into my life. In marriage, the couple will, for the most part, run their household based on the household they were raised. Marriage can be fun and beautiful if the couple takes the time to be friends first. It is so important that if you are contemplating marriage, that you don't let people rush you into it. Just because your mom wants grandchildren like yesterday, don't do it. This is a decision of you and your partner. Take all the time you need. Don't allow yourself to fall into the "Warning Signs of a Failed Marriage" that was discussed earlier in this chapter. Take time to talk about whether you want children and how you plan to raise them (family values). Enjoy the honeymoon and the honeymoon marriage. When children come on the scene, your life will be no longer your own. They will depend on you to lead and guide them. As they grow, they need tender loving care and at times, some tough love. If you are not sure about parenting skills, take classes, read books, seek out persons who have been successful in raising their children. This will be a valuable resource tool, one that someday your children will pass on to their children. The objective and goal is to break the cycle of abuse. Don't let your children have to contemplate suicide or even commit suicide like Chucky. Pressure is heaviness and a weight that will leave you confused, unstable and enviably you will make bad decisions. As you have read about my rape, it was a violation of my space and privacy. This was something that I know was not my fault. What gives a person the right to take your body without permission? This happens in domestic violence as well (marital rape). However, over the years, I have learned with the help of God that I can determine the outcome of my life by setting goals and boundaries. Had my husband and I known how to truly love one another as friends first and not lust, our marriage would have been easier and we would not have encountered the many pitfalls and tragedies. If we do not get a good foundation at an early start in life (childhood), we will grow up being angry boys, girls, men and women. If we don't understand the cycle of abuse, we will begin to operate in anger wanting power and control over others when we can't control ourselves and the ABUSE now begins.

Something To Think About!

Discussion: Take the time to digest all the stories and see whether or not there are signs of learned or generational behavior and whether the two sisters (my mom and Aunt Louise) both single female head-of-household moms, contributed to these tragedies and the death of their children.

Discuss how the cycle affected Chucky, Kevin, Tony, Vance, Michael and Gwen's life and ways you think these events could have been prevented.

What about the relationship between Cheryle, Chucky and dad? Was there pressure in that relationship? Name some of them.

Was this a contributing factor in his suicide?

How would you have handled the rape that Cheryle endured?

Let's Get Started – The Foundation has been laid!

CHAPTER 3

"THE ABUSE: POWER AND CONTROL"

"Man was not created to dominate humans – Man was created just to dominate the things in the earth."
Genesis 1:26
Dr. Myles Munroe

Over the last few years we have seen power and control at work. First, we saw the September 11th bombing of the World Trade Center. Then, there was a major shift in the economy – a recession. Individuals who had good paying jobs and benefits found themselves in the unemployment office and applying for help through social programs (food stamps and medical assistance). Then, there was the War on Iraq. Thousands of people from both sides of this war lost their homes and loved ones. Then there was the falling down of the giants in Corporate America (Enron, Martha Stewart and many others). Even in the White House, in the General Assembly room, the politicians that we have elected into office sit at their respective stations supposedly representing the people, only to find out that many are representing themselves. They are enjoying the power and control that we the people have given them. These political leaders cast their legislative votes on high-tech laptop computers. Yet, our children are expected to keep up with technology on antiquated computers and outdated textbooks. These are the politicians that we have given power and control to spend our tax dollars wisely. But, instead our teachers are under-paid; classrooms are overcrowded and there is a shortage of textbooks, supplies and meal programs for our children. What's wrong with that picture? I think that the Rev. Al Sharpton, Pastor and Political Activist said it best during a television forum. He said, "Politicians have asked their voters to come and go to them to the prom (Vote them in The Whitehouse), only to get to them to the dance and the politicians leave them on the dance floor." Government has cut numerous social funding programs like Boys and Girls Clubs and Domestic Violence programs. So even in the White House, Power and Control rules us.

    It is unfortunate that society has in so many ways failed us on how we should have relationships with one another and other countries. Depending on what side of the coin you are born on, society teaches in a subtle way that in order to be established or feel important you must have power and control no matter what the cost. As much as we want to think we are in control, the government let's us know that is not about "We the people." Consider this, you work for a living trying to provide for your household, but the government tells you how much money you will give them from your paycheck without your permission. To take it one step further, they even control how much money you will get back at the end of the year, if any from your income taxes. Governments officials ask voters to elect them into office, for the voters to find out they are not representing them at all. Look at how terrible the healthcare plan has affected our elderly. If the politician didn't take a raise for the next four years, then maybe our elderly would not have to choose every month between buying medicine and going hungry. Voters are being sucked in and controlled by those they trust to do the right thing. As my friend and mentor Dean Young says, "Most people aren't interested in doing what's right, but looking right." I contend, however, that this behavior has helped to perpetuate the outbreak of domestic violence abuse in this country. This teaching, I believe, gives some government officials the right to stomp on, walk on, under-mind and take from the hand that feeds them only to throw voters the scraps while they are living in there big mansion and eating $500 meals. It's about power and control. Think about this scenario? The people of California decided they wanted a change in government and elected a celebrity for governor. Why? Officials who had previously been voted into office had not represented people. Maybe the voters felt that these previous elected officials were amateurs. And, since they were just amateur's in their political roles, the people decided they wanted change and they hired a professional to do the job. They felt they needed to shift their former power and control and elected Schwarzenegger as their new leader.

As a child I could remember my grandmother praying to God to keep her in her right mind. I thought that meant that if she didn't ask God to help her that she would run around like a crazy woman and talk out of her head like what I had seen on television. Now that I am an adult, I better understand what that prayer meant. My grandmother was asking God to give her His mind and thoughts through reading the bible. She wanted to have love and compassion for all people. She did not want to be controlled by the cruel and disrespectful demands of others. This is what the batterer does to their victims. They demean them until the thoughts of the batterer are the thoughts of the victim. It is during this brainwashing process that warning signs, flashing lights and light bulbs are frequently ignored. Some call this intuition. These warning signs are good indicators that the batterer enjoys the control and power of manipulating their victim like a puppet on a string. In the world of domestic violence **Power and Control** comes in various forms:

- Use of coercion and threats
- Use of economics
- Use of intimidation
- Use of male or female privilege
- Using the children
- Use of emotional abuse
- Using isolation
- Minimizes, Denies, and Blames

Let's look at what happens during these various forms of Power and Control during the abuse.

- *Use of Coercion and threats.* Making or carrying out threats to do something to hurt him or her. They threaten to leave their partner, to commit suicide, to report their partner to social services if children are involved. Or, making their partner drop legal charges and do illegal criminal acts.

- *Use of Economics.* Preventing him or her from getting or keeping a job. Manages him or her by giving them an allowance. Takes his or her money. Not allowing him or her to know about or have access to the family income. The apartment or house is in one partner's name. No access to banking information. The partner has forged your signature on financial documents. The partner manages all the bills. The partner has to ask for money, which is humiliating and degrading, which the person who has the power and control loves.

- *Use of Intimidation.* Making him or her afraid by using looks, actions, and gestures, smashing things, destroying his or her property, abusing and displaying weapons.

- *Using male and female privilege.* Using him or her like a servant. He or she makes all the big decisions. Acts like the "king or queen of the castle"; this is okay if both individuals are being treated like royalty. Always being the one who identifies the man or woman's role.

- *Using the Children.* Making him or her feel guilty about the children. When possible, uses the children to relay messages. Uses visitation to harass him or her. The major power and control is threatening to take the children away and can be devastating. The custodial parent will bow down and worship the abuser just to protect the children. (See Resource Section – **Children**)

- *Use of Emotional Abuse.* Putting him or her down. Making him or her feel bad about himself or herself. Calling of names. Makes him or her think that they are crazy. They play mind games. They humiliate him or her and make him or her feel guilty.

- *Use of Isolation.* Controlling what he or she does, who he or she sees and talks to. They monitor what him or her reads, where he or she goes. They limit his or her outside involvement. They use jealousy or I'm deeply concerned about you to justify their actions.

- *Minimizes, Denies, and Blames.* Makes light of the abuse and not taking his or her concerns about it seriously. Denies that the abuse happened. Shifts the responsibility for the abusive behavior by saying that the victim caused it.

All of these ploys, plots and tactics are strategies for the batterer to gain control and power over their victim. For example, the batterer becomes angry or creates a scene at a restaurant because the victim did not order what the batterer wanted them to order. Or, the victim wears clothing that the batterer doesn't like so, they change their clothes to please them. Defiance from the victim can quickly turn into rage and anger from the batterer and can lead to physical abuse behind close doors or in public. This was mentioned in the chapter entitled, "My Story." First, the victim gets a slight push. Then they get a slight slap. Next, the victim gets beaten with a fist or an object. Frustration comes when the batterer can't gain power and control over their victim and the violence escalates.

There are many basic principles in the bible that help men and women deal with anger and emotions. Proverbs 23:7 says, "For as a man thinketh in his heart, so is he." Does the batterer purpose in their hearts to abuse? Is the objective of the batterer to get the victim to believe in their heart that what they say is the gospel truth and that nothing else matters? In the previous chapters and reported studies by others, we have slowly been putting the pieces of the puzzle together to see, for the most part, if domestic violence is learned behavior. Who really is the victim? Like a good play, there are many characters that make the scenes of domestic violence powerful. In this box office hit, the characters include victim, batterer, children, family members, friends, pastors and strangers. Together, we will look at why men and women batter and how society may treat the male batterer different from the female batterer. What drives them to anger, rage, hatred, power and control? These behaviors can have a significant impact on future relationships of both victim and batterer. The scars that are inflicted and embedded emotionally in these individuals can torment them for a long time unless they get professional treatment, positive nurturing, guidance and support. If this doesn't happen, I'm afraid that their healing and breaking the cycle of domestic violence may never happen. These individuals, however, **<u>MUST WANT</u>** to be set free from the cycle of abuse. The old saying goes, "You can lead a horse to the water, but you can't make them drink".

"THE WARNING SIGNS"

Imagine yourself driving along the busy streets of New York City. If you're not familiar with the city traffic patterns, many catastrophic things could happen to you.

- You could become involved in an accident.

- You could cause a major traffic jam or accident.

- If you're trying to cross the street, you could get hit by a car or truck and die depending on the impact.

This is why New York has numerous traffic lights, signs and people to direct the traffic. The lights and signs are there for a reason. You wouldn't cross the street during a green light or a do not walk sign. Traffic lights were put into motion to prevent accidents. **Green** light means go. A **yellow** light means caution. A **red** light means stop. As humans, we were designed with a built-in traffic light, sensors and instinct to alert us of danger. In domestic violence there are warning signs that are wonderful indicators that you may be in danger. Too often, however, we ignore the signs because we are in love, in lust, caught up in the moment or in denial hoping that things will get better in that relationship. For the most part, it doesn't get better. Unfortunately, because many of us have ignored the warning signs more times than we want to admit, it can sometimes end in death. Listed on the next page is a checklist that might help you recognize the warning signs.

Warning Signs

Place a check mark in all that apply to you or someone you know.

- ☐ Do you feel nervous around him or her?
- ☐ Do you have to be careful to control your behavior to avoid his or her anger?
- ☐ Do you feel pressured by him or her when it comes to sex (See Resource - Sex and Trust Page)?
- ☐ Are you afraid of disagreeing with him or her?
- ☐ Does he or she criticize you or humiliate you in front of other people?
- ☐ Does he or she always check up or question you about what you do without him or her?
- ☐ Does he or she repeatedly and wrongly accuse you of seeing other people?
- ☐ Does he or she tell you that if <u>YOU</u> changed that they would not abuse you?
- ☐ Does his or her jealousies stop you from seeing friends and family?
- ☐ Does he or she make you feel like you are wrong, stupid, crazy, or inadequate?
- ☐ Has he or she ever scared you with violence or threatening behavior?
- ☐ Do you often do things to please him or her, rather than to please yourself?
- ☐ Does he or she prevent you from going out or doing things you want to do?
- ☐ Do you feel that, with him or her nothing you do is ever good enough?
- ☐ Does he or she say that they will kill or hurt themselves if you break up with them?
- ☐ Does he or she make excuses for his abusive behavior by saying it is the alcohol or drugs or because he or she can not control their temper, or that he or she was just joking?

You may be thinking, Cheryle, this is ridiculous. No it's not. In the chapter entitled, "My Story", list the *"Warning Signs"* that you may think I ignored. You have my permission. My life really is an open book (Smile).

Warning Signs Cheryle Ignored

1.
2.
3.
4.
5.
6.

"WHO IS THE VICTIM?"

Webster defines a victim as:

"One that is injured, destroyed, or sacrificial under any or various conditions; one that is subjected to hardship, oppression or mistreatment; one that is tricked or duped".

In domestic violence, ultimately, everyone is a victim:

- **The Victim**
- **The Batterer**
- **The Children**
- **The Family**
- **The Friends**
- **The Society**

The shame and humiliation of being broken down mentally, physically and financially in the cycle of abuse has become a world-wide epidemic. You can talk to individuals in the USA and other countries and no matter what their native language; they probably can tell you that they know at least one person who has been battered. In Chapter 1, we explored how having a "Lack of Love" can lead individuals in a path of destruction, bad habits and death, if proper intervention is not provided. In Chapter 2, we explored how, "The Cycle Begins". When early interventions are not taken to nurture our children at an early age, the habits they may have learned from their family tree (generational) only reaffirms that bad habits not only harm them, but collectively puts our loved ones at great risk from the repercussions of domestic violence. All of these ingredients make for a lousy recipe for life, making all parties concerned, directly or indirectly victims.

When we recognize that someone we love, care about, or know, no matter what the gender, is a victim of domestic violence, we have now invited ourselves into their horrific and terrifying world. You and I become victims when:

1. **We see the abuse and don't address it.**

2. **When we don't educate ourselves to know how to respond to the person in the abusive relationship.**

3. **When we judge the victim for staying in the relationship.**

4. **When we prejudge the batterer for their role in the abuse.**

When we allow ourselves to become a part of the problem by judging and not becoming a part of the solution ---------- we have acquired a victim's mentality. Let's take this victim question one step further. How many times have you picked up the newspaper or seen on the television some man or woman embroiled or dying at the hand of domestic violence? How many innocent children do you know or have read about that have died or have witnessed one of their parents being murdered at the hand of domestic violence?

> *"Man, hostage dead after pursuit. Warfield, Va. – A man kidnapped his ex-wife Monday and fled to Va. From his pickup truck, he was firing at police and other motorists before killing himself. The man kidnaps his ex-wife and two children. The ex-wife had fled from Florida from her batterer because of domestic violence. The batterer eventually releases the children on the side of the road. He proceeds to drive him and his victim to VA. After a long chase he shoots his ex-wife and himself. (Herald-Sun, Durham, NC Sept., 24, 2002)."*

Did you know that most people who are in a domestic violence situation don't know that they are? They call it something else (lover's quarrel or spat). Even more alarming is that pastors and ministries have become victims too. We are hearing more now than ever about Christians who are becoming a batterer or victim. In most faith communities, women are far more likely to be the victim of abuse due to biblical teachings on submission and the Patriarchal Culture that has provided men with social permission to control women and children.

Here are some quotes…

"Scold your wife sharply, bully, terrifies her…then readily beat her. Wives should kiss the rod that beats her."
Rules of Marriage, 15th Century.

In 584 A.D. *43 Bishops and 20 other men representing bishops took a vote to declare if women were human. The result was 32 yeas and 31 nays.*

In June of 1977, Justice Donald Roberts of Franklin County New York said, *"Every woman needs a good pounding now and then."*

In some instance, the Christian batterer justifies his battering by saying such things as, "God told me to beat my wife or husband into submission". Or, because the batterer is knowledgeable of the Word of God, they use this as a smoke screen to keep others from knowing what they are doing behind close doors. Let's stop and look and how the Christian community could consider ministering to the cries of domestic violence from the pews so that the pulpits will not become a victim.

Because some people perish from a lack of knowledge, I contend that some seminaries have not prepared pastors and ministries for the real world that really exists outside the congregational walls. Many ministers preach about bringing in the lost sheep (people) – making the lay members (those already in the church walls) fishers of men-disciples (Matthew 5:18-19). Some pastors may even find it more comfortable to stick their heads in the sand like an ostrich than to confront the issues of domestic violence from their pulpits. Could it be that they themselves are battering in their own homes? There have been many reported cases. When a victim comes to the church and shares with the pastor that they are in a domestic violence crisis, the pastor's first trained instinct is to pray. However, the first question should be, "Are you safe"? Because some church leaders have been taught to, "Take everything to God in prayer," this is essential, but not the #1 priority for domestic violence victims. For victims, the sanctuary is presumed to be a place of safety from the abuse. You remembered in the chapter, "My Story", how I was battered on the church parking lot and no one helped me. Once the victim has divulged their shame and secret, pastors have a compassionate Christian obligation as the **Shepherd** to guard the **Sheep** (the victim). Recognizing that this concept may seem foreign to some, this book is designed to better help individuals understand that church folk are not only in financial crisis and healing crisis on Sunday mornings, but are also in domestic violence crisis. Ministries should begin to familiarize themselves with the resources available in their local area or they can call their local police station for a listing and assistance. Most law enforcement agencies have a specialized domestic violence division.

Once the pastor has gotten the victim and children to safety, it will become vitally important that the batterer (especially if a member of the same church), be held accountable for his or her actions. This process will take place through professional treatment programs mixed with spiritual counseling (prayer included). It should be noted that when pastors and ministers do not hold the batterer accountable, the batterer is ultimately saying to you, "That I don't respect you and I do what I want." So essentially, the batterer has power and control over you – the pastor. At **NO** time during the **accountability** process should pastors and ministers attempt to counsel the couple together. When doing this, you put the victim at greater risk for further abuse since there has not been enough time for the batterer to show signs of improvement. I know that this is tough to digest because you have been trained to hear both sides together (marriage or couple counseling). This process is okay – but not right now. The wounds of the victim and batterer are still fresh. Once you have gotten your victim to safety, make the batterer **accountable**. This process can and should take at least a minimum of six months to a year. Only then should restoration or reconciliation be considered if it is the desire of the victim without pressure from pulpit and pew.

In the bible, Jesus always met people at their point of need **FIRST**, then he disciples them. He began to show them how to live a disciplined life by teaching them biblical principles that could be used in everyday practical situations. Then, those who were healed through those teachings went out and told others about Jesus. When Jesus hand picked and trained the twelve disciples, He didn't just lay hands on them and send them out. Under the contrary, the disciples sat at His feet (got instruction – mentorship) for a significant length of time. I want you to know that I have a great respect for pastors and ministers because of the mandate and call upon their lives to look after the sheep. This task can be challenging and exhausting. This is why I purpose to partner with --- not persecute, to reach out and teach **prevention** so that together we will not have to continue to do **intervention** (put out the fire). Again, this process can begin when ministries educate themselves about domestic violence and its laws. The church is one of the best ways to begin because thousands and millions of people are sitting in the pews all across the country, especially on Sunday mornings. It is during this time of worship, that the teaching of domestic violence could be taught in a series. With the resources available in this book, powerful sermons could be written and preached to children and adults.

God never endorsed violence and neither should we (Psalm 7:9; Ezekiel 45:9). No victim should be encouraged to stay in an abusive relationship and asked to immediately forgive their batterer. Many victims, however, stay in the abusive relationships because of their spiritual commitment to their God. They stay for the better and the worst and take their vows seriously. While this is commendable, it is not wise. If God had intended for individuals to be a punching bag, He would have made them one. However, once the abuse has taken place, the commitment or vows have already been broken and that individual no longer has a marriage. They can pretty much consider themselves "shacking up". If husbands are required to love their wives as Christ loved the church (Ephesians 5:25-29), then verse 28 of that passage would stop the abuse. In verse 28 of that passage of scripture says, "Men should love their wives as their own bodies." This also applies to women who batter their husbands (See Resource Section – **What Churches Can Do**).

Forgiveness is a process and not something that happens overnight. As the batterer attempts to plead their case, they will come with a sob story, tears, falling down at the alter begging for forgiveness, do not be deceived. Abraham tried to deceive King Abimelech by telling him that his wife Sarah was his sister (Genesis 20). Judas betrayed Jesus by portraying that he was with Him (Matthew 10:4). And, the devil tried to deceive Jesus in the Garden of Gethsemane (Matthew 4). But, in the end, Jesus was crucified. This is how some victims may feel. As victims come into the sanctuary, many individuals will smile in their face pretending that they care about the victimization because it's the proper thing to do. It is important that victim and batterer are not made to feel betrayed by the one person they thought they could trust the most – Their Pastor – Their Leader. As ministers, we should **NEVER** encourage victims to stay in the abuse because of their vows. So, why do we punish the victim further?

In his book, "Adam Where Are You"?, Jawanza Kunjufu writes about three kinds of churches. They are the **entertainment church**, the **containment church** and the **liberation church**. Let's take a look at these different churches and see where you are as a ministry on the list. Ultimately, we strive for the last church for this is a church that trains, empowers and compels the people to reach out so that others will not become victims of abuse in the local congregation. We want to be people who were like Joshua in the bible who are not afraid to cross over the Jordan and possess the land (Joshua 3) - eradication of domestic violence.

- *The Entertainment Church* – A church where lots of whooping, hollering, and singing to the exclusion of teaching and working. The church makes you feel good for the moment, but does not address societal issues. The church administrators may have activities during the week, but does not empower the congregation to deal with the issues. In other words, lip service.

- *The Containment Church* – This church is similar to the Entertainment Church except they are only open 11am to 1pm on Sunday. Closed during the remainder of the week.

- *The Liberation Church* – This church is defined as a church in which Nat Turner, Harriet Tubman, Denmark Vesey, Sojourner Truth, Marcus Garvey and others were members. This church understands the liberation as described in Luke 4:18-19, Isaiah 58; James 2:26. Liberation churches normally have about 25% youth and 25% male. Young people and men respond better to the liberation theology.

Finally, as we close out this section entitled, "Who is the Victim", and I hope that you have gained a clearer picture of how your role in stopping abuse is vitally important. Just because you're not the one getting your head bashed up against the wall or being emotionally abused daily, does not excuse you from helping. Once again, educating yourself on, **"What to Say to Someone in an Abusive Relationship"** (Resource Section) can make a tremendous impact on the victim's life and maybe yours. As previously mentioned, our government has played a role in helping victimize those in abusive relationships by cutting out training programs and grant money. These funds could be used to provide long-term educational training to help break the cycle of abuse for both victim and batterer. I encourage you through this book not to be a victim whether family, friend, pastor or ministry, but a victor. Let's move on to the next section and tap into some of the batterers angry outbursts.

Let's Get Started!

"ANGRY OUTBURSTS"

Have you ever had someone angry with you? That person was screaming and yelling from the top of their lungs. They were like a balloon ready to burst because it had too much air. The primary reason a person displays angry outbursts is so that they can get what they want from you. We have seen this form of behavior too often in toddler's and young children as they have temper tantrums in the grocery store or the mall. During the wait in the grocery store check-out aisle, Little Johnny or Little Susie wants candy from the display as they sit in the shopping cart. As they continue to reach, whine, cry, hit and bite for candy, mom or dad says no. But, Little Johnny's or Little Susie's theatrical display continues until the parent gives in and Little Johnny or Little Susie get what they wanted -- the candy. Unknowingly, the parent is rewarding the child for bad behavior. Now, that one or two year old has just exhibited power and control over their parents. Remember that domestic violence is learned.

When our requests don't get the results we want from our partner, when our demands don't produce the results that we hoped for and our blatant disrespect does not work, our flesh rises and does yet another hideous or stupid thing. The ugly anger outburst magically appears. Because we can't get what we want (power and control) through anger, we tend to blame the other person for the anger. They will make a comment like, "If you would just do what I tell you (not ask), then I wouldn't get angry." Or, "He or she nags all the time", the angry outburst is now full blown and the individual displaying the anger in hopes of making their partner think twice about making him or her unhappy or angry again. Because the mind of the batterer is distorted, twisted and confused, they do not realize that their happiness is not based on how someone makes them feel, but that happiness begins with them.

So often we think that by controlling others, it serves as a wall to protect us from others hurting us. This form of display might offer some temporary solution to the problem, but doesn't fix the problem (Band-Aid). So, our defense mechanism kicks in and now we are programmed to hurt, destroy, or kill the troublemaker. How ironic it is that the person we have vowed to love and protect is the one individual that pushes us into angry outbursts. When we become angry with our partner, we not only threaten their safety and security, but our own as well. We may not realize it, but the fear that we have placed within our partner because of our angry outbursts can push them to protect themselves by killing. Punishing our partner by showing angry outbursts doesn't solve the problem. The individual displaying the angry outburst doesn't realize that in the end they have nothing to gain by getting angry. During this tit for tat, the cycle never ends. They may find themselves feeling like a merry-go-round. When angry outbursts are in motion, they don't care about the other person. Once again, it is the "All about me" mentality (power and control).

Each one of us carries an arsenal of weapons (anger, love and hate). When we are angry and think that someone deserves to be punished, we unlock our vault, which contains our weapons and we select the appropriate weapon for the appropriate situation, in this case ANGER. Sometimes the weapons are emotional abuse (verbal – ridicule- sarcasm). Sometimes they are plots to cause suffering and as in the case of domestic violence, physical abuse. No matter what anger weapon is in motion, they are all designed to hurt the partner. The more dangerous the weapon, the more important is to for the batterer to control their temper. It is important to understand that when anger wins – love loses.

Let's take a break here and discuss some of these emotions and their causes.

EMOTIONS AND CAUSES EXERCISE

Picture in your mind the time in the last year when you were angry?

1. Describe what provokes your anger?

2. Describe the physical sensation you felt.

3. Describe the thought you had at the time.

Picture in your mind the time in the last year when you were the happiest?

1. Describe what provoked your happiness (job, clothes, house, sex etc.).

2. Describe the physical sensation you felt.

3. Describe the thoughts you had at that time.

There are ways to help keep anger under control. They could count to ten, attend anger management classes, or find someone to talk to. The classes are designed to teach angry people how to control themselves and not others. While 12-week classes are helpful, these individuals need more long-term counseling to help them understand the root of their anger (See Chapter 2 – Generational Behavior). As humans, we have been programmed or conditioned to have instant gratification, fast food, microwaves, deferred payment plans, artificial insemination and quick sex just to name a few. When we can get to the point where we can learn how to have patience and fix the things that are broken within ourselves, then we can effectively deal with our emotions, especially, **Angry Outbursts**. Let's move on to the angry person who is called, "The Batterer."

Let's Get Started !

When you don't know the purpose of a thing, you will ultimately abuse the thing.

Dr. Myles Munroe

"THE BATTERER"

The batterer is like a walking time bomb. On the outside they are smiling giving the appearance that they are under control. They put on this persona that life is good. However, on the inside there's a war brewing. The batterer is always strategically planning and calculating ways they will attack their victim. They are waiting in the wings like a vulture waiting to descend upon their prey (the victim). There are many reasons why they batter. Some of those reasons were addressed in Chapter 1 and 2. Previously, we looked at how it's not good to put Band-Aids on situations that really need to be dug up at the root. There are various primers that ignite the fuse of this walking time bomb that drives them to mentally and physically torture their victim. I will attempt to explore some of these primers in the next section entitled, "Why?"

What if you knew absolutely nothing about the world of domestic violence and the impact it has on the victim, batterer, children and others? To help you visualize what the batterer is capable, of consider this scenario. I will refer to the batterer as a male since this abuse is the most commonly reported.

> *"He walks into the room and the crowd stands in awe of him. You would think that royalty has just arrived. He graciously walks over and greets his many colleagues and friends. They have all gathered at one of the most prestigious political events of the year. This is where anybody who wants to be somebody and somebody who thinks they are all that are under one roof. As he makes his way around the room socializing with his charming smile, suave mannerism and champagne glass in hand, some the guests inquire where his beautiful, petite and lovely wife is at*

tonight. With a soft and convincing smile he replies, "She's not feeling well tonight and sends her apology."

His friends find this somewhat unusual as the couple is always together at every function. What his friends didn't know is that their well-respected friend and colleague is a batterer. He is a wife beater. He left his wife at home not feeling well for another reason. That pathetic reason was she didn't lay out his tuxedo like he told her and she decided not to wear that new dress he bought her for the event. He immediately put on his Dr. Jekyll and Mr. Hyde personality and the beating commenced. As he began to beat her, with every word from his mouth, he expressed his unhappiness about her disobeying his commands. As he continued to thrust himself upon her, the words got louder and harsher. With her soft-spoken voice, she apologizes to him, but this did not satisfy him. He grabs her by the arm and throws her to the floor. He is 6 feet 5 inches and 215 pounds. She is 5 feet 4 inches and 105 pounds. She continues to apologize and a slap comes across her face leaving his handprint deeply embedded. He tells her that he will go to the party alone because she looks a mess and he didn't want to have to explain what she made him do.

So, he gets dressed leaves her lying on the floor balled up in a fetal position. As he exits from the bedroom, she tries to get up and realizes that her arm is broken and she can't call anyone for help. She would have to explain what happened to the people at the local hospital. Her husband, after all, was the CEO there. Although she is use to her husband's temper and mood swings, she always blames it on the stresses of his job. Lately, however, the beatings were getting worse. Her husband is an angry man, a batterer and a product of learned or generational behavior. As she sits in *the sitting room of their $4 million home holding her arm, she asks herself, "Why does he take his stress out of me."*

Something To Think About !

Discussion: What were some things that you picked out about the batterer in this scenario?

Do you think she asked for that beating by deliberately not putting out his tuxedo and wearing the new dress? She knew it would make her husband angry.

What could she have done differently?

Discuss how you think the staff at the local hospital would have responded if she chose to go? Consider if the hospital is trained in handling and if not trained in handling domestic violence cases.

As you can see from this scenario, the batterer is not just some unemployed or low income- individual. They come from all walks of life, all races and religious backgrounds. This is why it is helpful for you to stay focused on the primary objective of the batterer (power and control). Remember, that batterer is good in planting fear, intimidation and always finding ways to be the master of deception and manipulation. The batterer doesn't abuse every victim the same. Some victims are physically abused; verbally abused (threats of violence) and others are emotionally abused. The batterer believes in their mind that they are entitled to control another. Or, they have a fear of lack of control in their own life. They believe that if they can control the situation, they will not be hurt. But, the more they seek to control, the more they hurt themselves. Domestic violence, assaulting and battering is a crime. The legal system is trying hard to enforce stiffer punishment; however, we need to find ways, not the problem, before the legal system gets involved. These punishments vary based on the state in which you live. Some states do not recognize common-law marriages thus, allowing a batterer to walk away with just a slap on the wrist from the court system. Or, because the batterer has planted fear and intimidation in the victim, they may drop the charges and the batterer is free to continue the abuse. Recently in a Durham, North Carolina local newspaper, a woman was arrested for not appearing in court for her domestic violence hearing.

Domestic violence no-shows common

Woman arrested after she fails to come to court

BY JOHN STEVENSON
jstevenson@heraldsun.com; 419-6643

Court officials say two-thirds of domestic violence victims in Durham don't turn out to testify against their spouses or mates, and they almost always escape any consequences.

But one no-show victim, ███ █████, paid the price Tuesday by being arrested and spending about 90 minutes in detention.

The jury in █████' domestic case was chosen Monday, but because she wasn't in court Tuesday to testify against 35-year-old ████████, the jurors had to sit around with nothing to do from 9:30 a.m. to 3 p.m.

Superior Court Judge Abraham Jones then sent deputies to apprehend ██████, who had accused █████ of violating a court protective order by calling and harassing her. The case was on appeal from a District Court conviction.

Once in detention, ██████ was ordered to explain her absence. She told the judge that she had taken her sick child to the doctor, avoiding a contempt-of-court citation and a jail term of up to 30 days or a fine of up to $500, or both.

When you don't know the purpose of a thing, you will ultimately abuse the thing.

Dr. Myles Munroe

For the world of the batterer, it is like their drug. For pregnant women who are in an abusive relationship, the batterer may begin to punch her in the stomach hoping that she will abort the baby as the baby poses a threat. While pregnant, she is focused on the care of the baby growing inside and the batterer becomes jealous. In other words, he is no longer the focus. Also, by punching the stomach area, the batterer can leave bruises that can not be seen by others. Most pregnant women of domestic violence do not get proper prenatal care because the batterer refuses. I remember a young lady in Baltimore who lived in our neighborhood; we will call her "B". "B" had her first son, like me when she was a teenager. Later "B" found the man of her dreams and married. "B" found the man of her dreams and married. "B" found herself in the cycle of abuse just like her mom (learned or generational?). Well, "B" got pregnant again. Like most victims, she thought her marriage would get better by having a baby. During a domestic violence episode, "B" was beaten while pregnant to the point where she had to have her mouth wired. Yes, her husband, the batterer, had broken her jaw in several places. Because of the fear and intimidation by her husband, "B" didn't press charges and did not leave him. You see, she liked her new lifestyle and she didn't want to return to the life of living in the projects and back on welfare. Well, not too long after that beating, she went into labor. When she arrived at the hospital, while trying to be assessed by the medical team, her husband spoke for her. You may be wondering why. Remember that "B" couldn't talk because her mouth was wired. Imagine how she felt having to be in labor and not being able to scream from the pain of giving birth and the abuse.

When we hear that someone is being battered, especially if it is the man doing the battering, we may say things like:

- **The nerve of him or her**

- **He or she must be on drugs or something**

- **He or she must be sick in their mind**

- **If he or she would only get a job**

- **If he or she would just do what I tell them**

- **God told me to beat my wife into submission**

No matter what we hear or say, the batterer has his own way of rationalizing their abusive behavior. He's a batterer who is angry and out of control. As I continue to educate myself about domestic violence, I found out that there are many categories of a batterer. Let's look at the chart to help us understand some of these characteristic and categories.

CHARACTERISTICS OF THE BATTERER

Characteristics	Category One	Category Two	Category Three
History of Violence	No previous violent relationships with men or women	Some previous violent relationships with men or women	All previous relationships with men or women were violent
Premarital Abuse	No premarital abuse	Some premarital abuse	Frequent premarital abuse
Precipitating Factors	External triggers	External/internal triggers	Internal triggers
Frequency of Violence	Isolated violence	Sporadic violence	Chronic systematic violence
Probability of Homicide	Low	Moderate	High
Use of Weapons	No use of weapons	Some use of weapons	Frequent use of weapons
Degree of Remorse	Great remorse	Limited remorse	No remorse
Treatment Prognosis	Good	Guarded	Very Poor

This was fascinating. I though that a batterer was just a batterer. But, in reviewing the chart, I discovered that the higher the category, the more dangerous the batterer. With regards to the chart and my abusive situation, I could put my batterer in categories two and three. I was fortunate to get out because according to this chart, I was in serious trouble.

Unlike registered sex offenders, the batterer normally is not ostracized in their communities, even if the neighbors know that the abuse is occurring. Again, most people think that the only people who get battered are women of low socioeconomic status. This is far from the truth. Batterer's come from all walks of life and from all types of backgrounds. They have various personality profiles and occupations. Some are doctors, lawyers, CEO, preachers, deacons, sanitation workers and cafeteria workers just to name a few. Here is a profile of some general characteristics that fit a batterer:

BATTERER PROFILE

- *A Batterer* objectifies men and women. He or she doesn't respect the man or woman as a group of individuals. Overall, he or she sees the man or woman as property or sexual objects.

- *A Batterer* has low self-esteem and feels powerless and ineffective in the world. He may appear successful, but inside he feels inadequate. This may have come from not being taught responsibility and accountability as a child.

- *A Batterer* externalizes the cause of his or her behavior (ex: using scripture or I'm the captain of this ship mentality). He or she blames his or her violence on circumstances such as stress, his or her partner's behavior, a "bad day," alcohol, Unemployment or other substance abuse factors to numb the pain that is associated with these circumstances which they feel they have no control.

- *A Batterer* may be pleasant and charming between periods of violence and is often seen as a "nice guy or sweet girl" to outsiders.

- *A Batterer* will show some behavioral warning signs. They include extreme jealousy, possessiveness, a bad temper, unpredictability, cruelty to animals and verbally abusive. They have no respect for those in authority whether from the preacher, law enforcement, supervisors or government.

These are just a few characteristics of the batterer to help you understand the complexity and seriousness of what takes place in their private world of battering. Once again, the goal of this book is to help educate and together we can promote prevention instead of intervention. Let's journey a little further to try to understand "Why"?

Let's Get Started!

"Why"

In the introduction of this chapter, I mentioned primers that can precipitate why the batterer victimizes. They include **selfishness, frustration** and **anger**. First, let us look at what a primer is as defined by Webster New College Dictionary:

"One that precipitates a process of event."

Usually *selfishness* is the major primer for why they batterer. It's normally "My way" or "No way at all." In Chapter 2, we discussed how we have seen children in the grocery store performing their temper tantrums to get what they want (candy). This type of behavior we expect from toddlers and some children, but as adults, we tend to adjust ourselves to accept it. But, when this type of behavior is exhibited in adults, we tend to say such remarks as, "Oh well that's just how they are." So, just like the toddler and the child, the adult gets what they want and other adults tend to accept the behavior. The problem with this behavior in adults is that sometimes other adults are afraid to bring this unacceptable behavior to the person who is displaying this selfishness.

Recently, during an emergency consultation with our protégé's Mr. and Mrs. Harris, before Mrs. Harris had arrived, Mr. Young and I had an opportunity to observe a behavior that Mr. Harris had tried to suppress, selfishness. Mr. Harris had previously communicated with Mrs. Harris about getting Little E at church this particular Sunday morning. They both still attend the same church. The arrangements had been set the night or couple of days before. When the time came, Mr. Harris changed the plans moments before the exchange of their son was to happen. Mrs. Harris became furious because she now had to change her plans of an afternoon quiet-time (something she rarely gets). Later, when she arrived at the meeting, we learned that Mr. Harris could have easily eliminated this conflict by simply taking Little E with him to his appointment. But, Mr. Harris decided to put his feelings (selfishness) before spending every opportunity of quality time with his son. What this behavior revealed was that Mr. Harris wanted what he wanted regardless of how his decision affected Little E. Furthermore, his attempt to rebuild trust with Mrs. Harris was yet again being blown out of the water. When talking with other mentors, especially those, who mentor males, they agree that it is much easier to mentor or train a child than a teenager or adult. This is why it is important for the batterer to have good role models or mentors who are good examples to help them understand their identity early, making them accountable and responsible for their behavior. If this does not take place, then that individual will always stay in the mindset of *selfishness* and grow up to become "Little People In Grown-up Clothes."

The next primer is *frustration*. It's amazing how in the cycle of domestic violence, how one thing precipitates another (like the building blocks). Have you ever noticed how selfish people are easily frustrated? People are normally frustrated because they are (trusted) in a world with a partner who expects them to be accountable and responsible. But, most individuals have never been taught these attributes, especially men for they are required to be leaders. For the batterer, however, power and control is their form of wrong or addictive behavior. When this behavior can't be satisfied, they immediately become frustrated. That frustration is activated because they are not getting their needs fulfilled to their satisfaction (selfishness). Or, there is the possibility that they have not been taught how to effectively communicate those frustrations. Their frustration comes alive like a Picasso painting on canvas, vibrant and full of life. During a weekend visit with his parent's mentors, Little E was instructed to go and get a small table from the yard so that he could put his snacks on it. While carrying the table, he fell numerous times as we saw the frustration on his face. As much as we wanted to run to his rescue, Little E successfully carried the table to its destination. How proud we were of him and gave him praise for not giving up. On the other hand, had someone taught these skills earlier to Little E's dad, maybe he could have effectively worked through his frustration in communicating to Mrs. Harris. Let's revisit the emergency meeting with the Harris' and see how dad's frustration came alive like that Picasso painting.

While waiting for Mrs. Harris to arrive to the session, I discussed with Mr. Harris my observations and concerns in some areas in his life that needed his attention and improvement. I relayed to him that lately he had been a man of words and not much action and that this affects his relationship with his son. What concerned me even more, he had never acknowledged or discussed with his mentor or Mrs. Harris his role as a batterer. Without this acknowledgment, his total healing would not take place. He felt that he could sweep that part of his life under the rug just because we love him, embrace him and our continued mentoring support. Mr. Harris became very quiet during this conversation as I watched his countenance change. Because of my own experience with abuse, I recognized that change immediately. I shared with him that his decision at the last minute to change pick-up plans for Little E was selfish. Once, again it was all about what he wanted. I asked him if what he had to do could have included his son. With some hesitation, he replied," Yes."

During our conversation, Mr. Young (mentor) was standing in the background listening and observing. I informed Mr. Harris how important it would be to his healing and growth as a former batterer to take these reoccurring behaviors seriously. Well, in an abrupt tone of voice, he asked me if I was finished talking as he proceeded to stand and walk towards me. As he spoke, I could hear the frustration and need for him to justify his actions. As expected, his Dr. Jekyll and Mr. Hyde surfaced and this confirmed what I had been feeling for months. My grandmother use to say, "What you do in the dark will come to light." What Mr. Harris had tried to keep hidden (smoke and screen mentality) for over a year, had now been revealed (anger and frustration). When Mrs. Harris arrived, we listened to her side of the story and as usual the information was conflicting. In essence, Mr. Harris couldn't communicate properly what he wanted to do about rescheduling with Little E and chose to become abrasive in his communication with Mrs. Harris.

Finally, when he decided that he did not want to address the issue any further with Mrs. Harris, he immediately blocked out any further discussion for an alternative for that day. This could have been attributed to the fact that Mr. Harris was raised in a single female head-of-household where his mom took care of everything and anything that he did not want to tackle. Mr. Harris, at the moment, expected Mrs. Harris to once again fix the situation, as was the custom during their relationship. Thus, Mr. Harris' communication, responsibility and accountability skills were null and void.

These primers, **selfishness** and **frustration** can also lead to the next primer, *anger*. Anger becomes apparent when superficial efforts to walk in the other two primers fail. Have you ever been angry? If so, you could feel the transformation happening, but you couldn't stop it. This is how the batterer reacts when they have lost power and control over their victim. When the batterer observes that they can't intimidate their victim, they tend to become nervous and immediately find a way to control the situation. Not only the batterer, but individuals who do not batter use this tactic to also gain power and control over their situations. Normally, victims can sense when this primer starts to ignite. So, in order to avoid their anger, the victim gives into their demands just like the mom who gives the child the candy to keep it from having a temper tantrum.

Finally, let's see how our emergency meeting with the Mr. Harris' ended and how this ties into the primer of anger. When Mr. Harris' countenance changed as he stood up to me in an attempt to give his excuses, I sensed the anger of "How dare you question me attitude." Because I had triggered some of his hidden emotions, he became angry and became disrespectful to me with body language and tone of voice. At that moment, Mr. Young stepped in as reinforcement and took over the meeting. Later, with tears in his eyes, Mr. Harris apologized for his disrespect towards me and in love I accepted. What this anger confirmed was that this primer can destroy the individual and those around them if not dealt with properly. At that very moment, I too became angry (video clips of my past) and I wanted to knock his head off. So, even the person with the best of intentions can be affected by the anger of the batterer. Sometimes, while attempting to remove some of these primers, this doesn't stop the batterer from committing other acts of violence. Individuals who batter at that very moment may find it satisfying to beat down and gain power and control over their victim. They usually don't suffer any adverse consequences as a result of their behavior.

In closing, let's move onto the next section to see how the primers of *Selfishness, Frustration,* and *Anger* can produce and Angry Man or an Angry Woman who batters.

Let's Get Started !

"The Angry Man"

There are numerous reasons why men are angry and why they take that anger out on their partner in the form of physical abuse. Because they are numerous, we will only have an opportunity to explore a few of them. In Chapter 1, we explored some of these reasons (absent father and single female head-of-household). I have had numerous opportunities to listen and speak with couples, especially the men. The major question that I ask is, "Tell me about your family history" (your parents)? More importantly, I want to know about their childhood. One of the leading reasons why men abuse their partners is because of their anger towards their fathers for being absent from the home or they have witnessed the abuse in their in environment (learned behavior). Or, if raised by a single mom, she may be devoting more of her attention on dating and less attention on the son.

There has been a conspiracy to destroy man since the beginning of time. Whether you believe in God or not, there have been set into motion certain spiritual principles to help man impart goals and dreams not only for himself, but his family. Man was created to lead his household and take dominion over the earth (land, houses, business, etc. Genesis. 1:26-27), not to control mankind. This does not mean that man is to be boss, be dictator, while others in the household not have a voice. Man was created to instruct his household in love, wisdom and understanding. He is to provide for their basic needs first, such as shelter, food, clothing and guidance. Man was created to nurture his wife and to build her up, not tear or knock her down. He was created to help her to be all that she can be. When man focuses on all these things (building an empire and nurturing his family), then he will not have time to inflict harm on his partner, but he will become the best *king* to her (his queen).

The angry man, if he takes a retrospect of his life, will see that his anger could be traced back to his absentee father. When dad is absent from the home (work or death); son's run to mom for instructions or approval. The two-parent household is essential in the process because agreement is important. Sometimes children in these households tend to run to mom when they can't get what they want from dad. However, if mom resents the fact that dad is absent from the home, she will tend to say things like, "Your father is no good" or "Your father is always working and never has time for us." Although mom's advice maybe noble, she can't be a substitute for the positive wisdom of dad. And, if her feelings are ill ones against dad, then her advice to the son may not be good advice and could hurt him further down the road of his life. This is why it is important to have strong male role models to help fill-in the gap (coaches, pastors, teacher, Boys Clubs, etc.). As a single mom of two sons for many years, I understand that boys require a substantial positive male influence to help them develop successfully. In Africa, there are tribal rituals that take place to welcome boys into manhood. This ritual is called, "Rights of Passage." In the Jewish community, this ritual is called a "Barmitzph". Boy's who are fortunate enough to have these manhood rituals, tend to have strong and healthy family values. However, if these manhood opportunities are not available, they will tend to gravitate to the male figure that spends the most time with them. For instance, most everyone is acquainted with Michael Jackson. In a scene in the movie, "The Jackson's", Michael tells his record producer, Barry Gordy that he wishes he were his dad. Barry Gordy asks Michael why and Michael says, "Because you spend time with me." We all pretty much know about the relationship of Michael and his dad from what we have heard or read. The point is, while fathers maybe in the home, sons long to have the affection, approval and attention from their fathers and may look for it elsewhere. Why? The father is absent from the home in spirit and body.

If these affirmations of their boyhood and manhood are not achieved, the news article mentioned earlier about the hostage situation could happen.

> *"Man, hostage dead after pursuit. Warfield, Va. – A man kidnapped his ex-wife Monday and fled to Va. From his pickup truck, he was firing at police and other motorists before killing himself. The man kidnaps his ex-wife and two children. The ex-wife had fled from Florida from her batterer because of domestic violence. The batterer eventually releases the children on the side of the road. He proceeds to drive him and his victim to VA. After a long chase he shoots his ex-wife and commits suicide. (Herald-Sun, Durham, NC Sept. 24, 2002)."*

As mentioned earlier, man was created to nurture and instruct his family in wisdom, knowledge and provision of the basic necessities of life. Unless boys grab a hold of their identity early, it will be hard for them to learn about building character, responsibility and integrity. Boys should learn early that while accomplishing material things in life is important, it is better for them to understand who they are and learn skills on relating to others and work on delayed gratification. In the bible, Mark 3:14, Jesus appointed the twelve disciples. We read earlier that before Jesus sent the twelve out to do the work of the Lord, He spent quality time with them giving instructions on what to expect when they got ready to go out into the world. The word disciple means, "discipline." This same school of thought should be taught to our sons at an early age. Before we send them out into the world to do great and mighty things, we should prepare them for the many highs of lows that could possibly happen, including managing money. We see these pitfalls in our young athletes who choose NBA drafts straight out of high school. They sign million dollar contracts, but have not been taught financial principles to handle the wealth. Or, individuals who win the lottery are normally broke within a few years because no one taught them how to handle the wealth. Father's should first teach their sons how to love and respect their mother's and sister's as training ground for how they should treat their girlfriends and may be wife one day. Father's should tell their sons that women are a precious gift and should be handled as such. However, fathers can't teach what they haven't been taught themselves.

Women should observe how their partners, especially during the dating process, treat their mother, sister and other females (family, friends, workplace, etc.). This will be a good indication of how they will treat you. If dads are out of place in their role, consequently, sons will turn out to be just like their dads and the cycle begins all over again. For example, Little E is now two and a half years old. He mimics everything his father does. If he father puts his hands in his pockets, he does the same thing. If his father takes off his shoes, he takes his shoes off. When Little E comes to spend time with his fathers mentor, Poppa Dean, he does whatever Poppa Dean does. If Poppa Dean is working in his workshop area, Little E has his tools working as well. If Poppa Dean is out working in the garden, Little E has garden tools. See how important the father's role is in influencing the life of their sons (learned behavior). If boys are raised in a single female head-of-household, she may not be able to teach him certain things (changing a tire, oil, cutting the grass, plumbing, etc.). She may tell him not to play with dolls, but she never presented to him other options for him to choose from. So, in many instances she is unable to nurture her son in certain areas.

If the angry man has to struggle with his identity or masculine role, he becomes frustrated. He has not been taught how he is to respond to the issues of life. The angry man seeks to have certain questions answered.

- **Am I a man?**

- **Am I competent?**

- **Do I have any worth beyond my paycheck?**

- **How can I accept my limitations?**

- **Do I have meaning beyond the things I have accomplished (material things, career, etc.)?**

Society thinks that they are helping men when they put on such events as the Million-Man March; Promise Keepers and Annual Men's Conferences. What are our young boys and men to do once they leave all the hype? Who will help mentor them through the principles they have learned at these meetings? Changing the way people think does not happen overnight or at weekend conferences. Men become angry and frustrated trying to figure out how to make it in society. The rules keep changing. Is society set-up to help men fail or succeed? Well, it depends on what side of the coin you flip (heads or tails). Angry men make poor friends, poor husbands, lousy fathers, unhappy co-workers and frustrated church-goers. Angry men need right answers.

Another shortcoming of society in helping to perpetuate the anger in men is teaching them at an early age not to cry. This makes them look weak. If they fall, we say things like, "Boy stand up and shake it off, and that didn't hurt." Blood could be streaming from everywhere. They are also taught to play with rough toys (guns) as a child. We teach them how to play cops and robbers. Unknowingly, by doing this, we are telling them that it is okay to point guns at people and shoot them because the robber is the bad guy. As these early childhood behaviors are being taught, we teach our sons to "Want what they want". So, when he doesn't get his way because he can't buy the toys and gadgets he wants, he displays those angry outbursts. As an adult, when he has more than he needs and it no longer brings him pleasure, he gets angry because it doesn't satisfy him any longer. Boys and men need a positive outlet. They need someone they can talk too. This in no way means that they are weak because they are sharing their feelings. When men are angry, they need someone that they can trust and be accountable to regarding their failures, hurts, temptations and get him focused once again. Men need a target for their anger other than beating on their partner.

Over the last year, Mr. Harris has become very special to me. His biological dad was an absentee dad who was in and out of his life leaving the burden of raising him solely on mom. I have been fortunate enough to watch him grow threw his anger, hurts and disappointment. He has partnered with mentors, Dean Young and I, who are committed to helping young men reach their full potential if they are willing and committed. This has been Mr. Harris' personalized "Rights of Passage"program (a year + and counting). Although Mr. Harris is not presently living with his wife and son, he has been afforded this opportunity to dig up those deeply rooted primers that ignite his anger. At times when his anger it lit, that's when he takes full advantage of having access to Dean as a source of support. Mr. Harris purposes to call his mentor regularly. Although at times he may fall short in these attempts, he continues to be diligent and accountable for child support to his son and whatever support Mrs. Harris needs. This is a great accomplishment for him. This is why it is important that men have these positive role models so that they don't explode from all the drama that being a batterer and angry man can bring.

In the Introduction of the book, I talked about how I expected this book to have some controversy and that some women may feel like I am a traitor. It is sad to say, but some women have encouraged the behavior of the angry man. How dare you say that Cheryle? Well, think about this. As mothers, we tend to take over the household because the husbands are workaholics or have abandoned their families. We encourage the behavior by once again saying things like, "You are just like your father", and these remarks could be positive or negative. Or, we say, "Your dad works hard to give us a big house, fine clothes and good schools." Although this may be commendable, he is never home. Therefore, moms have a tendency not to push their sons into the role of responsibility as she would her daughter. Mom will ask Susie to perform household tasks and she will not tolerate her procrastination. However, when mom asks Johnny to perform chores, she has to tell him over and over again. Enviably, mom will find it easier to do it herself than to teach him this responsibility. When Johnny marries, he will expect his wife to do all the household chores because mom never made him. Thus, echoes the expression from wives across the country, "I am not your maid."

"Kissing the Boo Boos"

When my son Kevin was very small, I use to have him come to me when he was hurt. Like most toddlers, Kevin had his share of boo boos. He would fall, scrap and even broken limbs. He'd coming running to have me clean, kiss the wounded area and place a Band-Aid on the area. During one particular instance, Kevin was about three-years old. He was outside playing and had fallen on his butt. He came in the house crying and pulling down his pants. He said, "Mommy I fell down." He proceeded to pull down his pants and he asked me to kiss it. I was shocked and did not know how to respond. In actually, my little three-year old had just asked me to kiss his a__ __. Well, I had to do something because I had trained him to come to me whenever he got hurt. So, I kissed my finger and touched his butt and said, "All better." My point here is that our sons will have some boo boos and scraps that we can't always kiss away. We could be hurting them in the future from this natural nurturing behavior when they are children. So, when he becomes a man, will he be prepared to be the man that he should be? Women tend to look for the following qualities in a man:

QUALITIES WOMEN LOOK FOR IN A MAN

- **Someone who can be a leader in their household, not a boss.**

- **Someone they can be intimate with both mentally and sexually.**

- **Someone that can be a best friend.**

- **Someone who can be a spiritual partner (walking in agreement).**

- **Someone who will be a nurturing husband and father.**

Many women have been codependents for the behavior of abusive and angry men. What is codependency?

"A codependent person is one who has let another person's behavior affect him or her, and who is obsessed with controlling that person's behavior."
Author, Melody Beattie

You maybe saying, that's not me, but remember women by nature are nurturers. So, the angry man needs to take responsibility for his own actions, not you. Don't be a codependent for them. It's not your job to fix him. When we are codependents and the man is unable to control his anger and feels that he is losing control and power, he may batter. Because some women teach their sons at an early age to be "macho men" or "the king of the castle", he may not like to be challenged in any area of his life. In relationships, he likes to handle all the money, sign all the checks, monitors what she wears and is always very critical of others. He dislikes those in authority over him. While he thinks he is in control, superior and confident, underneath he really has low self-esteem and depends on the status of his partner to validate him. He feeds off the dreams and aspirations of his victim. He has poor social skills and many times suffers from depression, anxiety and suicidal thoughts. He has no goals and dreams of his own. If dad is absent from the home, he probably did not receive any affirmation from his dad during childhood. Therefore, it is important that he digs up the root of his anger that is buried deep and not just prunes it (Band-Aid). Remember that society has helped to shape his anger by the developing the rule that, "Boys don't cry and men don't share." Eventually, all his anger will become like a pot of water waiting to boil. This boiling pot of anger will push him into domestic violence behavior.

Therefore, in order for men to effectively deal with their anger that makes them batter, they need to know that they can trust someone in helping them break the cycle off their life. In his book entitled, "Trusting Heart, Dr. Redford Willliams of the Duke University Medical Center believes that the trusting heart says, *"That hostility begins with mistrust of others and is reduced by developing a trusting heart."* In other words, it will be frightening for the individual to learn new behavior, but their angry heart, with commitment to acknowledge that change is needed, can succeed in this process. When this happens, there are twelve steps that can help him acquire trust in others." They are:

1. He monitors cynical thoughts by recognizing them.
2. He confesses his hostility and seeks out support for change.
3. He stops cynical thoughts.
4. He reasons with himself.
5. He puts himself in the other guy's shoes.
6. He laughs at himself.
7. He practices relaxing.
8. He tries trusting others.
9. He forces himself to listen more.
10. He substitutes aggressiveness (firmness) for aggression.
11. He pretends that today is his last day.
12. He practices forgiveness.

The primer that exists within him takes us into the next question, "Why does he abuse? The angry man feels frustrated and powerless in society and takes it out on his partner. He feels that if his partner were different or treated him differently, he wouldn't be frustrated. This is one of the downfalls of the angry man; there's nothing wrong with him, it's everyone else. It's that denial syndrome which is part of the cycle. The angry man feels that he is the one to keep his partner in check. So, he hits or slaps her around. He believes that what their partner is saying is outrageous and has no validity and that she deserves to be slapped for saying something so stupid. He believes that when he is drinking or doing drugs, it's harder for him to control his emotions, yet another form of denial. Or, he batters because believes his partner nags too much. He says that this nagging feels like their partner is taking a hammer and pounding a nail into them. So, the only way to make them stop is by striking them. Although substance abuse may be a contributing factor, these are just excuses for a more underlying problem.

There are some ways that the angry man can release some of this pressure. Men need to confess or express how they are feeling. In the bible, **James 5:16 says, *"Therefore, confess your sins to each other and pray for each other so that you may be healed."*** However, we do not want the angry man to think that prayer is the cure all. Prayer mixed with professional treatment and a good mentor or spiritual advisor is a great start. Prayer, however, can help him to control his anger since God is the one who created him. God knew that man would have trials, tribulations and frustrations. The pressure of battering can be relieved and healing can come as a result of confession, accountability, commitment and prayer. This is a process that will and should take time as the angry man seeks out his own positive identity that is not based on unhealthy learned or generational behavior. Angry men can be nurtured and healed like women when they are real with themselves and when they allow themselves to become transparent to those who are committed to helping them.

Other ways that he can recover from his anger is by growing through the pain. Pain let's us know that something is out of order or not working properly. Pain can have an important positive affect and plays a major role in our personal growth. If things were always good, how would you grow? If we did not have any bad feelings, how would we appreciate the good ones? God is in the transformation business. The angry man should talk about his losses (self-respect, wife, children, job, home, etc.) (See Resource Section – **Mourning The Loss**). His growth through his pain should be shared with someone he trusts. God encouraged people to carry one another's burdens if that individual is serious about breaking the cycle (Galatians 6:2). Having someone who is a good listener can make a difference in the angry man's progress. The pain and pressure that he is feeling is mixed with lots of ingredients. They may include betrayal, neglect, rejection and maybe acknowledgment of their own personal abuse. Listening sometimes will be hard to do because we may want to put our two-cents in and give our opinion. Listen to what the angry man is saying - it is important. He is trying to pour out from his heart. He may want to know if his pain will ever end. My answer to that question would be, *"When he learns how to control his pain and not let the pain control him."* Yes, he does have a heart. He may feel like a baby taking its first steps. Try holding his hand. It is then; he can begin to put his trusting heart into your hands and his life into perspective. It takes courage and commitment from the angry man, mentor or spiritual advisor to accomplish this task. Finally, for the *Angry Man*, true peace can come from having a personal relationship with God. God created him, so He knows what needs to be repaired on him.

Don't Give Up !

"THE ANGRY WOMAN"

- *He attends church every week.*
- *He has a college education.*
- *He weighs 195 pounds.*
- *He is six feet tall.*
- *He is athletic.*

And

HE IS A BATTERED SPOUSE.

It has been said that behind every great man there is a great woman. However, the other side of that coin can be interpreted as "Behind every man's downfall there was a woman". According to the National Coalition Against Domestic Violence (NCADV), every year about 1,800 women are killed and more than 500,000 are badly injured by a spouse or lover. There's this gentleman at my church named Brother Peacemaker who has this theory that the devil is a woman. Brother Peacemaker believes his theory is somehow connected with the biblical account of Adam and Eve. Although he has not produced any biblical support for his theory, many men who have been abused by women may agree with Brother Peacemaker. Many years ago there was a television program called, "The Flip Wilson Show." In this comedy sitcom Flip Wilson plays a character named Geraldine. Geraldine was always getting in trouble and justified her actions by saying, "The Devil Made Me Do It." Sometimes we will hear men say to women, "You act just like the devil." Is this fact or fiction? You be the judge. In this section we will look at three important issues:

1. Why is the woman angry?

2. Why does she batter?

3. How does this abuse make her male victim feel?

This unspoken abuse is a very serious issue. For years we have focused on the woman who is battered and the many resources available to her. Yes, whether you want to believe this or not, men are victims of domestic violence. According to the U.S. Department of Justice, in 95 percent of all reported assaults, the female is the victim and the male is the perpetrator. In 3% of reported assaults, the male is the victim of battering in a homosexual relationship. In the remaining 2% of reported assaults, the female is the perpetrator. Due to the shame involved, it is possible that many men may not report the abuse to anyone.

Battering can also occur in same-gender relationships, which is an especially difficult situation because there are often no safe places for the male victims to turn. Just like the angry man who comes up with excuses for battering, the angry woman has a list of excuses to justify battering of her partner. Some women even use crying as a way to manipulate law enforcement officers and others to see her side and thus, she gets what she wants. Unfortunately, the angry woman rarely goes to jail for her abusive behavior. Have you ever stopped to think about how women can perpetuate or initiate domestic violence and has her need to be heard ignited the abuse? These are good questions that I hope to address. So, to the male victims reading this section, I want you to know that you are not forgotten. I care about you and your pain. To the women who are battering, I hope that this chapter will not only help you dig up the root of your problem and abusive behavior; hopefully, it will help you to understand why you batter. If you search your family history, you may find that it was learned or generational behavior. Women who batter are not held to the same legal statues as men who batter. The angry woman should be required to seek out help just like the men. They should be subjected to the court system just like the male batterer. Did you know that domestic violence took place in the White House? Some historians believed that Abraham Lincoln was a victim of domestic violence? It was said that his wife Mary Todd Lincoln threw firewood and other objects and that the President and was physically assaulted on numerous occasions. Times have changed in our response to domestic violence since Abraham Lincoln's day for the women, but not so for the men. Guess what, men normally don't tell. Maybe Mrs. Lincoln just wanted to be heard and get her husband's attention. I'm sure it was a difficult task being the wife of a president.

In an exclusive 20/20 series by Barbara Walters, "Battle for Sexes: Spousal Abuse Cuts Both Ways". She stated, "That women commit some 800,000 acts of violence against men every year according to some surveys." These are only the reported cases. This is largely due to the fact that men feel uncomfortable about sharing with others that a woman beat them or assaulted them. In her interview she noted that women who battered consider themselves victims (self-defense). Dr. Claudia Dias, an attorney and psychologists who runs batterer programs for men and women states, "Women who batter are much harder to treat. They start from a place where everyone sees them as victims." The angry woman will lie, extort and use coercion to get people to believe that he (the victim) is at fault. This is the same pattern the male batterer uses.

At the closing of Barbara Walter's interview she said, "That women should get equal time for equal crime." I agree with Ms. Walter's. Interestingly, most angry women who batter find this punishment hard to digest.

"Why Is The Woman Angry?"

While researching about angry women, I discovered that the majority of these women were molested at an early age or seeking affection because they never had an opportunity to be daddy's little girl, thus causing them to be angry. This form of anger gave the women, in their minds, justification to batter. They have this need to prove they can have power and control over their men. This could be attributed to the Women's Liberation Movement and the burning of bras. Noting that this is learned behavior, the women I spoke with had two main reasons why they batter men. One, because their mother battered their dad or partner and two, they are so bitter from past hurt relationships, they feel the need to control the relationship, she feels justified. Still, there are more reasons why she is angry. So, let's explore some of them.

- *She can't have her way.* How many times have women stomped and threw a tantrum because their husband or partner would not give into their wants. For instance, she may want a new living room set. Her husband informs her that they cannot afford one at the present time, but if she would just wait until they can pay cash for it, then she can get what she wants plus a few extras. She gets angry because she has invited her girlfriends to the house and does not want them to see her living room empty. She wants what she wants now. So in retaliation, she holds back sex from him or doesn't prepare meals. Why? Because she can't have her way -- she's an angry woman.

- *She calls him names.* Just like children, we call our partner's names when we are angry. We say things to insult him like, "You're stupid", "You don't know anything" and the most hurtful remark to him, "You're not that great in the bed anyway". While name calling at that moment, this gives her a since of power and control, it weakens his inner spirit and breaks-down his manhood. This form of abuse is called emotional abuse. Dr. Mike Murdock, motivational speaker and teacher has said that there are two types of spirits in a man, the **king** and the **fool**. According to which one the woman speaks to in his inner spirit, will determine what he will become. So, if you speak to the king in him, he will walk or talks like a king. However, if you speak to the fool in him, that's what he, will become, foolish in all his ways. Keep in mind that the women have been able to influence men since the creation of time (Adam and Eve, Genesis 3). Names and words are powerful. They can either make him or break him. She calls him names because she is an angry woman.

- *She instigates silly arguments.* Angry women have to have someone to pick a fight with. She has no other point of contact but him. She argues over little things that really are insignificant. For instance, she starts an argument because he did not pickup the name brand cheese from the grocery store. He decided to get the generic brand because it was cheaper. Or, she wants him to drive her to the mall to pick up some stockings. He really doesn't feel like it because he has had a hard day at work. She becomes angry and starts an argument. Because she does not want to understand or accept the fact that most men don't like going to the mall and because she wants what she wants now, she picks a silly argument. Why? Because she is an angry woman.

- *She needs to get her point across by using physical force.* The angry woman is so set on having her ways; she will use physical force to get her point across. How many times have you heard men sitting around talking about how they were trying to watch a football or basketball game? But, she wants him to stop watching the game and take out the trash. The game is very intense and he doesn't want to miss any of the final plays. What does she do? She stands in front of the television to get his attention so she can be seen and heard. Or, if he's reading the newspaper, she will knock the paper out of his hand while he is trying to read. She may continually interrupt him while he is working on a project in the garage or working on his car. Most frequently, she will stand in his face nagging, screaming and sometimes pushing. Why? She's an angry woman trying to get what she wants from him.

There was a time in my life after being raped that I used sex as a tool to manipulate men into getting what I wanted. I wanted to be the person who was in control and to get my point across. As mentioned earlier, angry women feel justified by their actions. I certainly did. I felt like I had a great excuse to take control. Why not, someone had taken control over me by raping me. Society has also greatly influenced this type of behavior. Television has become a powerful influence on women and how we treat men. It portrays that it's okay for women to strike men. How many television shows have you watched lately, especially the Lifetime Channel, where the woman expresses her dissatisfaction with her male partner by slapping him. However, on that channel, you rarely see the men hitting back, although she hit first. Remember, during the childhood years boys were taught never to hit girls back no matter what. I remember when I use to annoy my brothers and hit on them. But, he couldn't hit me back. I liked taunting them. A few times, however, my brother, Tony, would hit me pretty hard when our mom wasn't around. Some parents instill that behavior in us. The double standard in this type of thinking is that women hit and don't go to jail. While men, on the other hand, hit and get hauled off to jail. And, men don't tell because this makes them look weak to their peers. With all this anger deep down inside of her, it causes her to batter and abuse her partner. Remember that she feels justified.

"Why Does She Batter?"

In a report called, "Psychological Reports", the authors believe that there are some immediate reasons why she batterers:

- ***My** partner wasn't sensitive to my needs.

- ***I** wanted to gain my partner's attention.

- ***My** partner wasn't listening to me.

- ***My** partner was being verbally abusive to me. (Why?)

- I did not believe my actions would hurt my partner.

*Bold denotes all about her

Some deeper reasons that explain why women batter according to this report were:

- **I believe that I am in charge in a domestic violence situation and I have a right to strike if he breaks the rules.**

- **I have found that most men have been trained not to hit women therefore, I am not fearful of retaliation from him.**

- **I believe it is important and healthy to physically express anger particularly in my personal relationship.**

- **I believe men can readily protect themselves; therefore, I don't worry when I become physically aggressive.**

- I believe if women are truly equal to men then women should physically be able to express anger at men.

Although the statistics on the women batterer is not a true representation of the actual cases, some argue that domestic violence battering by these angry women is done in self-defense. This is not necessarily true. Researchers in this area have stated, for the most part, the women admit that they initiated the partner assault at least half the time. Because this book purposes to deal with both sides of the coin (victim and batterer), sometimes the woman who batter's her partner may do so because she feels disrespected. This disrespect invites anger and causes those primers (selfishness, frustration and anger) within her to set the bomb off, as this is dangerous for both sides. Now that we have looked at some of the reasons why women are angry and batter their partners, let's journey into the world of the battered man and try to understand how he feels. This area will be both educational and life changing. It was for me.

"How Does the Male Victim Feel?"

The male victim has feelings and emotions just like the women who are battered. How often do we dismiss their feelings because they are men? Just because they may have been taught to be rough and tough, we snicker when we think that a man would consider crying over a woman. Is he some kind of wimp? When God created male and female, He created both of them with mind, body and emotions. This beautiful creation was also packaged with a spirit. It has been said that when you break a man's spirit you have broken his will to live. For example, a horse trainer who finds a horse in the wild and tries to tame it because the horse's spirit is used to roaming free, domestic violence is no different. The victim whose spirit has been broken physically and emotionally will have to be retrained like the wild horse in order to have a good, healthy, acceptable and productive lifestyle. This is why many men and women die to this type of violence and more often than not, the batterer may commit suicide because their inner spirit has not been changed. Our emotions allow us to cry, be sad, be angry, feels pain and happiness. As hard as it may seem for you to grasp, men were created with these characteristics. Because most men don't like to be called sensitive, this makes it extremely difficult for them to communicate with others that things are not going well in their relationship department. Men like to brag, flex their muscles and stick out their chest. They want people to believe they have their household under control and that they are nice guys.

When male victims of domestic violence are faced with the dilemma of what side of the coin (relationship) to reveal to their family members and friends, they will, for the most part, choose the side that looks and sounds good. Women, who are physically abusive, can strip the male victim of his pride and self-worth. Remember, he has been taught not to hit back. Some women have battered their partners to the point that they needed hospitalization. Don't laugh, it's true. In the movie, "Thin Line Between Love and Hate" with actor Martin Lawrence, his batterer was a woman who was angry and bitter because he said **NO** to her controlling ways. In the movie, while Martin Lawrence is hanging out with the boys, he never thought that a bet, attempting to pick up a classy woman in a club, would cause him so much pain. She beat him until he was hospitalized and was bandaged from his head to his feet. You may be saying that it's only a movie. Stop and think if she brought baggage from a previous relationship into her involvement with Martin, then it would not take much to trigger her anger and rage. But, this type of physical abuse takes place everyday in real life all over the world. Most men and women normally don't call this domestic violence abuse. They prefer to call it a lover's spat ----- a misunderstanding.

Male victim's who are battered, through all their pain, will not go to the gym and share with other men that he is being battered at home. He has his manhood and reputation to protect. What most people fail to realize is that maybe these men are in the abusive relationship because it was witnessed in their home as a child. During those instances, dad did whatever mom wanted just to keep down strife. Or, dad gives into mom because this shows that he is a good provider and loves his wife. However, this type of control by women can chip a little piece of him away every time this occurs. When men say **NO** to women, immediately she begins the put him down by calling him names (fear and intimidation). Because she may be small in stature, she may threaten him by pushing or beating him with objects. With the intense pain and drama he feels, he will, for the most part, still defend his partner to family members and friends. Defending or denial of the abuse is normal in the cycle. Men who are battered carry physical and emotional scars just like women. They normally find it very difficult to trust in a new relationship if they so desire. If he decides to stay with his partner, it's out of fear and intimidation, especially if children are involved.

Further research studies on domestic violence have shown that angry women who batter are normally the initiators of the abuse. No one likes to invite pain to take up residence in his or her lives. Men normally don't handle pain well. Unlike women, men have not had to endure the experience of childbearing, which not only is painful, but life-threatening. However, men go through labor pains in other ways. For instance, every time he has to endure one more harsh word one more sleepless night, humiliation or a physical object (knife, gun, frying pan) to their body, they have gone through the pain of labor. Men who are battered endure these labor pains because they believe they love their partner and they want to protect their children, if any. The angry woman's behavior can cause major catastrophe for the household. While the man is supposed to be the protector and bread-winner of the home, she is constantly stripping power and control from him, putting the entire family in crisis. Although he may wear the pants – she controls the home and everything in it. So, his pain gets buried deeper and deeper. I commend those men who had the courage to step forth and say, "Help, I'm a victim of domestic violence." I apologize that society has not been kinder to you by making equal resources available for you, especially government and the justice system.

In conclusion, the angry woman's agenda in her role as batterer is to get what she wants no matter what the cost (power and control). This is just as wrong as the man who batters. In times past and present, some women have used sex to control and mind manipulation (a game) with men to get what they want. From their need to have control, power, no more failed relationships and manipulation, they have acquired such things as:

- passing grades in high school or college
- job promotions
- new clothes
- new homes
- new cars
- vacations
- money

Don't laugh. I am sure you know of people like that. I use to be one of them. Whatever their motive to obtain these things, they want what they want irregardless of the cost. Have you ever stopped to think how prostitution can apply to married and single women in relationships? How dare you call me a prostitute or ask me to consider the notion? This is just my personal opinion and does not mean that you are something nasty or filthy. But as women, we want something in return for services rendered to our partner.

Webster defines prostitution as:

"One who solicits and takes payment for sexual intercourse; to offer oneself or talents for sexual hire."

Cheryle's definition:

"You give me something – I give you something."

The only difference is that married women have a legal piece of paper to solicit from her partner and the single woman does not. Thus, for the most part, she's not on the street looking for a pickup because she has a husband, boyfriend or lover. My view on this is that some wives do perform sexual pleasures with their husbands because of their vows, for personal sexual gratification or as an aphrodisiac, to get what she wants. Some single women, however, are hoping to impress their partner, especially if the potential to marry one day exists. In essence, "You give me something, "I'll give you something." If scorned, some angry women do not walk away from relationships easily. The planning and plotting of how to get revenge with the person they believe has wounded them becomes an obsession. In actuality, I believe that what angry women fail to realize, is that she could be her own worst enemy. The angry woman needs to remember that when she batters her partner, she is hurting and damaging someone's son. How would she feel if a woman was abusing her son? There are truly no major differences among female and male victims of domestic violence. They both have feelings. Men who are victims of domestic violence, with little success, will try to walk away from the abuse. If this happens, the angry woman will attempt to find ways to stop them. There are some ways that the angry woman can teach herself to control her anger. In the November 2003 issue of Essence Magazine, an article entitled, *"My Woman Beats Me: The Painful Secret Brother Keep,"* this was an article about a man who was battered by his woman. The article listed a few ways to help women control their anger in an attempt not to batter.

- **walk away**
- **be aware of what triggers your anger**
- **develop a support system**
- **take responsibility for your actions**
- **get counseling**

In conclusion, when the angry woman can begin to look in the mirror and examine why she is angry, instead of her beating down her partner, she will learn how to control her own emotions and begin to break the cycle of abuse. Because women were created to be emotional creations, we like having our needs met (mentally, physically, sexually and financially). However, there is a way to have those needs met without battering. Until the angry woman learns how to control her anger, she will not attract a good, healthy and romantic relationship. She will continue to bring her baggage into someone's life, thus, the abuse starts all over again. So, *Angry Woman*, you need to consider your actions and break free from the behavior. It is important to remember that the male victim of domestic violence will need love, support and the nurturing of a good healthy woman, not an *Angry Woman*. Finally, just like for the *Angry Man*, the *Angry Woman's* true peace will come from having a personal relationship with God. God created her, so He knows what needs to be repaired on her.

CHAPTER 4

"TRANSITION"

"Sometimes in life you get dealt a bad hand of cards. Sometimes it's the joker. If you don't like the hand you have been dealt ----- throw it in and get dealt a new hand of cards."

O. Dean Young

"The things we have to learn, we learn by doing them."

Aristotle

It's A New Day!

"Everything that you were doing is different from this day. You've got to change or you may die (physically, financially and spiritually)".
                                                          Bishop Eddie L. Long

Wouldn't you like to have abuse towed away from your life?

The transition phase will sometimes make you feel like you are on a roller coaster. It will require the following actions by you:

1. **Letting go of the old.**
2. **Gathering new information to generate new direction.**
3. **Considering the options and taking action.**

In the beginning your transition will be difficult to adjust while *Ending* the relationship. The victim or batterer will exhibit feelings of *Denial* that the relationship is ending. Sometimes they may even convince themselves that the abuse is not that bad and the victim may consider rejoining the batterer. However, if both decide to close the door, seal it up with bricks and never tear it down or reopen the relationship, they should expect some emotional change. As they move through the transition, they may experience *Anger*. For the victim, they will be entitled to be angry and express those emotions as long as it does not endanger themselves, children or others. They should let their anger be used in a constructive way by being determined to break the cycle of abuse. They should remember that they are only responsible for their own actions. Transition will bring an array of emotions (fear, confusion, frustration and stress). These emotions can have a tremendous physical impact on the body causing them to seek medical attention. They both will need to stay focused and surround themselves with a good support team. Tighten your seat belt, as the roller coaster ride of transition is about to move to the next stage of the track.

As they begin to move forward, their exploration into a new life will become chaotic at times. Many individuals will try to advise them of what is best. They should be careful. Although their intentions may be good, their advice could delay their progress. The efforts towards making that new exploration will be scary. Again, stay focused and do not get off course. The goal is to work towards a wonderful new positive and healthy life. Most individuals have some mode of transportation to get from one destination to another. For domestic violence victims, moving from their present form of slavery, bondage, or imprisonment to freedom is a major struggle. As they attempt to move forward, little video clips of the past will begin to play in their head to try to discourage them from leaving the abuse. For the batterer who is attempting to transition, the video clips of how their partner took care of all their needs may replay over and over. Now, he or she has to learn how to handle problems, situations and circumstances on their own. They may or may not succeed and just move onto another relationship. Transition from domestic violence requires focus, courage, assistance from others and finances. The victim recognizes that they need to escape for their own personal safety and the safety of their children (if any). Who can they trust to help them make the transition? Is it the government, civic organizations, churches, family or friends? The transition out of this imprisonment can be very dangerous. Sometimes the escape can lead to death. It is vitally important to understand that having a safety escape plan is necessary (See Resource Section – **Your Safety Plan**).

In the bible, God speaks about writing the vision and making it plain (Habakkuk 2:2). In the English language this means, that if the victim has a safety plan then the person(s) they trust can read it and help them implement that plan. A safety plan will help the victim prepare for a safe exit off the roller coaster of abuse. It will be their road map. Once the victim has made the transition from the abusive relationship, they should be warned that the batterer will come looking and will begin to stalk and harass them. We will look at some of the things that the victim can expect when they decide to leave their violent partner. The batterer may be an emotional wreck because they have lost power and control over their victim. There are judicial laws set into motion that will help protect the victim from the abuse and stalking. Through a local abuse shelter or local magistrate's office, the victim may take out a court protection order (restraining order) for protection against the batterer. This order attempts to protect the victim from being approached by the batterer in various places that the victim requests in that protective order. It should be noted that sometimes these protection orders work and sometimes they don't. These orders, for the most part, only serve as legal proof in a court of law as a good defense for the victim should the batterer violates that court order. In the Resource Section, I have prepared a sample of a "**North Carolina Protection Order**" and a section on "**Knowing Your Rights**." I will share with you two personal situations on why these orders are not a sure thing. Finally, while this chapter primarily focuses on the victim's transition, it should be noted that these principles are available to the batterer if they are serious about transitioning. It is my desire that this chapter will help both victim and batterer try to take control of their lives and make a smooth and healthy transition.

"GETTING OUT"

In a visit to Duke University, Durham, North Carolina, Dr. Maya Angelou, noted author and speaker, spoke to a group of incoming freshman. She told the students that, *"Courage is the most important of virtues because without it they could not produce any of the other virtues."* As I read the article I asked myself what is the definition of virtues so that I could fully understand her statement to them. Webster defines virtue as:

"Conformity to a standard of right; morality; a beneficial quality or power of a thing."

So, without it, nothing can really happen. Dr. Angelou motivated and encouraged the students to go out and change the world using their courage. This is exactly what it takes for victims to transition out of domestic violence. It will take them courage to boldly go to a place that they have never been before. It's the new uncharted and unfamiliar territory. Just in case you maybe wondering if I really know what I'm talking about, in 2002, Dr. Ann Brown, Director, Women Health Lecture Series, Duke University Medical Center invited me to speak. The audience was clinicians and social workers who had an opportunity to hear my experience with domestic violence. There was a question and answer period and I responded by being open and honest. Now that took courage,

Babies are a great example of how transition works. First, they are born. Then, they are breast-fed or bottle-fed. They are weaned slowly from the bottle to the cup and sometimes a straw. From there they begin to learn how to drink from a cup. Then, they transition from crawling to learning how to walk. In learning how to walk, they may fall down many times. However, they get back up holding onto furniture or any finger or hand that is available. Eventually, they are walking on their own. Once they learn how to walk and form words, parents begin to teach them how to go to the potty. Potty training is a very scary moment in a child's life. Parents are excited about saving money from the expense of Pampers. Then suddenly, the parent wants the child to stop stinking in their pampers and become friends to the bottomless pit (the toilet). That transition is not only hard on baby, but parents too. Everyone is now making transitions to the child's new schedule of trying to time when Little Johnny or Little Susie may have to sit on the pot. For victims of domestic violence, like the baby learning all of these new skills, they too now must learn new skills that are healthier and productive for them.

Another example of transition is when children go to elementary school. In grades K-5, they begin to learn the basic skills in reading, math and science. The students will take weekly, quarterly and end-of year tests to see if they are equipped to advance to the next grade. Without this preparation, when they arrive to middle school, they will be like a fish trying to swim out of water. Transition, while sometimes frustrating, will enable victims to prepare to be able to stand on their own in hopes that they will be at least able to tread the water. Transition is an opportunity for them to display what Dr. Angelou described as **COURAGE**! This courage gives them an opportunity to prove to **themselves** and no one else that they can do this. It is this type of test in life that we all must pass. During a Wednesday night bible study presented by the late Bishop Mack Timberlake of Christian Faith Center in North Carolina, he and his wife Pastor Brenda shared the following lesson about passing life's test.

PASSING LIFE'S TEST

- *Testing always precede promotion.* For the victim, having to endure the abuse is a tremendous price to pay. However, promotion into their newfound freedom is well worth the fight. Testing and promotion will enable victims to effectively help someone else and one day becomes a powerful motivational speaker, advocate and author. When victims don't take the test with courage, pride and pass, they will have to retake the class, sometimes THIS WILL MEAN staying in that abusive relationship a little while longer. If they refuse to take the final test with courage, they cannot advance to the next level --- **freedom**. This is hard medicine. But, it is well worth it.

- *The goal of every individual no matter what their religious background is to be a leader.* When you were created, you were already given an assignment on earth that only God knew you could fulfill. In order to fulfill the assignment, victim and batterer MUST pass the test. We were born to do great and special things in life. In the bible, Ephesians 4:1c puts it this way, **"Walk in a manner worthy of the calling with which you have been called."** So, you will have obstacles and setbacks. They are just roadblocks because you were born to be a leader. So, make the necessary detours.

- *A test has no value if lessons are not learned.* Cartoonist Charles Schultz once had Charlie Brown carefully building a sandcastle on the beach. Standing back to admire his work, Charlie Brown was soon engulfed by a downpour, which leveled the castle. Standing before the smooth place where his artwork had once stood, he said: *"There must be a lesson here, but I don't know what it is."*

In that powerful teaching, an important thing stood out for me, which was:

"Without the tests and trials in our lives, we never would have taken time to think through these truths about who God really is and who you are to become."

Domestic Violence storms may sweep down upon you from different directions and for different reasons. Sometimes the storms are brought own from others (the batterer) or sometimes we have caused them ourselves (not having the courage to leave). Or, sometimes they may show up like that hurricane I mentioned earlier in the chapter entitled, "My Story". No matter the reasons they are in our lives to help us learn valuable lessons and help us to transition out of them. Here are some things that a test will reveal:

- *The development of your character.* You will be able to develop who you are through your failures and not your successes for without the failures --- you can have no successes.

- *The nature of your faith.* This faith will determine if you have faith in **yourself**, others or God.

- *The strength of your commitment to get out of the storm.* This will determine how bad you willing to chart a new course for your life are. Also, it will be a determining factor in deciding how bad you want your life back.

- *The level of your maturity.* In the bible, I Corinthians 13:11 states, *"When I was a child, I talked like a child; I thought like a child, I reasoned like a child. When I became a man, I put childish ways behind me."* Wow, that's powerful and something to feast on.

- *The health of your attitude.* What you meditate on the most will determine the quality of your health. When you allow those bad video clips to continue replay in your mind, eventually it will affect your mental and physical health.

- *The measure of your ability to learn.* These are the tools, skills and people that are placed in your life to transition out of the abuse (mentor and protégé).

From my personal freedom from domestic violence, I would have never imagined that because I choose to past the test (with many retakes) and endure the storms that I would become the author of two books, motivational speaker, mentor, counselor and advocate for domestic violence. This transition was extremely difficult.

The transition from my home to a shelter; from a shelter to another new home made me learn how to walk, talk and think on my own. Oh boy, that was a challenge. All of these transitions have empowered me to become who I am today – strong, but in a loving, tender and caring way. I shared with my mentor that although I've come a long way from my abuse, there's still much for me to improve upon. He replied, "You're *just a diamond in the rough.*" I could hear Dr. Murdock saying, *"Your mentor is not your cheerleader, they're your coach."*

Noted author and motivational speaker, Dr. Spencer Johnson, published a book entitled, "Who Moved My Cheese." It is a powerful practical teaching about how transition can be made easy. It depicts how transitional circumstances were happening (warning signs) around the characters in the book. Some of the characters choose to just sit and wait to see what would happen and the other characters went out and made change happen. It is a book that I highly recommend. It is one of the best written easy to read books that I have ever bought (See References Section). The characters of the story are two mice and two little people. Cheese is used as a metaphor as to what you want in life (peace, joy, home, success, etc.). The maze in the story represents where you look for what you want in life. For victims of domestic violence, the maze would represent trying to gain freedom from the abuse. In order for the victims to get through the maze, it will take courage, persistence and reading the warning signs for them to take back their life as the maze will have many dead ends and detours.

The characters of the story were faced with some unexpected changes in their lives just like domestic violence victims. As the characters try to find ways to deal with the transition in their lives, one of the characters gets out successfully and begins to write what he has learned on the wall of the maze. While the batterer could utilize these writings, keep in mind that they want to keep their victim under their power and control, thus, keeping their victim at a dead end just like the maze. Listed below are some of those writings and how it applies to domestic violence, especially the victim.

Change happens. **They keep moving the cheese.** In domestic violence, things are always changing (moods, finances, homes, jobs, etc.). Always find ways to keep yourself safe. Have a backup safety plan.

Anticipate change. **Get ready for the cheese to move.** Victims of domestic violence, for the most part, can anticipate when their batterer is about to strike. They have learned their body language and tone of voice as a warning sign that they are about to experience another beating. For this reason, it is important that victim's are not caught off guard as this could lead to fatal injury or death.

Monitor. **Smell the cheese often so you will know when it is getting old.** When the victim leaves, the batterer will make every attempt to lure their victim back under their control. The victim will, over time, recognize those same old lines and tricks. Once the victim is out of immediate danger, it will be easier for them to see the forest for the trees.

Adapt to change quickly. The quicker you let go of the cheese (domestic violence), the sooner you can move on and savor new cheese (a new life - freedom). During the transitional period, the victim may find it difficult to get their life on track. They may be concerned about having to leave the comforts of their home for less suitable living arrangements. I left my abuse with just the clothes on my back. I lived in a shelter. Slept on an air mattress for months, ate off paper products, ate lots of canned foods, especially peanut butter and jelly and had enough clothes to take me through a week. This went on for six months. However, the pain I experienced was worth it for me to spread my wings and sore like an eagle. I don't ever want to be a chicken. Now, I have gained more than ever, especially, peace of mind.

Change. **Move with the cheese.** Change from domestic violence is a good thing. While the transition is taking place, the victim may find themselves having to move many times before they are settled in that perfect place of peace. Don't be discouraged because that peace will happen.

Enjoy the cheese. **Savor the adventure and taste the new cheese**. Once out of the violence, take the time to notice the beauty around you. Enjoy the well-deserved quietness and peace. Do not be quick to get involved with new cheese (relationship). Give yourself time to heal (one year or more).

Be ready to quickly change again and again. **They keep moving the cheese.** Remember that situations will occur during your transitional period from domestic violence. Be prepared for the change because some people will be jealous that you have acquired enough courage to take a stand and say, "**NO MORE**." Just when you think you have settled in, someone will try to come alone and move your cheese (joy, peace and happiness).

    Now that you have made the decision to have courage to make the transition, while it is a good step forward, it's not the final step. Let me share with you some things as a victim you can expect as you begin to leave the abusive relationship. Because the victim is now out of the household or anticipating leaving, this does not mean by any shape or form that the abuse is over. Guilt, shame and doubt will try to consume the victim's mind. Stay encouraged. Don't look back. The individual that has abused can be read in several predictable ways. The batterer knows things about their victim that can push their buttons (emotions). They will try hard to persuade and intimidate the victim to return to them. They may try to persuade them with gifts and promises to seek professional help. However, the victim's time away from the abuse is very crucial in order for them to make decisions without fear. This is especially crucial in the domestic violence situation where religion is a factor (See Resource Section).

THE BATTERER'S ATTEMPTS

- *The batterer will attempt to locate their victim.* During this time of transition, the batterer will make every attempt to locate their victim. They will not leave a stone unturned. The batterer will contact and harass family members and friends. They will either attempt to gain sympathy or threaten them. If the batterer uses the sympathy line, much of their story may be a distorted version of what really took place. This is typical of the cycle of abuse. They will try to convince family members and friends to help them get their victim back. It is recommended, unless the victim has a strong family and support team that is willing to stand up to the batterer, the victim should attempt to transition to a place not familiar to their batterer. Remember that the batterer can be very charming and persuasive, but yet have the Dr. Jekyll/Mr. Hyde personalities. Always be prepared for him or her to use these tactics on others.

- *Apologies and Promises.* If the batterer does make contact with their victim, they will first try an apology line. This will include promises of better behavior, gifts and items for the children or home, promises to get help with their anger and the ultimate, counseling or going to church. He or she believes this might bring their victim back to their sphere of dominance, thus the honeymoon of the relationships begins. Remember that the batterer truly believes that the victim is their possession to do as they please and not a gift to cherish and adore. The ultimate objective of the batterer is to establish and maintain power and control and they will use apologies and promises to hinder your transition. Don't fall for it.

- *Threats and intimidation.* When apologies and promises don't work, the batterer will move to the next level that includes threats and intimidation. This behavior often includes threats to attack family members and friends, threats to kill him or her or have his or her family members, especially the children and friends. Keep in mind that he or she alone is responsible for his or her actions and the results of those actions, not you. Take the necessary precautions and refuse to listen to any additional threats from the batterer. These precautions will be discussed further in the section entitled, "**The Protection Order.**"

- *Using the children.* During the transitional period children are often used by the batterer to keep the victim under their power and control. While the victim and children are out of the home, whoever has custody will use this to lure their victim back. Remember, for the most part, the law will always side with the woman. It is extremely difficult for male victims to gain access of the children. Because the batterer is manipulative and cunning, know that he or she may not be as smart as they think. Eventually, they will pay for the consequences of their actions. Advocates for children of domestic violence are working hard with the courts to be a voice for the children to hear their side of the story without being fearful of the batterer. There are numerous community agencies that are available to help victims deal with the problems (male victims are not as fortunate) of being a single parent.

- *Counseling and the Religious Approach.* As mentioned, during the transitional phase apologies and promises are made. Suddenly, he or she may become religious and want to attend church in the most obvious manner. Most pastors and ministries often doubt these sudden conversions. He or she may begin by taking counseling sessions. Unfortunately, many clergy encourage the victims to go back to their batterer to sort out their problems mixed with prayer and counseling. It has been my experience over the last two years of counseling that once separated from the household, especially the victim, they should allow themselves time to heal. This process should take a minimum of one year apart from one another to work on them and it should be the victim's choice to reconcile in the relationship. This allows the victim an opportunity to see if they are able to trust their partner again.

"YOUR SAFETY PLAN"

Congratulations on considering and getting enough courage to leave the abuse. It will be vitally important without any hesitation that the victim begins to work on a safety plan secretly. Most often victims have one person whom they trust that will be able to assist them. Whether they stay in the abusive relationship or plan to leave, they victim must consider their safety and the safety of their children.

Listed below are some important things the victim should know about developing a safety plan. More detailed information can be found in the Resource Section,**"Developing A Safety Plan"**.

- *Gather all important papers.* Put together all important documents for you and your children. These will include social security cards, birth certificates, passports, immigration papers, etc. Sometimes it's hard to secure the original documents. When this happens, make copies and give to a trusted friend.

- *Try to set aside extra cash, checkbook or credit cards.* Realizing that having extra is sometimes impossible; hide cash and financial records in a safe place if possible. The victims may want to consider opening a separate account at a different banking institution.

- *Hide an extra set of car and house keys.* If you are considering staying in the home; I strongly suggest changing the locks or purchasing a security system immediately after the batterer has left. Or, you can have your local police patrol the area for a designated period of time.

- *Pack a suitcase or bag containing the essentials of what you may need for yourself or children.* Because I did not receive this valuable teaching, I had to leave with just the clothes on my back and start all over again. The victim can consider placing clothes at someone's home. If the batterer monitors the clothing, considering purchasing clothing from a second-hand shop since finances may be tight.

- *Plan ahead about where you could go when possible.* If you plan to stay with relatives or friends, discuss your plan with them ahead of time. If you are planning on going to a shelter, contact the agency so that they can help you get out safely. Most of the time when networking with a shelter, you can receive a police escort.

- *If danger is imminent, leave immediately.* Your safety is very important. Please do not try to take anything with you.

- *Talk with your children if they are old enough about the safety plan.* Take the time to help the children understand what is about to take place. Teach them how to call for help, 911, should the need arise.

- *If your phone has a re-dial or caller-ID, make sure you clear all calls.* Your batterer will always try to find out whom you are talking to.

Finally, in the Resource Section, **"Personalized Safety Plan"**, you will find an outline that will be of great benefit in helping the victim tailor a plan for themselves. If you are a victim, you have just made a major step in your future to become a victor. So, stay prayerful, stay focused, stay encouraged and stay safe.

"THE STALKER"

Definition – *Stalker*

"To walk with a stiff, haughty, or angry gait. To move threateningly or menacingly. To track game (the victim)."

After leaving my batterer, I thought that I was free from the physical abuse. Having beaten me until my face was distorted and other areas bruised, I though that he would leave me alone. But, he located me at the shelter. That was frightening. When I left the shelter and secured a Protection Order with the help of a domestic violence advocate, even with those actions, he still stalked me. When I was at work, when I turned around he was there. At the store, when I turned around he was there. Although the protection order stated that he was to stay fifty feet away, this did not stop the fear and torment that I felt daily knowing that he was on the street. By the time I would call the police and they would arrive, he would be gone. This process went on for a while. After transition into my new home, he located me and began tampering with my mail. As Dr. Angelou stated in her address to the Duke students, you need to have courage. Well finally, I got enough courage to prosecute him for harassment and tampering with mail. This broke his future stalking of me.

Stalkers are out of control. Most people believe that men who batter stalk their victims more violently than women who batter. This is far from the truth. Women who batter stalk their victim in more vindictive ways. The women will slash tires, bust out windshields, follow their victims, and call the other woman (girlfriend) threaten and harass her if this scenario is in motion. Also, some women who batter and stalk bring along a whole posse of their girlfriends who are normally male bashers and male haters to be a part of their conspiracy to get revenge. Women stalkers, in my opinion are just as dangerous as men stalkers. Victims, whether male or female, should beware of this vicious stalker. They are angry and frustrated because they have lost their power and control over their victim. There are several kinds of stalkers.

- **Simple Obsession**
- **Love Obsession**

STAY AWAY FROM ME !!

- *Simple Obsession Stalkers.* These stalkers have been intimate with their victims. Many times the victim has tried to end the relationship. The stalker refuses to accept this. The stalker normally suffers from:

    - **Personality disorders**
    - **Emotional immaturity**
    - **Extreme jealously**
    - **Insecurity**
    - **Low self-esteem**
    - **Feels powerless if not in a relationship**

Getting reconciled with their victim is the ultimate goal of this stalker. If they can't get their victim back, they believe they can't survive without them. These stalkers have previously been abusive to their spouses or intimate partner. During the relationship, the stalker has used domination as a way to bolster their shortcomings and low self-esteem. This form of domination gives them a sense of control and power they can't find elsewhere. The stalkers worst fear is losing people whom they have had control over. Without this power and control, the stalker feels that they have no self-worth and identity. In desperation and with courage, the victim has left the relationship, thus, the batterer becomes nobody and begins the stalking process.

It's this total dependence on their partner for identity that makes the stalker dangerous. The stalker will stop at nothing to get or win their partner back. Life is not worth living if they can't exert their dominance. Unfortunately, most stalkers become suicidal and want to **KILL** their intimate partner.

Simple obsession stalkers do not always begin with violence right away or try to terrorize. It normally starts with:

- **I just want to talk to you or meet you for one last time?**

- **If you talk with me, I promise to leave you alone.**

- **They will appear that they show up out of nowhere, but the truth is they have been there all the while.**

The stalker desperately wants their partner back. When this doesn't happen, like a full pot of water coming to a boil on the stove, the stalker boils out of control and spills out of control many times assaulting and sometimes killing. Far too often, law enforcement officers and advocates find that the stalker follows through on their threats. Sometimes for the stalker, death is better than having to face the humiliation of the victim leaving them for someone else. The humiliation of having to face their own powerlessness is too overwhelming.

- *Love Obsession Stalkers.* These stalkers have had no intimate or close relationship with their victim. The victim could be a friend, business acquaintance, a person they only met once, or a complete stranger. An example of this type of stalking was in 1994, when I was raped in my home while my children were asleep. When asked by the police officers to come down to the station to look at pictures of sexual offenders, it stunned me to see men who lived in my old neighborhood in the mug shot books. The officer informed me that the person who brutality raped me could have been someone I knew as they had been watching my every move. This stalker was obsessed by something they couldn't have. You can read about this in my book entitled, "**Abused, Battered, Brokenhearted and Restored.**" The stalker truly believes that a special, often mystical relationship exists between them and their victim.

Contact with the victim whether far or near becomes a positive reinforcement of the relationship and any wavering of the victim from an absolute **NO** is seen as an invitation to continue the pursuit. Like the cartoon character, Pepe Lapue, a male skunk, from the Warner Bros. Merry Melodies, Pepe was always determined to win the affection of another female skunk named Barbara Ret. When she refused his stinky and obnoxious affections, Pepe became persistent about getting the beautiful female skunk and followed her everywhere. Barbara Ret's turning away, turned Pepe on. Like Pepe Lapue, the more the *love obsession stalker* can't have, the more they want. These stalkers will often read sexual meanings into neutral responses from the victim. These stalkers are often loners with some type of emotional void in their lives. Any type of infatuation, even negative, helps them to fill this void. As mentioned earlier, actor Martin Lawrence in the movie, "Thin Line Between Love and Hate," is a typical example of this emotional void. The woman in the movie perceived in her mind that the relationship with Martin Lawrence was a perfect relationship. After Martin got what he wanted from her (sex), he began to back off. The relationship was only a bet to win a classy woman with his friends and he won. When he later refused other affections from her, because she had not let go of previous baggage of hurts and disappointments from another relationship, she became unstable towards him both physically and emotionally. It's a good movie to watch to get a feel of how women can stalk and hurt men too.

Many of these stalkers suffer from what is known as "Erotomania" (sexual desire). They believe in their mind that the other person truly loves them. Usually, the other person is of a higher socio-economic status than they are or some unattainable public figure. When these stalkers are apprehended by police officers and questioned, the stalker has fantasized a complete relationship with the victim. When no affection is returned from the victim, the stalker often reacts with threats and intimidation. For example, male fans stalked Christina Applegate and Madonna. When this form of intimidation does not work on the victim, the stalker may become violent and even deadly.

In closing this section on stalkers, it should be noted that some stalkers harass their victims not out of love, but hate. Most often, stalking becomes a matter of revenge especially with some women. However, most often, men tend to swallow their pride and suck up the loss and move on to the next available woman. Stalking is a serious form of abuse that keeps the victim living in constant fear. The idea of having to look over their shoulder is enough to make them a nervous wreck. Keep in mind that the stalker is a person who is out of touch with reality. The anger that resides within them eats away at them like terminal cancer. Listed below are some traits of a stalker. A more detailed description can be found in the Resource Section – **"The Stalker."** As the victim transitions out of the abuse, I urge them to be careful and do not take their surroundings for granted. Stalking is serious and can cost the victim their life.

- Stalkers will not take NO for an answer.

- Stalkers display an obsessive personality.

- Stalkers do not display the discomfort or anxiety that people should naturally feel in certain situations.

- Stalkers often suffer from low self-esteem and feel they must have a relationship with the victims in order to have self-worth.

- Stalkers, like rapists, want absolute control over their victims. Stalkers are cowards.

- Stalkers many times have a mean streak and will become violent when frustrated.

"THE PROTECTION ORDER"

Unfortunately, this section will be somewhat short. Why you may ask? Because as much as law enforcement agencies are working diligently to get officers trained to assist these victims, they are not always able to bring a peaceful resolution. Keeping in mind that the angry man or angry woman has no respect for those in authority, these types of angry outbursts, at times, makes the officer's job more difficult, especially if they have to discharge their weapons to bring the situation under control. The protection order is the victim's legal proof that abuse is happening and that they may fear for their life. This protection order legally identifies the batterer as a potentially dangerous person allowing law enforcement officers to act quickly and without question on the behalf of the victim. The Protection Order can provide the following:

- **Prohibits further abuse.**

- **Prohibits contact with the victim.**

- **Prohibits the batterer from the home, school or workplace of the victim and children.**

- **To order spousal support or child support for housing of the victim and children.**

- **Whatever other items the victim and judge deem necessary.**

- **The batterer may be ordered to attend counseling or some other form of anger management classes.**

This sounds good doesn't it? Remember, previously we discussed the different types of stalkers. Normally, the stalking will begin after the victim leaves or after they leave the courtroom. Earlier in this section, I mentioned that we would visit two courtroom situations that I witnessed. Let's visit the courtroom.

While visiting the domestic violence court session with a young lady who was being battered by her husband, it was shocking for me to watch the court system at work. While sitting in that courtroom with a judge who looked like he should have retired twenty years ago, I was quickly reminded that the fate of the victim's lives were in one man's hands. But, for the majority of the cases, the system works if victim and batterer do their part. There will always be a few incompetent lawyers, judges and police officers. That is why it is so important to seek the help of a trained domestic violence court advocate. In the one case, there was a woman who had put the boyfriend out because of his physical abuse to her. They had a son who appeared to be about eight or nine years old. The judge ordered the man to stay away from the victim for one year. The batterer agreed. The batterer asked the judge if he could be allowed to see his son, at least at school. The judge asked the victim if this would be okay. The woman replied, "No Your Honor." The judge asked why and she replied, "He has a temper and I don't trust him alone with my son." She relayed to the judge that the batterer owned a gun and she was fearful for her life and the safety of her son. The batterer acknowledged to the judge that he had a license for the gun. The judge wrote in the protection order that he could keep his gun. Now, that's scary. Could it have been that because North Carolina doesn't recognize common-law marriage that the judge didn't take the abuse seriously because he was just a live-in boyfriend? In essence, the judge could have just given the batterer a license to stalk, kill and even commit suicide.

In court case number two, a Christian couple appeared before this same judge. The husband, during a counseling session, admitted that God told him to beat his wife into submission. He had been ordered to take a psychiatric evaluation, but he never adhered to it. Apparently, this couple had appeared before this judge before in previous domestic violence incidences. This time, however, the victim was fortunate enough to have an attorney represent her. The victim was concerned that her batterer would walk away again and be aloud to continue to harass. After listening to the case, the judge ordered that a protection order be reinforced for a period of one year. The order stipulated that he was not to appear on the premises of her home, job, church or any other area were she was. This was a man who beat his wife, punched holes in the walls, stalked, harassed, snatched telephones out of the walls, intimidated and tormented this woman until she was an emotional wreck. The husband asked the judge if he could still attend the church where they both were members. The judge wanted to know if this was a large church. The husband replied, "Yes." The judge okayed the request and changed the order. This put a big hole in the victim's faith in the legal system. It was apparent to me that church was doing him any good. The batterer was out of control and had violated other protective orders, which the judge had in front of him when he rendered his decision. What would have stopped the batterer from pulling a gun on the parking lot or in the sanctuary of the church and shoot the victim? In this case, the victim opted to attend another church for safety reasons. That's scary too. Now, the batterer had won again. He got what he wanted, church and more intimidation to his wife. Not only that, he was saying to the church that he didn't respect the preaching or teaching enough to make a change. In essence, the church has become his new victim as well.

Some victims, after receiving a protection order, will purchase and learn how to use a firearm. The victims are so fearful and intimidated by their batterer that they will not take chances for their safety. Personally, I believe that the only way for a batterer to stay away from his victim is when he or she knows that the victim has total support from family, friends, support organizations, churches and the legal system. My brother Tony would say to me when I was a teenager, "A man will only do to you what you allow him. Unless he has a knife to your throat or a gun to your head, he will move onto to another woman (victim) when you don't give them what they want." The batterer will eventually get tired of the chase and drama and move onto a new target.

Although we appreciate the legal system for its efforts, it doesn't always work for the victim or batterer in its effort to provide what is needed to stop domestic violence cases. Men who are battered and try to prove their case before a judge get very little support because of the labels imposed on them as a wimp or cry babies. Victims of domestic violence should keep their protection order with them at all times and give copies to their supervisor, family members and friends. If the victim should spot their batterer or stalker, call the police immediately and tell them that you are a victim of domestic violence and that you have a protection order. Consider your safety at all times.

In conclusion, as we close out this section on Transition, I realize that it will be difficult, I've been there. As Aristotle wrote: *"The things we have to learn, we learn by doing them."* With this in mind, getting out will take courage and I believe that Dr. Angelou has said it well in her address to the freshman student at Duke University. Remember that in order to have a smooth transition, you will have to **"Pass Life's Test."** If for some reason you don't pass the test the first time (leaving the abuse), don't be discouraged – retake the test and try again. Once you have successfully made your way through the transition, if you are the victim, develop your **Safety Plan**, if possible, a head of time. This will be important because in most cases, victims have to leave immediately with their children with what they have on their backs. Be prepared for the **Stalking** to commence. I have outlined for you the various stalkers and their characteristics. When possible, familiarize yourself with what to expect or share with a trusted friend so that they may help you through the process clearly. Let the law enforcement officers, domestic violence advocate and court system assist during the **Transition** process. Like any system there are plus and minus. However, these individuals are there to assist and protect you. Trust them to help you. Once the coast is somewhat clear, then you can begin to work on "**Breaking the Cycle: The Healing Process**" and continue through the process toward freedom.

During the **Transition Process,** sometimes you may have to take the **stairs** instead of the elevator.

By: Vincent A. Allen

Let's Get Started !

Chapter 5

"BREAKING THE CYCLE: THE HEALING PROCESS"

"How long must I wrestle with my thoughts and every day have sorrow in my heart? How long will my enemy triumph over me?"

Psalm 13:2
New International Version

Wow! It may seem hard to believe, but you are now one step closer to your healing. Matters of the heart with regards to domestic violence should be taken as seriously as having a major heart attack. Now that you have taken the courage to transition out of the abuse, the pain you are experiencing is real. However, like any other medical symptom, given the right treatment, you can live a healthy, happy and productive life. One thing I have come to realize is that only God can go into the very deep places of the heart and massage it and reshape it from all of the stress, hurt and abuse it has taken. I think that the hip-hop gospel artist, Kirk Franklin said it best on his God's Property CD, "He'll Take the Pain Away." In the cycle of abuse, victims tend to neglect themselves and care for the needs of the batterer. Our aim and mission during this cycle was to be caregiver's to others. Unfortunately, this form of giving has been thought by society to be a noble and nurturing experience for others. But, in actuality was an act of destruction for both victim and batterer. The good news is that because you have made it through the transition process, you have the ability to be generous, loving and nurturing to yourself.

Whether victim or batterer, you have just opened yourself up to numerous possibilities of breaking the domestic violence cycle off your life and your children. All the stories you have read are true and were shared to help you understand the seriousness of domestic violence from both sides. No one has the right to beat you or belittle you. However, before you can begin to heal, I know that you really don't want to hear this, but you MUST forgive YOURSELF and consider forgiving the BATTERER (Luke 11:4). Cheryle, I don't know if I can do that. Well my friend, if you don't then you will never walk in total freedom and peace. Don't forget about those video clips that will continue to play and keep you in bondage. You will never be able to step into your destiny. Why? You have been carrying the baggage of others too long. If you don't to forgive it's okay. Unloading the baggage of abuse at the check-in counter will help you to heal and break the cycle. For example, I have a friend named Jackie. Because of her stressful job, every night she would have a bowl of Hagen-Diaz ice cream to unwind. She carried the baggage of the ice cream, bowl and spoon to her mouth nightly. After a few months, the ice cream became a weight on areas of her body that no longer pleased her. Eventually, Jackie had to let go of that baggage, the ice cream and begin to find healthier ways to handle her stress. Another example is that I had no control over my finances. This was a heavy weight (baggage) and burden for me after every payday. My mentor talked to me about a budget. When I began to put the budgeting principles into motion, the heavy baggage of bills was removed from my life. So, when the attendant asks you to take your claim ticket for your baggage (unwanted abuse), tell them, "No thank you" because you won't need it. As I began to let go of the baggage in my life, I was led to attend a Christian Women's Conference in 2001. Although the lesson during the conference was targeted towards Christian women, I recognize that everyone who reads this book may not be a Christian. So, the teachings that were presented could be applied in making everyday decisions to help alleviate the pain and stress from the abuse.

UNLOADING THE BAGGAGE

- **You will only be what you see yourself becoming (strong and self-sufficient).**

- **Begin to map out your destination.** The new directions you will begin to undertake will require goals and a plan of action. Your destiny is on God's mind. Suggested readings: Jeremiah 29:11 and 3 John 1:2

- **God's word goes beyond your human understanding.** As a victim of domestic violence, you may not understand why bad things happen to good people or why good girls like bad boys. But know this, what you have endured will pass if you are willing and obedient to having a mentor or spiritual advisor that can help assist you. Suggested readings: Isaiah 1:19 and Jeremiah 1:5

- **God will come to your rescue.** When no one else was available to help me out of domestic violence, I spent a lot of time in the Word of God in my quiet place. I now can thank my family for not being able to assist me. If they had, I would have depended on them for my source and not God. In doing this, He proved Himself to me that He will always supply all of my needs and He will do the same for you. Suggested readings: Psalm 91:1-16

- **Never be fearful.** When you walk in fear, it will hold you back from your destiny. When leaving your batterer, they will stalk you. Fear will try to grip you to keep you from breaking free. Please, don't look back. Suggested readings: Isaiah 46:9 and Isaiah 55:11

- Dare to believe that something good will happen for you – never doubt.

- To be healed you will have to deny some people and things in your life.

- Your healing will cost you something (pain, fear, anxiety, insomnia, etc.). Don't be afraid to tackle those feelings as you launch out into the deep.

- You can not put a dollar amount on your healing and destiny.

- Put yourself around successful people who can pour into your life. This does not necessarily mean people who are just materialistic.

- Be willing to face all opposition.

- Getting rid of the old baggage will be crucial.

- You will begin to have a new level of confidence once the baggage is unloaded.

- You will be able to help others who are going through their abuse. Suggested readings: Numbers 23:19 and Isaiah 46:9

- You will need a place and people to help you unload the baggage and get to your place of healing.

- God has given you the power and ability. You may not feel like you have much strength to unload the baggage and move on, but you do. Once you begin to set the wheels in motion you will be surprised how much strength, courage and stamina you have. Suggested reading: Luke 10:19.

So, to sum it all up, in order for you to begin the healing process and break the cycle of abuse, you MUST let go of the baggage. Don't waste your energy on trying to fix the abuser for this will drain your strength. The next phase of breaking the cycle is the mourning or grieving the loss. Let's look at what can happen to an individual during this phase.

"MOURNING THE LOSS"

"Sometimes in life we may have to die, loved ones may have to die and relationships may have to die. Sometimes death is necessary so that others may live."
                               Cheryle E. Dawes

Feeling sad and depressed is a part of the transition from domestic violence. The emptiness that victim and batterer face, especially the victim, is called, ***mourning the loss***. It is their grieving process. These emotions are much like those of a loved one who has physically died. However, for victims of domestic violence the mourning process can be extremely difficult because the person they are mourning is still alive. Some victims do slip back into the cycle of abuse in order to avoid the pain of completing the mourning process. This is why it is important to allow yourself to go through the healing process no matter how longer it takes. Depending on the individual and the intensity of the relationship, the mourning process can fluctuate. If the loss of the relationship is considered significant, the loss will be harder to work through. However, if the loss was not significant, the loss will hardly affect that person at all.

While mourning the loss, the individual may experience some of the following symptoms:

- **loss of ability to sleep**
- **loss of sense of safety**
- **loss of ability to trust themselves or others**
- **loss of self-esteem**
- **loss of confidence**
- **loss of physical health**
- **loss of mental health**
- **loss of freedom from chronic pain**

- **loss of freedom from anxiety, panic, flashbacks and hyper-vigilance**
- **loss of nurturing needed to grow and thrive**
- **loss of ability to make good life choices**
- **loss of family and friends**

If these symptoms persist for a long length of time, this could cause serious mental, physical and psychological problems. These complications could contribute to dysfunctional family members for future generations. Once again, this could also delay the healing process. If victims are still in the home experiencing the abuse, it is difficult for them to grieve because they are constantly confronted with the abuse. Another problem is the acknowledgment by the survivor (victim or batterer) and society that the victim has the right to grieve the loss of the relationship. Most times the victim is too ashamed to talk about how they feel about the loss. Those survivor's who are able to talk about what has happened, tend to blame themselves for how they responded or didn't respond to the abuse. Feelings of guilt when they are around others, who don't understand, sometimes become intensified. Again, this mourning process can be extremely difficult for victims, especially where church-goers tend to push towards marriages staying together. Victims will tend to beat themselves up for not healing faster. If the victim grew up as a child witnessing domestic violence, they have grown accustom to hiding their emotions from others. This behavior sometimes is called "numbing" and is difficult to break. A noted author once wrote, "Healing our grief is a journey, not a destination". The journey into healing asks the victim to weave their losses into the fabric of their lives. This is commonly referred to as, "Good Grief."

Individuals who try to assist survivors of domestic violence through the mourning process should recognize that each person has a right to grieve in their own way. There are no specific rules. They should accept their thoughts without interjecting their opinion of what they should or should not do. The survivor needs lots of time. Don't box them in by saying, "You should be over this by now." Survivors sometimes may revisit the place where the abuse happened. These familiar places may cause them to trigger their sensory. The olfactory is related to the senses that will trigger the taste. It could be a particular food or the smell of their cologne or perfume of the batterer. The cerebrum sensory is the part of the brain that takes you down memory lane. This is when the victim may remember a particular room (where the abuse occurred) or the sound of a particular song that connects them to their abuse. Also, remembering holidays and anniversaries are particularly traumatic. Recently, a young lady that I mentor, we will call her "J", decided to take back her life and not take her husbands abuse any longer. Although her stance was the right thing to do, the abuse is still very vivid and fresh in her mind. "J" currently resides in the apartment were her abuse occurred. Needless to say, her sensory triggers are activated more frequently. "J" was having difficulty sleeping in the bed where she slept with her husband. She repeatedly had to deal with the reality of her unborn child (miscarriage) due to the abuse. Her insomnia became difficult for her to function at work and school. As her mentor, I advised her to get rid of the baggage (things in the house) that reminded her of him, especially the mattress. She had informed me that she had been raped many times by her husband on that bed. So, my colleague, Dean Young and I decided to go and buy her a new box spring and mattress. Now "J" sleeps like a baby and I don't get those 2am and 3am telephone calls anymore. "J" is learning how to deal with the loss of a failed relationship and baby. She is doing better with rebuilding her self-esteem and life, but has a long way to go. Sometimes she feels like she is on a roller coaster, but she manages the ride well. It is important that you name your loss. Whatever emotions the survivor feels, they should say it (anger, hurt, fear, etc.).

Victims of domestic violence must go through this mourning process. Dr. Elisabeth Kubler-Ross is a well-known researcher and has implemented important strategies in helping individuals deal with grief. The present emotions of the survivor are very high in this stage of their life. Family members and friends may find it difficult to understand. It should be noted that everyone involved is affected by the "Mourning the Loss" phase. Dr. Kubler-Ross identifies these stages as denial, anger bargaining, depression and the last phase, acceptance of the loss. However, the acceptance phase will only be seen in those individuals who have allowed themselves enough time to work through the stages of grief. Let's look at what the stages involve.

Denial and isolation are usually the first reactions in the grief process, but not always. All human beings are individuals and do not go through the stages of grief in the expected order. Denial and isolation reactions are shown when the affected individual:

- **talks only about the future**
- **avoids talking about their or their loved one's illness or problem**
- **avoids family and friends**
- **blames others for their illness or problem**
- **refuse to return phone calls to friends and loved ones**

How do you help someone in this stage?

It is difficult to know what to do when talking to anyone that is grieving. Remember that denial acts as a buffer against the shock of dying or losing a loved one even in a domestic violence relationship. Sometimes friends and family members think it is best for the person to face reality. Pushing the person in this direction, too soon, is unfair. Denial and isolation may well be the individual's way of learning how to cope with traumatic support to someone in this phase: So,

- be nonjudgmental of their behavior
- do not take anything personally
- be a good listener when they want to talk

Anger of all the stages in the grieving process can be the most difficult for friends, family or advocates to understand. Typically, an individual moves from the denial stage to the anger stage when they realize that death or loss is probable. During this stage the person may:

- ask "Why me/my relationship?"
- may question religious beliefs
- accuse family members or friends of uncaring attitudes

Family members also go through intense anger, during this phase. Like all the stages in the grieving process, anger can occur after any traumatic event. I have seen situations where anger can cause alienation. Dealing with an individual in this phase can cause feelings of anger in you. You may feel "dumped on" unfairly.

How to Cope with this Stage

The best way of handling this situation is to:

- remember that the anger is not directed at you, but at the situation
- visualize how hurt you would be in the same situation
- accept the behavior as part of a process and a sign of change
- not allow the anger to alienate you from those who are important in your life
- allow yourself a break from the person, but assure them that you are not deserting them

Bargaining. After the grieving person or family member has vented their anger at friends, family and at God, they enter the bargaining phase. This stage is seen as an attempt to enter some agreement or to finish an important task to prolong life.

During the bargaining stage, the affected person:

- makes promises to God or other higher power
- agrees to change their lives if allowed to live
- agrees to change their behavior

After going through the bargaining stage, the individual or family member usually enters a state of depression. Psychologists reference two types of depression, reactionary and preparatory. Let's look at the difference between the two depressions as they apply to domestic violence.

Reactionary depression. This occurs because there are additional losses such as finances, family role and intimacy.

Victim: If the victim is use to living a more substantial lifestyle, they may become depressed because they can no longer shop at Nordstrom's. The thought of having to shop for clothing at Wal-mart is repulsive. If children are involved, they may look upon mom as not too special because she can no longer afford $160.00 tennis shoes. She now has to shop for everything at the neighborhood thrift store.

Batterer: The batterer is depressed because they have relinquished their role as king of the castle when their victim decided to leave the abuse. Once the batterer realizes that their apologies and fancy gifts will not win them back, sometimes they will go into a state of depression momentarily. Then, more often than not, they will move own to another victim whom they can have power and control over.

Preparatory depression. This is when the individual knows that the loss can happen at any moment.

Victim: When the victim finally reaches the point in their life that they don't want to live in the abusive relationship any longer, mentally they are on edge about how will they survive. Their batterer will threaten to withdraw all financial support from them, thus causing them to become depressed by constantly thinking in their mind over and over again when it will happen. Will it be today? Will it be tomorrow? They know in their mind that it could happen any moment.

Batterer: When the batterer begins to realize that things are changing with their victim, they become on edge trying to figure out what they are thinking and what's their next move. They begin to plot like moving chess pieces across the board. Like the chess pieces, they are not sure when they may get checkmated. The thought of the batterer not being in control, for some, can cause this form of depression.

How to Help People in this Stage

The first reaction that caregivers generally have toward this stage is to cheer the depressed individual up and encourage them to look at the bright side of things. This may work somewhat for reactionary depression. However, preparatory depression is more complex. A grieving person will find more comfort in expressing him or herself. Often, this just means sitting with that person and listening. This stage of grief tends to be a quiet one and sometimes all someone needs is your presence.

Acceptance is considered the final stage in the grief process. Some family members and friends see this as a happy time of resolution. This stage is usually only seen in individuals that have enough time to work through the other stages of grief.

As we close-out this section, "**Mourning the Loss**", I hope that you have a better understanding that the process is essential to the healing process and breaking the cycle of domestic violence. Unless the victim is allowed to experience the loss and work through the pain, the cycle of abuse will continue for both victim and batterer (Resource Section – **The Journey Through Grief**). More importantly, I want you to understand the many components to the loss and the healing process. Once again, just like the person who has been diagnosed with cancer, alcoholism, drug addiction, gambling, shop-a-holic or any other kind of addiction, it can cause the loss of life. Domestic violence has the same affect if we remember that the individual they are mourning is still alive thus, making it more difficult to grieve.

THE MENTOR

"Mentors are people that you should respect."

"Mentors are trusted teachers."

"Mentors are people you should be willing to submit to or be accountable to."

One of the most fulfilling habits I could have ever acquired was that of a good Mentor. This is the person whom you can go to for advice and guidance. The mentor is your greatest cheerleader. They will let you know when you are right and when you are wrong. A mentor is what parents are supposed to be for their children, someone who they inspire to be like. In the introduction of this chapter, "Breaking the Cycle: The Healing Process", in order for healing to take place; you must recognize that the mentor who pours into your life will be a determining factor in who and what you will become. A mentor can either help you be a success or a failure. In domestic violence, the batterer influenced who the victim would become by lowering their self-esteem, introducing them to crime or substance abuse. This is a true statement. Think about it? When victims are in the abuse, they listen to everything and did whatever the batterer told them. This was partly due to the fear they felt of being battered. Finding a mentor who has a heart and passion for you and your creative talents and gifts given by the Dream Giver (God), is important. I have been fortunate over the years to have dynamic and extraordinary mentors, Dean Young, Jackie Goodwyn, Dr. Mike Murdock and most recently, Dr. Myles Munroe pour into my life. Some have poured through books and audio-visual materials, while other have poured into me in person. All of these mentors have a heart and passion for helping to heal and mend the hearts of broken people and helping them to become successful in every area of their life.

In his Wisdom Commentary, Dr. Murdock shares what the relationship should be between the mentor and his or her protégé. Let's hear what Dr. Murdock has to say. This information can apply to both victim and batterer. Remember that it is my desire to help you see "Both Sides of the Coin."

- **Mentors are trusted teachers.** Various teachers will enter and exit you life. Your inner spirit (your conscience – still small voice) will always be the most important dominant teacher. But, your mentor's advice should always be trusted.

- **Wisdom, knowledge and advice determine the success of your life.** Mistakes and Mentor. For example, mistakes that were made by the victim by listening to the batterer didn't bring a successful or healthy life. But, if both victim and batterer would attach themselves to a mentor, mistakes can be turned in to miracles (no more abuse).

Mentors will determine the difference between poverty, prosperity and freedom from domestic violence. Some other differences between mistakes and mentors are decrease and increase; loss and gain; pain and pleasure; deterioration and restoration. Dr. Murdock goes on to give twelve qualities of an uncommon mentor.

1. **An uncommon mentor is the master key to the success of the protégé.** With the help of God, mentors are one of the most important master keys to total success, spiritually, emotionally, physically and financially. The problem, however, can be that there are not enough people who want to invest their time and energy into mentoring.

2. **An uncommon mentor transfers wisdom through a relationship with the protégé.** Just like the disciples who sat at the feet of Jesus as He prepared them for ministry, the protégé should be willing to sit and submit to the mentor acquiring wisdom, insight and knowledge to help them become a better individual in every area of their life.

3. **An uncommon mentor guarantees your promotion.** As the protégé continues to seek out the wisdom and advice of a mentor, some of the advice will not be easy to swallow. If the protégé accepts and acts upon the mentor's advice, they will get further ahead in life than they could have ever imagined. This will happen based on the protégé's determination to never return to the abusive relationship.

4. **An uncommon mentor can determine your wealth.** Grab hold of the principles of living on a budget. When I took the advice of my mentor, I went from having no money on payday after paying my bills – sometimes there was not enough; to having more than enough and some left over to help others. Expect your financial picture to get better. Living on a budget works.

5. **An uncommon mentor can paralyze your enemies against you.** Mentors can see things in certain areas of your life that you may not be able to see clearly. I had an employer that tried to fire me after just receiving an excellent evaluation. Because of my mentor's wisdom, he was able to share with me a head of time a plan of action. I followed his advice, escaped the plot to ruin my excellent reputation and consequently walked into a better job that gave me the flexibility to finish this book. How? The new job allowed me to work from 6:00 a.m. to 2:30 p.m. Thus, allowing me to come home, nap and begin another 8 hours on this project.

6. **An uncommon mentor can cause influential people to listen to you.** Because of my connection with Dr. Murdock, at times, all I need to do mention the teachings of him and people sit up and take notice and listen.

7. **An uncommon mentor will require your pursuit.** The lives of mentors are very busy. For this reason, you should seek after them in person, books or tapes. Their time is very precious and as protégé's we should be mindful and respectful of this.

8. **An uncommon mentor is more interested in your success than your affection.** This may sound harsh, but this is necessary for the protégé's success. Mentors are concerned about you. For this reason, they do not have time to watch you get all emotional about the things that are surrounding you. They are concerned about helping you reach your fullest potential.

9. **An uncommon mentor is not necessarily your best friend.** They are your coach.

    - Your best friend loves you the way you are.
    - Your mentor loves you too much to leave you the way you are.
    - Your best friend is comfortable with your past. Your mentor is comfortable with your future.

    - Your best friend ignores your weakness.
    - Your mentor removes your weaknesses.
    - Your best friend sees what you do right.
    - Your mentor sees what you do wrong.

10. **An uncommon mentor will become an enemy to the enemies of his protégé.** Mentors are concerned about your success, those who try to set traps for you. A mentor can help to place a hedge of protection around you and keep a watchful eye on those whom set out to destroy you.

11. **An uncommon mentor sees things you cannot see.** Mentor's see weaknesses in you before you experience the pain of them. They have already experienced the pain of a problem you are about to create. For instance, when you were dating your batterer, others saw things in that person that you could not see. However, we tend to ignore the mentor's advice. Ignoring things often causes pain later that could have been avoided.

12. **An uncommon mentor can create an uncommon protégé.** Mentors help to create warm and teachable individuals who can reach out and teach others. Because of my past domestic violence abuse, I have learned how to become submitted and humble in a positive way. This has become a great learning tool for me and has proven to be beneficial. Previously, submitting to anyone was

not something I did with joy. However, with a mentor's advice, some individuals who knew of my past and called me stupid for staying in the abuse, now respect me for what I have become. This is all due to my uncommon mentor who has created an uncommon protégé.

Here is what Mrs. Harris, survivor of domestic violence and protégé, has to say about what her mentorship experience means to her.

Finding a Mentor!
From
Mrs. Harris' Point of View

I was serious about change. Finding a mentor was my next move once I decided to transition from the abuse. Unfortunately, it was not as easy as you may think. Most of the time when I was missing or lost something, it could be replaced (materialistic). But, when I was dealing with interpersonal matters, it proved to be more challenging. Here are some qualifications that I was searching for in having a good mentor.

- **Does your mentor set a good example?**
- **Is he or she nonjudgmental?**
- **Is your mentor consistent?**
- **Do they walk in the fruit of the spirit?**
- **Do they share with you their own failures and shortcomings?**

Setting a good example

Meaning, do they do what they are advising the victim (protégé') to do? One of the many reasons why people end up in domestic violence is due to a lack of having boundaries and limitations in their life. Does your mentor clearly have boundaries established in dealing with their own affairs? Is your mentor able to teach you how to say no, when normally you would say yes? Do they set goals and achieve them. And, are they showing you how to do the same.

Nonjudgmental

When dealing with domestic violence and relationships, a lot of times the victim can experience an array of emotions which can affect their judgment. A good mentor will know and understand this. They will be patient and the victim will feel comfortable when dealing with the mentor. Also a good mentor will not be judgmental of the batterer, their family, or friends.

Consistent

The words of a good mentor will always be consistent. Although no one is perfect, a good mentor's advice should not contradict itself from one week to the next. It should not contradict the word of God either. All wisdom, knowledge and understanding come from God. So, it should not contradict the principles taught in the bible. Finally, a good mentor is a man or woman of their word. What they teach the victim they will teach the batterer, but from a different angle. Every relationship, person and circumstance is different, but again the main teaching principles will be the same with a good mentor.

Walking in the fruit of the spirit

This does not mean that your mentor literally walks in fruit (strawberries, apples, peaches, etc.), but rather it is referring to Galatians 5:22-23. Walking in the spirit is a "religious" way of saying acting or one's behavior. The fruit of the spirit are *love, joy, peace, patience, kindness, goodness, faithfulness, gentleness, and self-control.* A good mentor is one that is full of love toward their protégé. Along with being consistent and lots of patience, a good mentor is consistent in these nine attributes.

Sharing failures and shortcomings

A good mentor will share what they have been through in their lifetime and what they are dealing with in their current day to day life. The significance of telling what they have been through is so they can speak from experience when dealing with the victim or batterer. Their reasoning behind sharing what they are currently dealing with is to let you know they are human too. When looking for a mentor it is important to get with someone who can express his or her own problems. It is nice to know a mentor can help you, but also that we all are a work in progress and no one has arrived to perfection yet.

Mrs. Harris is a college graduate with a degree in Psychology. Even with her educational background, she found not only herself in the cycle of abuse, but Little E. Although she had textbook knowledge, she could not see the warning signs. She is doing exceptionally well and as her mentors – Dean and I are proud of her.

Thank You Mrs. Harris for Sharing!

In closing, the mentor's role is very time consuming. It takes commitment to try to get individuals to change their learned and comfortable behavior. I guess this is what Jesus meant when He said, *"Unless you come as little children..." (Matthew 18:2)*. This means that as adults, we should have a child like attitude when working with a mentor. Children are trusting and have the ability to soak up information like a sponge. Like a loving parent, a mentor is a tough love parent to the protégé. For the victim and batterer, trust and respect of their mentor is a major key. Finding someone they can open up to is not as easy as opening a can of soup and pouring it into a pan. A mentor will not judge. A mentor loves. A mentor does not condemn. They commend. A mentor does not tear you down. They build you up. The mentor will help you to understand your strengths and weaknesses. Their goal is to help you not to return to a life of abuse and to become successful in every area of your life. Chapter 1 and 2 helped set the pace to understand why the mentor's role is important, especially when you are trying to change unhealthy behavior.

"SPENDING QUALITY TIME WITH YOURSELF"

Society portrays that if we are withdrawn, introverted or anti-sociable, that there must be something wrong with us. Or, that we need people and material things to make us happy. Some physicians and psychologists may prescribe medications to help keep their patients calm and stay in control of their anxiety. In some cases, these medications may be warranted for a short period of time. However, for the victim and batterer, spending quality time with a mentor and oneself is essential to healing and breaking the cycle. It's during this time that placing a Band-Aid to fix the problem(s) should not be allowed to stay on the open wound too long. Healthy quality time alone can help prevent both victim and batterer from ingesting the negative influences that will try to infiltrate the quality time needed to strengthen them. During this process, they will need to learn how to discipline their mind and body just like that newborn baby who gets on a feeding schedule. Spending quality time will allow individual's to self-exam themselves. It's during this time that they may feel like an ugly caterpillar, but they should not be discouraged because soon they will discover by spending quality time, that a beautiful butterfly will emerge. Since my transition, there is nothing in my life more important than spending quality time with God and myself. It's during this time that He gives me direction for my life. These moments give me an opportunity to build, rebuild and encourage myself by reading, taking long bubble baths, focus for writing and producing books and more importantly, fixing **my** broken emotional wounds. I don't feel guilty and you shouldn't either. During this time, I don't answer the phone or respond to emails. I've learned to set boundaries that will help me look at my goals and objectives. Here are a few suggestions that may help you:

- **Take a realistic self-inventory.** Begin to make a list of your strengths, weaknesses and limitations. This will be hard and painful, but necessary. Then, begin to refine your list (smooth or fine tune).

- **Share your list with your mentor, spiritual advisor, family member or friend.** Keep in mind that these individuals should be individuals whom you trust. You want individuals who will help build you up and not condemn you if you make a wrong decision. This list will reveal shortcomings and weaknesses and exposure of these for a positive change.

- **Be true to your values.** Getting out of domestic violence will require tenacity and courage. When you were born, you were given a special gift from the Dream Giver (God). That special gift was put inside of you at birth to make a difference here on earth. *"But we have this treasure in earthen vessels (your body) that the excellency of the power may be of God, and not of us (II Corinthians 4:7).* This is why trials and tribulations have come into the life of victim and batterer. You are on a special assignment from God that no one else can fulfill but you (breaking free from abuse to help someone else).

Spending quality time is an excellent time to begin cultivating that gift. Set and plan realistic goals for yourself during your quiet time. You should have the following:

- **obtainable goals**
- **one-day at a time goals**
- **one-week goals**
- **monthly goals**
- **yearly goals (1, 3, 5 year)**

Be very specific in setting your goals. This will become your road map for success. I had set goals for writing this book. However, it's okay to know that you may make some detours along the way. I had to make many detours, thus delaying the book for about six months. So, detours are fine because it puts you on a journey towards a new healthier and fuller life. The majority of my life was spent in disorder, very little discipline and very much out of control. Having goals and objectives has become a lifestyle for me, just like showering. So, consider purchasing a wall calendar or daily planner to help get you organized. A Franklin Covey organizer is a great tool. It has become my second bible and is a good way to help you stay focused and manage your time wisely. This organizer is extremely helpful for those individuals who are more visual. Below are some helpful hints to help assist you while getting organized and work towards spending quality time with you.

- Be assertive with yourself and others. Boundaries are essential.

- Stand up for what you believe about your values.

- Continue to believe in what is right and healthy for self. If what you see presently is not what you see for you in the future, then what you see now is just temporary.

- Be mindful to take into the account the feelings of others in a positive way. Learn how to sift through those feelings like flour in a sifter.

- Always accept the humanness of yourself and others. This is very important.

Another effective way of spending quality time with is by keeping a journal or diary. This method, I believe, is one the most effective ways to express and learn how to get in touch with your feelings. As a former victim, I encourage you to begin to examine yourself and write down anything that you could have contributed to the abuse and begin to fix what is broken (i.e., prayer of forgiveness, plan of action, etc.). By keeping a journal or diary, you will be able to express things on paper that you would not share with anyone else. After leaving my abusive relationship, I kept a journal for an entire year. It's amazing that when I began to write about my abuse, I discovered that the thing I hated most in school (reading and writing) came alive. Now, I enjoy the thing I hated the most. From that journal my first book was birthed, *"Abused, Battered, Broken-hearted and Restored"*. When keeping your journal or dairy, try the following:

- **Purchase a journal that is beautiful.** Something that represents you. This journal will become your best friend. The words you write down won't try to give their opinion. You will be writing **your** precious and valuable thoughts and emotions from the depth of **your** soul.

- **Always write the date and time.** As mentioned earlier in the book, sometimes the victim and batterer may lose track of time during the cycle of abuse due to the emotional merry-go-round. Documenting these important items will be a great resource tool later. It will remind you of how strong and victorious you have become in breaking the cycle of abuse.

- **Having a tape recorder available.** Another way of gathering notes and thoughts for your journal is with a tape recorder. There may be times that a thought may surface and you may not have time to write it down. A hand-held tape recorder on your person will enable you to record your thoughts that can readily be transferred later.

Something To Think About !

List YOUR Positive Qualities
1.
2.
3.
4.
5.
6.
7.
8.
9.
10.

List YOUR Negative Things YOU Want To Get Rid Of
1.
2.
3.
4.
5.

Go To the Next Page and Consider Doing the Worksheet !

THOUGHT IDENTIFICATION WORKSHEET

For the next 15 minutes leave aside everything you have been doing and try to write down all the thoughts that are coming into you mind in the space provided. Be sure to write down everything, even if it appears trivial or unimportant. I have provided a continuation page for you if you need more space.

THOUGHT IDENTIFICATION WORKSHEET

CONTINUATION PAGE

Not so long ago the trend was that because women were more emotional, that they were better at writing such books as romance and parenting than men. However, that concept has changed over the years. Bookstores and library shelves all over the world say otherwise. Because it has been the practice of men not to tell how they feel, just by searching the internet or buying a magazine, we will find that many men are writing emotional stories about their personal feelings and abuse. They are not being afraid to tap into those God-Given emotions and share their pain and progress with others. Those who have been incarcerated because of battering are writing and sharing about how sorry they are for the damage they may have afflicted on their victim, children, family and friends. No matter what method you may choose, writing is a good sense of healing. As mentioned previously, having a committed mentor or spiritual advisor in your life to listen and help guide you through the process will be instrumental. As you work through this process, remember that the instruction and advice that others may give to you may not always be pleasant to digest.

Remember, as a victim or batterer, you never had time for you. If you are a victim you catered to the needs of the batterer, thus, forsaking everything else. If you are the batterer, you never had time to keep a job or be with friends because all your time was consumed in finding ways to manipulate and control the relationship. Keep in mind that the idea of learning how to spend quality time with you will take some getting use to. But, be like the Nike slogan, "JUST DO IT." As in the case of the Harris' (Chapter 2), after one year of intensive mentoring and continued counseling, they are still developing and growing through their own personal shortcomings. Although they do not live in the same household, they have shown tremendous courage to take the advice of their mentors and break the cycle of abuse off their lives and for the sake of Little E. I must admit, that Mrs. Harris has excelled in leaps and bounds during this process. This could be attributed to that fact that she is a mom and primary caregiver 24/7 for Little E. Mom is learning how nice it is to have just one hour or one day alone. As her mentor, I try to make this happen for her as often as possible. Little E, however, has had to learn how to adjust to spending quality time without his dad in the household. He has made tremendous progress during the cycle of abuse. He loves basketball and spends his available quality time (everyday) shooting baskets (he's pretty good) and watching "Space Jam" starring Michael Jordan gathering knowledge on how to be a better basketball player. Most recently, Mrs. Harris has taken ample time and has developed goals and a plan of action. And, her mentors recently had the wonderful experience of seeing her and Little E move into their new home. During a visit to deliver a dryer, Little E greeted us at the door. He was the happiest two and a half-year-old that we have seen since this family was presented to their mentors. When they first came, Little E was an emotional wreck at home and in daycare. It brought tears to our eyes and joy to our hearts to see his progress today. He is smart and adorable. All of this has transpired because mom (former victim) has taken into consideration all the components needed for the healing process to be successful.

    Finally, nourish, accept and build a strong foundation. This will only happen by spending quality time with you. For some taking a long walk, riding a bike or taking a run is therapeutic while gathering their thoughts. Men may choose to go to the gym, play basketball or some other sport to clear their head and get a better prospective about their life. Women, however, may like to a take nice long bubble bath with candles burning. Whatever method you chose, be consistent, be persistent and be diligent until you get the desired results you want. Remember that you have mentors, spiritual advisors, family and friends to help you along the way. One of the contributors for this book has written a profound resource tool entitled, "**Redefining Your Image: Who do you see when you look in the mirror?**"(Resource Section) It is a compelling writing of how God sees you when you look in the mirror whether victim or batterer. Remember to daily cultivate your mind and spirit. Feed yourself good encouraging resource materials like, Cheryle Dawes, Zig Ziglar, Dr. Myles Munroe, Dr. Wayne Dyer, John Maxwell, Joyce Meyers, Kenneth Copeland and many others. Expose yourself to positive things. Avoid negative conversations, movies or television shows with violent scenes (rape or domestic violence) until you are ready. Avoid music lyrics that are degrading to men and women. Listen to tapes and read good books over and over again until it becomes a part of you– Smile. The keys of wisdom and knowledge are in your hands. Go and unlock the door as you *"Spend Quality Time With Yourself."* I believe that gospel recording artist Yolanda Adams and educator and motivational speaker Dr. Maya Angleou sums this section up by singing and reciting the following:

- See Next Page -

<u>Yolanda Adam Sings</u>

Wounded, but time will heal.
Heavy the load the cross I bear.
Lonely the road I try, I dare.
Shaken, but here I stand.
Weary, still I press on.
Long are the nights the tears I cry.
Dark are the days, no sun in the sky.

<u>Maya Angelou Recites</u>

"YET STILL I RISE"

<u>Yolanda Adam Sings</u>

Never to give in.
Never to give up against all odds.

<u>Maya Angelou Recites</u>

"YET STILL I RISE"

"REBUILDING YOUR SELF-ESTEEM

One of the most difficult things for human beings to endure is the self-examination process. Like a woman who has been taught by her physician to do monthly breast examines or the man that has been reminded to get a yearly colon examine; whether victim or batterer, we need to do a regular examination of ourselves. It's easy to blame others for the situations we find ourselves in. While this may be partly true, it's **YOUR** decision to change it. We can't treat our self-esteem like we do the symptoms for the common cold, plenty of rest, fluid and chicken soup. Or, like a cut on our finger by placing a cute little cartoon Band-Aid on it. Self-esteem must be a personal issue. While rebuilding, you may have to depend on others like a mentor, spiritual advisor and close friend or relative to help pour positive information into you until you are strong enough to stand on your own. Be very selective in your process. This could have either a positive or negative effect as you are rebuilding your mind and spirit.

In Chapter 1, we read how we are products of our environment. Our self-esteem is shaped and structured from many sources. From our birth to childhood, many individuals, especially family members, try to influence what you should become. Some people want to be like Michael Jordan, the basketball star. Some want to be a politician, like a senator or president of the United States. Some want to become a doctor like Ben Carson (Neurosurgeon), some want to win the grand prize on American Idol, while others may want to be a lawyer like Johnny Cochran. When my son Kevin was about six years old, I asked him what he wanted to be when he grew up. He replied, "A big old bus." What he meant was he wanted to be a school bus driver because he liked the big yellow bus because the children had fun on it. Our self-esteem sometimes can be motivated by competition between siblings. We are, at times, seeking the approval of those who are significant in our lives (parents, grandparents, etc.). Once again, this could have a positive or a negative impact on your self-esteem. For me, being in an abusive relationship had a negative impact on my self-esteem. The abusive environment of being beaten physically and emotionally had a tremendous effect on what I had become. My outer and inner beauty smarts and spirit had been zapped right out of me like a bug zapper. But, it was during my wilderness experience and spending quality time with me, which I learned how to rebuild. While rebuilding, there will be those who put others down. They do this to feel good about themselves. This gives them a feeling of superiority, power and control. But, it all depends on you. Beware of this, as you are working towards healing. There will be two kinds of people during this time and every time in your life:

- **Those who add to your life. The individuals will be a positive influence.**

- **Those who subtract from your life. These individuals always want you to give and never give back.**

In his book, "Full Esteem Ahead," Rob Solomon, quote's Gloria Steinem:

"I began to understand that self-esteem isn't everything; it's just that there's nothing without it."

This statement may be challenging, but the reward will be great. While rebuilding your self-esteem, you will have to let go of your past and grab hold of your future (unloading the baggage). As you grab hold of this concept (the idea), you will begin to see a beautiful self-portrait yourself. For both victim and batterer, it is here that they can begin to discover their dreams, vision and passion for life and the contribution they want to make. You will no longer want to walk in the shadow of others (generational or learned behavior). I learned what my assignment was through one of my mentors, Dr. Murdock. In his book entitled, "Seeds of Wisdom on Your Assignment", he lists the following clues that pointed me into my destiny.

- **Your assignment is any problem you were created to solve on earth.** This is that special gift from the Dream Giver. You were put here on earth to fulfill an assignment that no one else can do but you.

- **What you love is a clue to the gifts and wisdom you embrace to complete your assignment.**

- **What you hate is a clue to something you are assigned to correct.**

- **What grieves you is a clue to something you are assigned to heal.**

- **If you rebel against your assignment, God may permit painful experiences to correct you. You know, "Experience is the best teacher."**

- **Your assignment will require seasons of preparation.**

- **You will only succeed when your assignment becomes an obsession.**

Dr. Murdock's books along with Lester Sumerall's book entitled, "Embracing the Call", has had a tremendous impact on my life which has led me into the arena of authorship and motivational speaker. But, I had to learn how to tear down the old house (bad habits) and rebuild a new house (good habits). With this in mind, I could now begin to select the materials I needed to rebuild. For example, in order for a carpenter to build a house they would need materials like lumber, nails, concrete, etc.

Another important thing to know in rebuilding your self-esteem is recognizing that you have some things about you that are broken. These are things that are not functioning properly (mentally, physically, financially, etc.). This is okay to acknowledge and know that it is only temporary. In the case of the Harris', in counseling sessions, they recognized they both had made numerous mistakes in their relationship (dating and marriage). While mentoring and counseling them, Mr. Dean Young and I have readily learned their weaknesses. As their mentors, we instruct them on how to improve upon those weaknesses. It should be noted that it is very rare for victims of domestic violence to have any communication with one another. The Harris' really are the exception to the rule and Mr. Young and I praise them for their milestones. They have grown stronger in their communication skills (sometimes good and sometimes bad), parenting, financial needs, personal needs and spiritual needs. All these qualities are wonderful motivational tools in helping them rebuild their self-esteem, especially Mrs. Harris. As mentors, we do not disrespect their parents for not having the necessary skills to keep both victim and batterer out of the cycle of abuse. Once again, this process will take a long-term commitment from the mentor or spiritual advisor as well as positive commitment from the protégé's. This is how rebuilding can begin to manifest or come forward.

Here are a few important things to feast upon or digest while you try to rebuild.

- **Remember who your enemy is.** While rebuilding, understand that your number one enemy will be ignorance. This can be caused by learned behavior or failing to follow the instruction of your parents, mentor or spiritual advisor. What you learned previously didn't work for you. Now, you may find yourself sitting on the bench in the gym on the sidelines, learning how to get new information that will help build you and get you back in the game.

Don't get weary. You will be battling with your mind and your flesh (video clips) to turn your life around. Your family members may think you're strange because you no longer will accept the behavior that was past down to you from generation to generation.

- **Only judge yourself.** Don't waste your time and energy looking at what others have done to you. As a victim, remember that you no longer want to be a victim, but victorious. For the batterer, you no longer want to batter, but a bridge builder. When the victim dwells on what the batterer has done, those thoughts can and will to drain you mentally as well as physically. When you keep reminiscing on what you have been through, the batterer still has power and control over you.

- **Don't make people think like you.** People who have never been victims may not understand your sudden radical turn-around. Don't sweat it. When the victim was under the control of the batterer, they found themselves talking and think like them. Or, when the batterer tries to turn his or her life around, no one will believe them. They will always be labeled, flagged and tagged as a batterer. This can be infuriating. So don't make people do what you didn't like done to you. God is in control and you are only in control of you.

For the victim, days, weeks, months and years, which you were was predicated on what your batterer wanted you to be. So, being patient and learning how to spend quality time with you is important. Those little instant replay video clips will try to distract you from your course. Here is another suggestion that can be helpful while rebuilding your self-esteem. These suggestions are also applicable for the batterer.

- **The words that you speak will be an indication if you are a winner or a loser.** Everyday, speak greatness into your life. Say to yourself that you are special and that today will be a great day because you are on an assignment.

"Do not let this Book of the Law depart from your mouth; meditate on it day and night, so that you may be careful to do everything in it. Then you will be prosperous and successful."

Joshua 1:8
New International Version

Begin to get a **POSITIVE** mental picture of what you see yourself becoming. See yourself living a strong and positive life. Put up pictures of that sweet peaceful home you would like to have or that nice car and pictures of money (smile). What you see and hear over and over again is what you will walk into. But, you will be required to so some things to help with the process as mentioned in the scripture, Joshua 1:8. We are products of our environment. More importantly, remember that God created you and He thinks highly of you (Jeremiah 29:11). Because you have chosen a new path for your life, it will be of the utmost importance that you focus on your many opportunities and not your obstacles and failures. Don't let fear, doubt and unbelief be a part of your rebuilding. You can leap over these hurdles like a strong athlete.

 Recently, I had the awesome opportunity to hear a great teacher, motivator and mentor, Dr. Myles Munroe. Dr. Munroe says, *"What you are passionate about will eventually allow you to have visions and dreams of what you will become. "* Your vision, will come as you begin to rebuild your self-esteem and your source of confidence. Confidence, prayer and patience are essential to healing. To piggyback on Dr. Murdock's teaching on, "Your Assignment", validates what Dr. Munroe has to say about your vision being a motivating factor in rebuilding your self-esteem. Here's what Dr. Munroe has to say:

- Your vision chooses your friends.

- Your vision chooses your library.

- Your vision chooses your diet.

- Your vision chooses your to do list.

- Your vision chooses your associates.

- Your vision chooses your priorities (important vs. urgent).

- Your vision chooses your wardrobe.

- Your vision chooses your plans.

- Your vision chooses your spouse (it's not how much do you love me, but where are you going in life).

Finally, as you rebuild, you will need to hold onto the courage that Dr. Angelou spoke about in Chapter 4. Remember, that for everything there is a season (Ecclesiastes 3:1-8). Let's read what that scripture says.

A Time For Everything

Vs. 1 There is a time for everything, and a season for every activity under heaven:

Vs. 2 a time to be born and a time to die, a time to plant and a time to uproot.

Vs. 3 a time to kill and a time to heal, a time to tear down and a time to rebuild.

Vs. 4 a time to weep and a time to laugh, a time to mourn and a time to die dance.

Vs. 5 a time to scatter stones and a time to gather them, a time to embrace and a time to refrain,

Vs. 6 a time to search and a time to give up, a time to keep and a time to throw away,

Vs. 7 a time to tear and a time to mend, a time to be silent and a time to speak,

Vs. 8 a time to love and a time to hate, a time of war and a time for peace.

What is learned from the domestic violence experience whether victim or batterer will be valuable? Just like the farmer who needs his tractor to plow the field to get a good harvest; so will t need to plow through their personal fields in order to rebuild. So, I am encouraging both victim and batterer to lift their head up from the sand. Look up and enjoy the beauty around you. There are people out there who are depending on your breakthrough to help get them through. There maybe times while doing their very best to rebuild, that their steps may seem few and far between, but I encourage them to hold onto the hope that they can do this and rebuild with one brick at a time. Looking back will only delay their journey.

"SUBSTITUTING WRONG BEHAVIOR FOR RIGHT BEHAVIOR"

"There is a way that seemeth right unto man, but in the end it leads to death."
Proverbs 14:12
New International Version

As we open up this section, I am sure that there are numerous things that are running through your mind about right or wrong behavior (some may say addictive behavior) as it applies to domestic violence. I am quite aware that my opinions, suggestions and use of terminology used to describe the behavior may not be used in your vocabulary to describe your abusive relationship. But, know matter what words we use to categorize the behavior; it is still unhealthy for both victim and batterer. In the previous section entitled, "Spending Quality Time With Yourself", you were asked to make a list of **YOUR** positive and negative qualities to help you begin to work on moving forward in the healing process. If you have not done so, take a few moments to make your list from below.

List of Your Positive Qualities
1.
2.
3.

List of Your Negative Things To Get Rid Of
1.
2.
3.

I have attempted to establish that domestic violence is learned behavior. For me, I know that being in a domestic violence relationship was the wrong behavior for my life. But, I choose to treat my domestic violence as a form of addiction. So, I'm a *Recovering-Victorious Domestic Violence Addict.* Pretty hard label for myself, you think? Well, that's because domestic violence is a pretty hard lifestyle to break. Here's is Cheryle's definition of a **Domestic Violence Addict**:

"One who lives a lifestyle of being in repeated domestic violence relationships. One who will take the mental or physical abuse of her partner to please them – no matter what the cost."

This is what I had become and it almost cost me my life. This is why I treat my domestic violence like any other addiction, (alcohol, drugs, gambling, eating and shopping). Society has labeled these as "Addictive Behavior" which has many faces attached to it such as depression and sometimes suicide. I believed, based on my history, that there are many similarities. Have you wondered why the victim is attracted to the batterer? And, why batterers know how to attract or bait their victims. Why are they drawn to this wrong or bad behavior?

Addictive behavior as defined by R.C. Engs' papers on alcohol and drugs says:

"Any activity, substance, object, or behavior that has become the major focus of a person's life to the exclusion of other activities, or that has begun to harm the individual or other physically, mentally, or socially is considered an addictive behavior."

When someone thinks of an "addict" they immediately associate this with an alcoholic lying in the gutter or a drug addict stealing to get their next fix. But, according to Eng's definition, I believe, we could easily slide domestic violence on the list. This is why it is important to provide continued educational training for medical institutions in the area of domestic violence so they may better treat their patients when presented in their offices or emergency rooms. Some researchers believe that there are some similarities between physical addiction (ex. alcohol or drugs) and psychological dependence to things like gambling, sex work, eating disorders, shopping and **I** will now add **battering**. It is believed that these behaviors may produce-endorphins in the brain, which makes that person feel "high". In the case of the batterer, when they are abusing their partner, they appear to get this "rush" or "high" and will not stop until it is satisfied (power and control of the victim). If the victim or batterer continues in the wrong or addictive behavior, it can become a way for life, which can only lead to destruction. It can happen. I was one of those individuals ("My Story").

In this section, I will attempt to help you understand more clearly how wrong or addictive behavior can be changed by learning how to substitute it for good or positive behavior. In order to accomplish this, we will need to build a foundation by understanding the following:

- **Some of the characteristics of wrong or bad behavior.**

- **What can cause of the wrong or bad behavior?**

- **Is it bad behavior or a choice?**

Once this foundation is built, we can begin to recognize that the victim and batterer must purpose or believe in their heart (*"For as he thinketh in his heart, so is he." Proverbs 23:7*) to accomplish the task at hand (no more abuse) no matter how difficult it may seem (courage and determination). If they have purposed in their heart, then a positive change will take place. But, a **change** in them will be required. This change may sometimes require removing people and things from their life either temporarily or permanently. We discussed some of those challenges in the section entitled, *"Spending Quality Time With Yourself."* Many people may not admit that they are addicted to various things such as: shopping, eating, sex, drugs, etc. However, the **12-Step Recovery** process that has been implemented for Alcoholics and Narcotics Anonymous used to get individuals clean and free from the addictive behavior can be applied to domestic violence. I will list those 12-Steps for your information. If the individual chooses not to go through the entire process, they could be setting themselves up for continued **major problems** in the future.

The victim or batterer who is determined and has the courage runs the **race** of recovery or eradication of domestic violence, will have to run it at their own pace and not at the expectations of others. When this is accomplished, results will be a **good behavior and positive** lifestyle no matter what else is going on around them. This can be accomplished by setting boundaries and having supportive people in their life. Again, I believe that this section will be the most important. Without the acknowledging or addressing of the wrong or addictive behavior of domestic violence, society will continue to have unhappy, unhealthy, unproductive and uncooperative individuals trying to make it in a world without the proper tools.

Let's Get Started !

"The Foundation"

is always built from the bottom up.

Beware of those individuals who say, "I don't need anybody" or "I can do this by myself." As you can see from the illustration above, you can't get to the top unless you build a foundation from the bottom. As we begin to build the foundation, the characteristics provided on the next page in bold are used to describe those individuals who are in "Official Addiction Programs". I will use these characteristics to show how these "Official Addiction Programs" can be applied to the cycle of domestic violence.

Let's Get Started !

CHARACTERISTICS

1. **The person becomes obsessed, always thinking of the object, activity, or substance.** The batterer does this with their victim. They are obsessed about having that power and control. If the victim leaves or attempts to leave, stalking their victim (the object) becomes the obsession of the batterer. This can sometimes lead to the destruction of property or death of victim or themselves. The batterer may use substance abuse to ease the pain and frustration of not getting what he or she wants which also dulls his or her rational thinking. This causes him or her to act on the negative thinking.

2. **They will seek it out, or engage in the behavior even though it is causing harm (physical problems, poor work or study performance, problems with friends, family and coworkers).** The batterer, when they have lost power and control, will tend to slip either into depression or rage. When in rage, they will destroy structures (punching holes in walls) and personal items of their victim. If the batterer is fortunate enough to have a job, their productivity becomes poor which can lead to termination of employment. When this happens, the baggage of abuse and trauma from both victim and batterer can be imposed on family members, friends and coworkers making it difficult for them to function effectively on their jobs and personal lives.

3. **The person will compulsively engage in the activity, that is, do the activity over and over even if they don't want to and find it difficult to stop.** The batterer after they have abused their victim attempts to make apologies to the victim and the honeymoon stage of the relationship begins all over again. This honeymoon stage may last for a brief moment. Sometimes, the victim will also make apologies to the batterer even if it wasn't their fault out of fear for their

safety. So, in the mind of the victim and batterer, they both want it to stop, but don't know how.

4. **Upon the end of the activity (abuse), withdrawal symptoms often occur. These can include irritability, craving, restlessness or depression.** This characteristic can apply to both victim and batterer. They are both traumatized about the episode and both will seek out one or all of these withdrawal symptoms. This is especially common when the domestic violence relationship has ended. At this point, they are both "Mourning the Loss" as discussed earlier.

5. **The person does not appear to have control as to when, how long, or how much they will continue the behavior (loss of control).** For example, a woman may buy ten pairs of shoes when she only wanted to buy stockings. Or, he may drink six beers when he only wanted one. The batterer, when control of power is lost, will not stop victimizing until the adrenaline subsides. To the victim, it feels like the abuse it will never end. They may cry out, "How long and how much more must I endure."

6. **They deny that the problem results from engagement in the behavior, even though others can see the negative effects.** This is more noticeable in the life of the victim. Others like, family, friends and coworkers saw things in the batterer while they were dating that just didn't fit who they were. They would say, "*How did they end up with him or her.*" Many didn't say anything because they knew it would not change the victim's decision. Recently, while meeting with Mrs. Harris, Mr. Young asked, "Did your family say anything about your relationship with Mr. Harris while dating?" She replied, "*No, because they knew it would make me rebel.*" The negative effect was that she became a victim

7. **The person hides the behavior after family or close friends have mentioned their concern.** The victim and batterer both show signs of this behavior. Sometimes the victim will keep the abuse from family and friends because of safety reasons or fear. The batterer, however, will have others to believe that all is well in their relationship with their partner. At social functions, they both may personify that they are the sweetest and most romantic couple on the face of the earth.

8. **Many individuals with this behavior report a blackout time while they were engaging in the behavior (don't remember much about what has happened).** During domestic violence, the batterer, after the abuse, may not remember the episode of abuse. What they may remember is looking at the physical or emotional damage done to the victim or their personal property. For the victim, if they were to press legal action, when asked questions by law enforcement, their answers are vague and sketchy. As a former victim, as I took my final beating that night, there were many things when questioned by the police and domestic violence advocate that I didn't remember. Again, this could be the body's way of protecting us from the trauma. It wasn't until I wrote my first book that I began to remember bits and pieces of what transpired.

9. **Depression is common in individuals with addictive behavior. This is why it is important to seek immediate medical attention to find out the source of the depression.** Victims of domestic violence may experience many faces of depression (eating disorders, anxiety, insomnia, etc.). However, if they seek medical attention, during the triage of the patient (questions asked by a nurse during the visit), they may not share that abuse is taking place? Therefore, the physician may not be able to adequately treat their patient. Again, this is why education to the medical community

about domestic violence is important (See Resource – **"Domestic Violence Guide for Physicians"**. The batterer, however, may not seek medical attention, but may choose to self-medicate by using alcohol or substance abuse to deal with their depression.

10. **Individuals with addictive behaviors often have low self-esteem. They feel anxious if they do not have control over their environment and come from psychologically or physically abusive families.** The batterer normally has low self-esteem. They depend on their victim to help them feel and look important. They normally do not have an identity of their own and need their victim to validate them. These individuals may have been a witness to abuse in their home as a child, thus, this behavior seems normal for them.

As mentioned, here is additional information of what the **12-Step Program** uses to help rehabilitate their clients. I think that these affirmations could be applied to domestic violence. What do you think?

12-STEP AFFIRMATIONS

1. **I can't.** We admitted we were powerless over our addiction. That our lives had become unmanageable. Suggested reading: Romans 7:18-20

2. **God can.** Came to believe that a power greater than ourselves could restore us to sanity. Suggested readings: Mark 9:23-24, Romans 10:8-10

3. **I think I'll let Him.** Made a decision to turn our will and our lives over to the care of God as we understood Him. Suggested readings: Proverbs 3:5-6, Romans 12:1-2

4. **Make a searching and fearless moral inventory of ourselves.** Suggested readings: Ezekiel 36:26-27, 31, Lamentations 3:40

5. **Confession is good for the soul.** Admitted to God, to ourselves, and to another human being the exact nature of our wrongs. Suggested readings: James 5:15a, Psalms 51:1-4a, 7,9-10

6. **Accepting God's forgiveness.** Were entirely ready to have God remove all these defects of character. Suggested readings: Psalms 51:8-12, 14-17

7. **Humbly asked Him to remove our shortcomings.** Suggested readings: Isaiah 57:15, James 4:7-10

8. **Made a list of all persons we had harmed and became willing to make amends to them all.** Suggested readings: Psalms 5:16, Matthew 5:23-24

9. **Continued reconciliation.** Made direct amends to such people wherever possible except when to do so would injure them or others. Suggested readings: Matthew 18:15, Colossians 1:20

10. **Renewing a right spirit.** Continued to take personal inventory and when we were wrong, promptly admitted it. Suggested readings: I John 1:8-10, Romans 5:20b, 6:1-4

11. **Growing in the grace of God.** Sought through prayer and meditation to improve our conscious contact with God as we understood Him, praying only for knowledge of His will for us and the power to carry that out. Suggested readings: Isaiah 1:18, James 1:5, Romans 8:26

12. Giving Back. Having had a spiritual awakening as the result of these steps, we tried to carry this message to others, and to practice these principles in all our affairs. Suggested readings: II Corinthians 5:18-21, Galatians 6:1

Something To Think About !

Could you see from the list how Domestic Violence could be incorporated in a 12-Step Program? Discuss it and name some of them.

Keep Going There's An Assignment to Complete !

It is hard to tackle a problem if you don't know all the components. Understanding the characteristic is the first step to building the foundation to substitute wrong behavior for good behavior. Take a moment to fill in the chart on the next page and let's move on to the next foundation.

Something To Think About !

"The Foundation"

Discussion: Did you notice any similarities between domestic violence and other addictions? List them.

Example: Domestic Violence – Blackouts
Alcohol – Blackouts

Domestic Violence	Other Addictions
1.	1.
2.	2.
3.	3.
4.	4.
5.	5.
6.	6.
7.	7.
8.	8.

Let's Get Started !

"Causes of the Wrong or Addictive Behavior"

This section will attempt to look at some of the causes of this behavior. While there is no current research to show that there is a direct correlation between domestic violence and other addictions, the patterns and symptoms of the abuse are similar. In 1995, the economic cost of substance abuse in the United States exceeded $414 billion, with this health care cost, it was estimated that $114 billion was attributed to substance abuse. By eighth grade, 52% of adolescents had consumed alcohol, 41% had smoked tobacco and 20% had smoke marijuana. These numbers have climbed dramatically over the years.

I believe that although the batterer may use alcohol and substance abuse as an excuse to abuse, it is not the major cause. The alcohol and substance abuse is just yet another Band-Aid for a more deeply rooted problem. Some researchers consider gambling and alcoholism as diseases, while others consider these as learned or addictive behaviors. Because of this lack of agreement among the experts, it brings challenges for therapist, physicians and others regarding prevention and treatment of these individuals. So, what causes someone to batter? We really don't know. But, we all agree that whatever the debate or controversy of treatment, if victim and batterer are not willing to do the individual work to break the cycle of abuse, the prognosis is not good.

As an example of how researchers debate of validity of findings, in my research, I found a paper written by Dr. E. Comings entitled, "The Genetics of Addictive Behaviors", Dr. Comings posed a question. Although, I do not believe that domestic violence is genetic, his theory of why some become alcoholics and others do not were interesting. He wanted to know why some teenagers take a drink and not crave more, while others know from the instant of their first drink that the alcohol is going to cause them problems for the rest of their life. From his research he concluded that the most obvious reason for the susceptibility for the addictive behavior was an inborn or genetic trait. This was based on a study of alcoholism in children of alcoholics adopted away from their alcoholic parents at birth. This would provide researchers with powerful evidence that genes play an important role in the development of subsequent alcoholism. His colleague, Dr. Donald Goodman was one of the pioneers in this field. On the basis of the study, he found that the frequency of alcoholism, in adopted-out sons of alcoholic fathers was just as great when they were placed with non-alcoholic parents with alcoholic parents. The study showed that this form of alcoholism was predominately a genetic disorder. If this behavior is prevalent in individuals, when seeking medical attention, physicians should ask about history of alcoholism and substance addiction during the examination to help learn of any genetic disorders. This especially important for pregnant women as this may effect their unborn child.

In the journal entitled, "Psychiatric Times, Dr. Jeffrey A. Schaler wrote a controversial article called, "Addiction is a choice." He writes,

> *"Is addiction a disease or it is a choice? To think clearly about this question, we need to make a sharp distinction between an activity and its results. Many activities that are not themselves diseases can cause diseases. And a foolish, self-destructive activity is not necessarily a disease."*

With this statement, when we see this addiction (alcohol, drugs or domestic violence), we should think about not whether this behavior can cause physical or mental disease, whether or not it is foolish or self-destructive, but if it is something distinct or separate. In other words, is the pattern of the addictive behavior itself a disease? He believes that addiction is a behavior and is the decision of the individual. For these individuals, the use of alcohol or substance abuse could be a determining factor in their decision to continue the behavior. The person that is called an addict normally will monitor their consumption. They know how to reserve a little for that next habit. The same is true for the batterer. They are manipulative and calculating. They sometimes will monitor when they will attack their victim, while other times, spontaneous in their attack. If the victim and batterer choose to continue in the abusive relationship, then it becomes a choice no matter what variables were used in the equation to make them stay.

      In closing this section, whether domestic violence is addiction or choice doesn't really matter. What is significant that the outcome from this behavior is painful and causes great heartache for victim, batterer, children, family and friends? This could ultimately lead to the destruction of lives. As the foundation is being built, remember that starting at bottom is not necessarily a bad thing, especially for the victim. These individuals will need the help from a variety of positive and trusting individuals to help them break the cycle of the behavior. The victim and batterer should under the similarities and characteristics of those labeled or tagged as alcoholics or drug addicts. The principles of the 12-Step program can be utilized to help them break free. This will require courage and hard work. It is difficult to change comfortable behavioral patterns, especially as adults. But, **YOU CAN DO IT !**

Something To Think About !

Discussion: Write your views about whether domestic violence is addiction or a choice. Share with your study group or a friend.

What are some of the similarities in alcohol, substance and domestic violence? List them.

ALCOHOLISM   **DOMESTIC**   **SUBSTANCE**
                       VIOLENCE   **ABUSE**

As we close out this chapter on *"Breaking the Cycle: The Healing Process"*, remember that some people may try to dominate your space as you attempt to break the cycle of abuse and begin the healing process. Although in love their intentions may be genuine, you need to begin to set those boundaries and fight for what you haven't had – YOUR FREEDOM. Once you begin to set those boundaries, remember that those video clips will replay in your mind. As a victim, sometimes the words of the batterer will cry out, "No one cares about you like I do". But, once you have established those tactics from the batterer and the intentions from family member and friends, the mourning or grieving process will begin. Allow yourself time to mourn and grieve what has happened to you. For victim and batterer, they have lost something from the relationship. It is sometimes difficult to mourn because the individual is still very much alive. Find yourself a compassionate, strong, committed and supportive mentor or spiritual advisor. They will be able guide you from your pain into your destiny. They are concerned about who you are right now in the abusive cycle and what they want to see you become.

Spending quality time with you is another great benefit for the healing process. Try not to allow depression to set in. Remember that depression has many faces and distorts the truth. The mind is a powerful thing. The person who has offended you becomes the offense and their offense becomes your wrong or addictive behavior. Because of the offense or wound, we may tend to turn to behaviors that are not healthy for us (alcohol and substance abuse). Consider the various suggestions provided to help you break the cycle of abuse. Whatever positive outlet you choose, give yourself ample time to make a list of things that you like or dislike about you so that you can begin to fix them. Because my life is truly an open book, here are a few things on my list for your use as a sample.

CHERYLE'S LIST

LIKE ABOUT ME	DISLIKE ABOUT IT
Hair	Can only wear in a few styles. It's wavy and fine.
Hands	That I can't keep nice looking nails.
Teeth	Wish they were whiter.
Hips	Wish they were a little smaller.
Skin	Wish my face was not so oily.
Butt	Wish I didn't wobble when I walk so that it wouldn't be so noticeable.
Ears	I want to be a much better listener.
In Progress	Work on not being so defensive.

So as you can see, I'm still working on me. I didn't want you to think that you are out there all alone (Smile).

In closing, refine your list. Constantly make the need adjustments and alterations needed for your success. Make your list come alive in your life. As you rebuild your self-esteem, recognize that what you see on the outside may not a good representation of what you are on the inside. Embrace that warm spirit that you feel deep within you. The special gift inside of you give by the Dream Giver is waiting to be released. More importantly, don't forget to substitute that wrong or addictive behavior for good ones. Now is an opportunity for victim and batterer to stop blaming others – take responsible for their actions – release the pain – rebuild – MOVE FORWARD. Don't allow any more negative influences to dominate your very existence for why you were created, not even through medications (stress) if you can help it. As you cautiously and successfully mourn the loss, spend quality time with yourself, rebuild your self-esteem and substitute that wrong behavior for good behavior, know that you have what it takes to do this. You have the courage and strength to climb the mountain and break the cycle. Finally, I hear the words of R. Kelly echoing out to you, "I Believe I can Fly", and that you are well able to overcome the giant of abuse.

CONCLUSION

I trust that this book has been a source of enlightenment, inspiration, awareness, sensitivity, strength, support and a valuable educational tool for what transpires in the life of a victim and batterer of domestic violence. I hope that you were been able to see, "**Domestic Violence: Both Sides of the Coin.**" If both victim and batterer are sincere and committed about breaking the cycle of abuse, then it is my hope that the book has done this for them. As stated in the **Introduction**, I expected the book to spark some controversy. Some women may have branded me as a traitor because I have compassion for the batterer. I am not. Since domestic violence has been established, for the most part as a learned behavior, other has used various labels to describe the abuse. The motivation for writing this book is to promote prevention instead of intervention. I wanted to help educate schools, medical and religious institutions, law enforcement and social organizations about the seriousness of domestic violence.

The stories all were true from my personal experience, family mentor protégés and written to help you better go inside our world of abuse as well as understanding the dynamics this has on both victim and batterer. Chapter 1, *"In the Beginning"*, allowed us to see how having a lack of love as early as childhood could have a significant impact on the informative years of boys and girls. In my own personal story, *"My Story"*, I revealed how the rippling effects of having a lack of love played in my life as a young mother and wife. Ultimately, these rippling effects could have attributed to the suicide of Chucky. Individuals use alcohol, drugs and other devices to cover up their deep-rooted pain. When that deeply rooted pain begins to create problems and are not addressed, especially in girls, early promiscuity (sexual activity) can lead to teen pregnancy. We explored some reasons why these problems can exist: 1) absentee father and 2) single female head-of-household. Either way, the family structure has been broken. In, *"Impacts of Lack of Love"*, we examined my personal tragedy of dealing with the suicide of Chucky, that when some children are exposed to dysfunctional behavior in the home, especially domestic violence, the chances of suicide are greater. If parents begin to notice signs of Youth Suicide (Resource Section), it is important that they seek good professional counseling, support, love and guidance so that their child will not become a statistic. I encourage parents not to think that suicide of a child could not knock at their door.

However, if early intervention does not take place in the home, *"The Cycle Begins"* of abuse will continue. It can pass down from generation to generation (our children and grandchildren). As mentioned earlier, I was three generations of the cycle of abuse (grandmother, mother and daughter). In the case of Mrs. Harris, as far as she could trace her family history, she was second generation of domestic violence (mother and daughter). And, "J", because she was adopted at a young age, it was difficult to trace her family history, but she had been in several abusive dating relationships and an abusive marriage. If we dig hard enough, we could probably link "J" back a few generations as well. The story of Aunt Louise and her children was another good example of how generational behavior works. Aunt Louise was a single female head-of-household who loss all three children tragically. If the cycle of domestic violence is not eradicated early in the family structure, it will continue to leave an open door for the abuse to take resident in our children, their children and their children's children.

Once the door of is open, the individuals whether they are dating or married will begin to experience things in the relationship that in the beginning may seem charming and to good to be true. Then, at the moment of the twinkling of an eye, the red flags and warning signs begin to emerge --- *"The Abuse: Power and Control"*. These signs are significant because they help us to know that something during relationship may not be quite right. Unfortunately, many of the signs are ignored and then we find ourselves as victims. When the signs are ignored, victims especially, will find themselves involved with an "Angry Man" or "Angry Woman". This book, if taken seriously, contains enough valuable resource material to help keep victim, batterer or anyone you know from the power and control cycle of abuse. More importantly, it is a wonderful training tool.

The *"Transition"* process will be one of the most difficult of all. The victim will return to their abuse an average of seven times. But, since you have read the book this far, it is my hope that you are already out or you are contemplating getting out or preparing to help someone get out. Preparing a safety plan for the many ramifications of leaving the abuse is vitally important. This is why I have provided *"Your Safety Plan"* guide in the resource section of this book. This plan is not only designed to help victims get out of the abuse, but to help those who will assist in this process see how detailed this process can be especially if children are involved. Once to safety, the victim, for the most part, can anticipate being "Stalked" by their batterer. The stalker is out of control because you have decided to no longer be controlled. Although fear may grip the victim, they can be confident in knowing that the law is there to protect them through a *"Protection Order"*. If the victim is not comfortable with contacting their local law enforcement agency, they can contact their local domestic violence agency for assistance and support. They are wonderful and have valuable resources to help guide victims through the process. It should be noted, however, that male victims of domestic violence might not have as many resources available to them because society tends to support women.

Most importantly, *"Breaking the Cycle: The Healing Process"* is crucial to starting a new life. Bouts of depression and grief will begin take hold of their life. Like many who have lost loved ones (physical death), the mourning and grieving process is no different for individuals in the abusive cycle. Sufficient time to "Mourning the Loss" is important and should not be pressured by family or friends. This process is important for both victim and batterer as they both have lost something from the relationship. It should be understood that they may never forget the pain of the loss, but they will learn how to move on and have a successful and productive life. This is why *"Spending Quality Time With Yourself"* is okay. As the healing process is in motion, don't let others dictate to them how to chart their new course. They both should set their boundaries and limitations. The can enjoy the long runs, walks, baths, workouts and whatever positive means of relaxation. Meditation of readings and music are also a positive way for them to get in touch with their feelings. As they begin to appreciate and chart their destination, "Rebuilding Self-Esteem" will be a terrific start to boosting their confidence and self-worth. The victim and batterer should remember that for months and may be years, they were living in the shadows of others. Whatever the vehicle used to bring them to the abuse, this is now an opportunity for them to be what "The Dream Giver" (God) has made them to be (trailblazer to help other out of abuse). Don't forget to learn how to *"Substituting Wrong Behavior with Good Behavior."* Whether you choose to acknowledge domestic violence as learned, generational, addiction or choice, if not dealt with effectively, the results are the same, DESTRUCTION. I've learned how to pick and choose what is good and not good for me. This is because I have chosen to have **"The Mentor or Spiritual Advisor"** to help me gain focus and direction. The mentor will be one of the best investments that the victim or batterer could have ever make. Remember that it may not be easy swallowing the medicine or advice that they give them to take, but if taken as directed, they will become a much healthier individual.

Although this chapter is labeled **Conclusion**, in reality, it is the **Beginning** of a **New Beginning** for anyone who wants to learn more about domestic violence, especially the victim and batterer and how you can help if a domestic violence case ever came knocking at your door.

It has been an honor for me to expose my personal pain and pleasures as well as those whom God placed in my path to get this project completed. They were reluctant, but wanted others to hear their stories so that they would not have to endure the ugliness of abuse. I hope it has done that for you. May this book go around the world educating and helping people to be set free. Again, **thank you** for the opportunity to write this book for you. Remember that, *"We Need Each Other"*.

Please email me at godmbtcfc@yahoo.com and let me know how this book has been a source of encouragement for you.

Love, Cheryle

The Love We Desire Is Already Within Us

God is love. This is where we must begin. We cannot expect to have a loving relationship with our family, mate or children until we heal our individual relationship with God. In the ancient traditions of people of color, all life was centered on the Creative Force and its elements. Our ancestors had a wholesome respect for the Creator and all creations. They honored the earth for support, the sun for the life force and themselves as expressions of creation. Today, we relate to one another's ego. We want to please one another because of who we are or what we have. We hold people in awe; we want people to fulfill our needs. We demoralize ourselves and one another for what we believe is love (domestic violence). **God is love**. That's it! God does not give presents to make you love Him. God does not have needs, except that you love Him, but He will not force the relationship. God does not make threats like your batterer has. God does not feel abandoned. God does not deal with rejection. The only thing God does is **love you** and that is the only reason you are here. He has created you to fulfill an assignment here on earth. He has equipped you with everything you need in the world to make it.

RESOURCE SECTION

🗝 *Proverbs 4:7 – Wisdom is supreme; therefore, get wisdom, though it cost all you have, get understanding.*

🗝 *What you read and hear over and over will help YOU step into YOUR divine destiny.*

THE RIGHTS OF BATTERED MEN AND WOMEN

- **The right** to share equally with a partner all decisions and responsibilities related to the relationship, children, home and finances.
- **The right** to share equally with a mate in financial decisions.
- **The right** to grow and explore personally potential without feeling guilty, selfish, or afraid.
- **The right** to have friendships with both men and women outside of the relationship as long as you do not violate the privacy of the relationship with your partner.
- **The right** to express opinions and have them given the same respect and consideration as those of your mate.
- **The right** to have and express sexual needs and desires without feeling selfish, demanding or aggressive.
- **The right** to have emotional, physical and intellectual needs be as important as the needs of a mate.
- **The right** to expect a mate to give at least 50% to resolve difficulties in the relationship.
- **The right** to hold a mate responsible for his or her behavior rather than assuming that responsibility yourself.
- **The right** NEVER to be physically attacked or psychologically degraded by a mate and the right to terminate.

FACT vs. FICTION

Fiction – Abused men or women can always leave home.
Fact – His or her level of danger increases when they try to leave.

Fiction – Abused men or women are crazy or mentally ill.
Fact – Battered men and women seldom suffer from mental disorders.

Fiction – Abusers are unsuccessful and lack resources to cope with the world.
Fact – Many abusers are successful with economic and social power.

Fiction – Abused men or women enjoy being beaten, that why they stay.
Fact – No one enjoys being threatened, beaten, pushed, shoved, kicked, etc.

Fiction – Battering only happen to poor young women with low self-esteem and lots of children.
Fact – Battering can happen to any man or woman regardless of race, age, socioeconomic status, sexual orientation, mental or physical ability and religious background. All women are influenced by religious, social and cultural messages.

SEX and TRUST

Having a good relationship is very important. However, having a relationship does not mean that you have to have sex. But, whether you are kissing, touching or having sex, it should ALWAYS be something that you both want to do. Sex and trust are very meaningful in a relationship. Consider this:

Sex is meant to be:
- Something that you decide to do when you are ready
- Something that makes you both feel good
- Something that you can stop or interrupt at any time
- Something that is safe (you both have protection to prevent unwanted diseases or pregnancy)

Sex is not meant to be:
- The only way to prove that you love someone
- Something that you feel pressured or forced into
- Something that you do because everyone else is doing it
- Something that makes you feel used

Trust and Communication:
The most important thing in a sexual relationship is that you trust the other person and you feel like you can communicate with them. If you are considering a sexual relationship, or if you are in a sexual relationship, ask yourself:
- How much do I trust this person to respect what you do and do not want to do?
- How comfortable would I feel talking with them about safe sex and contraception?
- How comfortable would I feel saying to no to them if I changed my mind?

Sex and Pressure:
- What if someone has touched you or made you touch them in a sexual way, and you felt like you had no choice?

You might have:
- Felt scared to say no
- Felt pressured into having sex, because they made you think that if you did not, they would break up with you, or they would not like you
- Been asleep, drunk, or high and did not really know what was going on
- Been forced into sexual contact (this happens a lot in domestic violence)

Extra Special Note: No one should force you into any type of sexual contact. In fact, this is sexual assault, and it is a crime that can be reported to the police. Remember, talk to someone about it. Do not hold it in. There is help out there for you.

****This section is directed for those who can't hold out.

FIVE STEPS TO SAFER SEX

1. *Communicate* – You can't practice the other four steps without this one.

2. The only 100% safe sex is abstinence.

3. Next to abstinence, the safest sex is with a clinically monogamous partner (both have been tested for STDs and have vaginal or anal intercourse or oral sex only with each other).

4. If you choose to have sex with multiple partners, use a condom each and every time you have vaginal or anal sex or oral sex on a male.

5. Also, use a latex dam anytime you perform oral sex on a female or have oral-anal sex.

ABSTIENENCE

Abstinence means choosing not to engage in oral, anal or vaginal sex

It's a choice you can make for one night or a lifetime

HOW FAR DO YOU WANT TO GO? DOES YOUR PARTNER AGREE?

TALK ABOUT IT FIRST !

I CARE ABOUT YOU !

People don't care how much we know until they know how much we care.

Types of Abuse

Here are some examples of how abusers get power and keep control.

Physical abuse: The abuser's physical attacks or aggressive behavior can range from bruising to the ultimate, which is murder. It begins with what is excused as trivial contact that can escalate into more frequent and serious attacks. These include hitting, pushing, kicking, biting, scratching, slapping, shooting, punching, stabbing, pulling hair, breaking bones, choking, burning, throwing objects, pinning down, blocking exits to rooms and buildings or death.

Sexual abuse: In some domestic violence situation, rape does occur. Sex is normally pretty rough and not sensual at all. For the most part, the women who are victims are forced to have sex with the batterer or take part in some illicit act. This may include forcing the victim to have sex with others, inserting objects into them without permission, forcing the victims to satisfy them without the victim being satisfied and accusing them of having sex with others.

Although there have not been recent reports that show that men are raped, they are not excluded. They normally don't share this information publicly.

Isolation: Controlling whom he/she sees and talks to, what he/she does, where he/she goes. Moving him/her away from family and friends.

Economic Abuse: Controlling finances, trying to keep him/her from getting or keeping a job, making harassing phone calls to him/her workplace, controlling access to the car, keeping her pregnant so she can't work. Making him/her ask for money, making him/her live on an allowance, making him/her account for all the money that gets spent. Taking his/her money, failing to provide adequate support for him/her and his/her children, trashing his/her clothes and belongings, running up, and ruining his/her credit.

Emotional or Psychological abuse: This abuse can include constant verbal, harassment, excessive possessiveness, isolation, deprivation of physical and economic resources and destruction of personal property (spiritual literature, pictures, clothing, etc.). Calling the victim names, lying, using obscenities toward them, and telling them they are worthless. Telling them they are crazy, playing mind games, subjecting them to the "silent treatment" making them responsible for how they feel or act. Directing negative or ugly body language toward them, insulting or putting them, especially in front of others.

Using "Male/Female Privilege": Treating him/her like a servant, making all the "big" decisions, acting like the "master of the castle," making him/her feel total responsibility for housecleaning and child-care.

Intimidation: Putting him/her in fear by smashing things, destroying his/her property, using looks, actions, gestures, and a loud voice.

Threats: Making and/or carrying out threats to do something to hurt him/her emotionally or physically, threatening to take the children, commit suicide, and report her to child welfare, have his/her committed to a mental hospital.

Using Children: Making his/her feels guilty about the children, using children to give messages, using visitation as a way to harass him/her.

CHARACTERISITICS OF RELATIONSHIP ADDICTION
Men and Women Who Love Too Much

- Typically, we come from a dysfunctional* home in which our emotional needs are not meet.
- Having received little real nurturing ourselves, we try to fill this unmet need vicariously by becoming caregivers, especially to people who appear, in some way, needy.
- Because we were never able to change our parent(s) into the warm, loving caretaker(s) we longed for, we respond deeply to the familiar type of emotionally unavailable person whom we can again try to change, through our love.
- Terrified of abandonment, we will do ANYTHING to keep a relationship from dissolving.
- Almost nothing is too much trouble, takes too much time, or is too expensive if it will "help" the person you are involved with.
- Accustomed to lack of love in personal relationships, we are willing to wait, hope and try harder to please.
- We are willing to take far more the 50 percent of the responsibility, guilt and blame in any relationship.
- Our self-esteem is critically low, and deep down inside, we do not believe we deserve to be happy. Rather, we believe we must earn the right to enjoy life.

*Homes in which one or more of the following occur (effectively disrupting and preventing contact and intimacy)

- Substance Abuse
- Compulsive behavior (eating, working, cleaning, gambling, etc.)
- Physical abuse of spouse and/or children
- Inappropriate sexual behavior of parent toward child (from seductiveness to incest)
- Constant arguing and tension
- Extended periods of silence between parents
- Conflicting attitudes or values of parents
- Display of contradictory behaviors that compete for children's allegiance
- Parents competitive with each other or their children
- Parent who cannot relate to family member and actively avoids the, blaming that member for avoidance.
- Extreme rigidity and/or obsession about money, religion, work, use of time, display of affection, sex, television, housework, sports, politics, etc.
- We have a desperate need to control people and our relationships, having experienced little security in childhood. We mask our efforts to control people and situations as "being helpful".
- In a relationship, we are much more in touch with our dream of how it could be than with reality of our situation.
- We are addicted to people and to emotion emotional pain.
- We may be predisposed emotionally and often biochemically becoming addicted to drugs, alcohol, and/or certain foods, particularly sugary products.

- Being drawn to people with problems that need fixing, or by being enmeshed in situation that are chaotic, uncertain, and emotionally painful, we avoid focusing on our responsibility to ourselves.
- We may have a tendency toward episodes of depression, which we try to forestall through the excitement provided by an unstable relationship.

- We are not attracted to people who are kind, stable, reliable, and interested in us. We find such "nice" people boring.

HIGH RISK INDICATORS FOR SERIOUS INJURY OR DEATH FROM DOMESTIC VIOLENCE

- Access to or ownership of guns.

- Use of a weapon in a prior abusive incident.

- Threats with weapons.

- Threats to kill.

- Serious injury in prior abusive incidents.

- Threats of suicide.

- Drug or alcohol abuse.

- Forced sex of female partner.

- Obsessive.

- Extreme jealousy.

- Extreme dominance.

WARNING SIGNS WHILE DATING

If you answer <u>yes</u> to any of these questions, you could be in an abusive relationship, or your relationship could become abusive. Check the box if one or more items apply to you or someone you know.

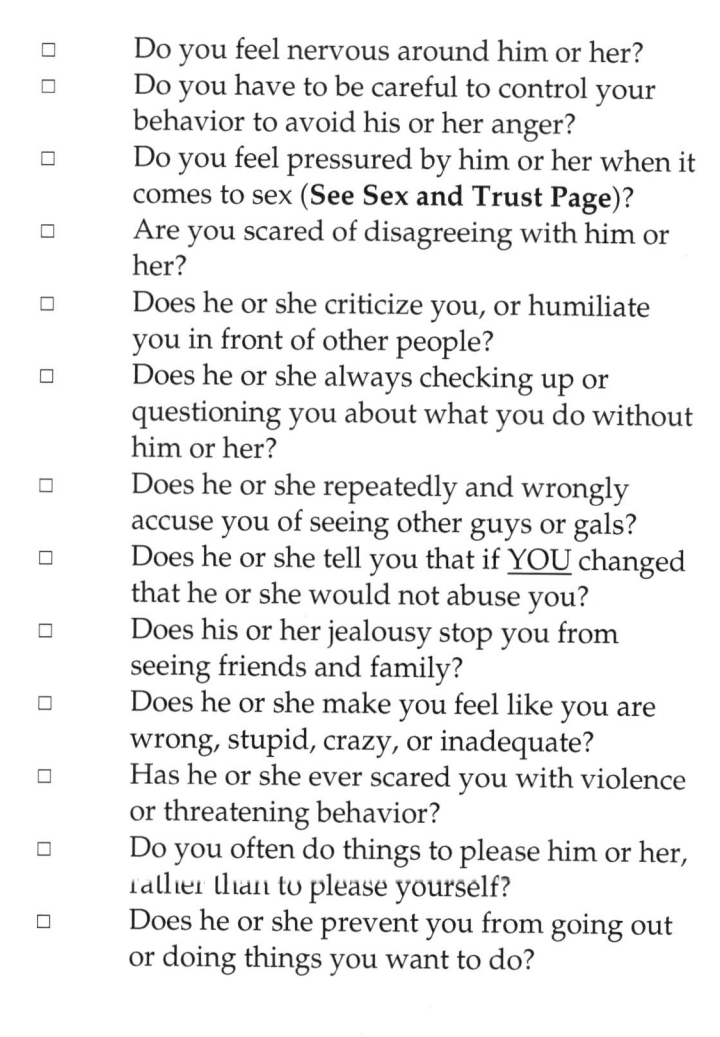

- ☐ Do you feel nervous around him or her?
- ☐ Do you have to be careful to control your behavior to avoid his or her anger?
- ☐ Do you feel pressured by him or her when it comes to sex (**See Sex and Trust Page**)?
- ☐ Are you scared of disagreeing with him or her?
- ☐ Does he or she criticize you, or humiliate you in front of other people?
- ☐ Does he or she always checking up or questioning you about what you do without him or her?
- ☐ Does he or she repeatedly and wrongly accuse you of seeing other guys or gals?
- ☐ Does he or she tell you that if <u>YOU</u> changed that he or she would not abuse you?
- ☐ Does his or her jealousy stop you from seeing friends and family?
- ☐ Does he or she make you feel like you are wrong, stupid, crazy, or inadequate?
- ☐ Has he or she ever scared you with violence or threatening behavior?
- ☐ Do you often do things to please him or her, rather than to please yourself?
- ☐ Does he or she prevent you from going out or doing things you want to do?

- [ ] Do you feel that, with him or her nothing you do is ever good enough?
- [ ] Does he or she say that they will kill or hurt themselves if you break up with them?
- [ ] Does he or she make excuses for his abusive behavior by saying it is the alcohol or drugs or because he or she can not control their temper, or that he or she was just joking?

Even if you just answered yes to a few of these questions, do not think that it is not bad. These are warning signs are a clue for you that you maybe in an abusive relationship. If you are in an abusive relationship, it is likely that it will get worse over the course of time. Do not think that you are able to help them change. This is a myth. You can only save yourself and children if there are any.

REINFORCED POSITIVE HABITS

"You Decide Whether You Will Be Victim or A Victor"

- **Become God conscious.** Search out God for yourself. Spend time in studying the bible. There may be many ministers, preachers and teachers who will try to feed into your life. This does not mean they can not pour wisdom into you. However, you must remember that they are human and walk in the flesh like you. So remain God conscious and not man conscious.

- **Have a personal intimate prayer life.** Domestic violence victims will at times feel all alone. But, you are never alone. There is a great host of angels that know where you are and are standing watch over you (Psalm 91). Take time out daily to communicate with God. He does not need any big fancy words. He knows the very desire of your heart and He would love to hear from you.

- **Get yourself some Godly friends.** You will need to surround yourself with people who love God and you unconditionally.

- **Have a sweet, humble and teachable spirit.** For the men, this does not mean that you are weak. This characteristic in essence makes you strong. This is where your mentor and/or spiritual advisor comes in handy. They will provide you with instructions for you to adhere to. This will enable you to walk boldly and proudly into your destiny.

- **Have a winner's mentality**. Speak powerful words into your life. Begin to speak powerful words into your life and post them around your home, in your car and at your desk. The bible says, "That out of the abundance of the heart, the mouth speaketh." You can prophesy your own future. You are a victor.

WHAT CHURCHES CAN DO

Victim Safety: Safety for the victim and any children that are involved in the relationship must be the top priority. Without safety there can be no restoration of the marriage covenant. Making sure that she has a place to stay during an episode of violence is CRUCIAL. Getting acquainted with your local domestic violence program and keeping shelter phone numbers handy is imperative.

Accountability: Abusers should be held accountable for their violent behavior and should be encouraged to seek professional counseling from a certified abuse intervention program. Many abusers feel remorse after a violent incident. Feeling remorse and seeking forgiveness is a typical phase within the cycle of domestic abuse, but this is actually another method of control on the part of the abuser. Couple's counseling is NEVER appropriate when there is violence or threat of violence in a relationship. Churches and clergy need to remember that the remorse phase is only temporary and that true repentance requires sacrifice and the desire to make long-term changes.

In Acts 26:20 we read: *"Repent and turn to God and perform deeds that are worthy of repentance."*

Restoration: The restoration of the relationship can happen only after the first two steps are accomplished. If the abuser refuses to take the necessary steps for change, then clergy should assist the victim in mourning the loss of the relationship. Again, safety must be the top priority of those assisting victims. Some victims of domestic violence do not feel comfortable with the idea of divorce, but at the same time, cannot safely continue to live with the abusive partner.

SUGGESTIONS FOR CLERGY DEALING WITH ABUSIVE MEN

- Be very clear that the violent behavior is unacceptable.

- Do not accept his rationalization of blaming his victim. Even if he is under pressure at work, the house is not clean, the dishes are dirty, violence is not acceptable.

- Hold him accountable. Promises to change are part of the cycle of violence. Accountability requires concrete actions, like going to an abuse intervention group. In order to change he MUST accept responsibility for his action and seek appropriate help.

- Do not take his word that the violence has stopped. Check with his abused partner (without his knowledge) and ask her if the abuse has stopped. Remember: Abuse is about one individual gaining power and control over their intimate partner. Even if the hitting has stopped, you should ask her if he continues to attempt to control where she goes, who she sees, etc. *NEVER TELL THE ABUSER ABOUT ANY CONVERSATION THAT YOU HAVE WITH HIS VICTIM.*

HOW TO APPROPRIATELY ASSIST VICTIMS OF DOMESTIC VIOLENCE IN YOUR CONGREGATION

- Listen carefully to her story. Take her seriously.

- Be concerned for her safety and the safety of any children involved. If she is worried about the spiritual implications of seeking a divorce, do not discuss this aspect. Just emphasize to her that safety should be the top priority and all of the other things that are of concern to her (such as divorce, child-support, etc.) can be worked out later.

- Do not criticize her for not having left sooner. Battered women leave their abuser an average of seven times before making the final break. If she does decide to leave, help her identify her options for going to a very safe place where the abuser will not find her.

- If she decides not to leave right away, then encourage her to prepare an emergency exit kit (See Safety Plan). This kit can be as simple or as elaborate as she chooses. The following items should be considered: Extra cash, any medications that are required on an ongoing basis, social security cards, immunization records, important bank records, phone numbers, at least one change of clothing for herself and the children, along with one or two special toys. Help her to identify a safe place for her to hide the kit, such as at the home of a friend, the church, her place of work, etc.

- Never blame the victim for the violence. Even if she blames herself (and this is often the case) do not reinforce this blaming pattern.

WHAT ABOUT FORGIVENESS?

Some quote King Lear ("forgive and forget") as though it were scripture. But quick forgiveness is not helpful to anyone in a violent relationship. Forgiveness is a process that enables us to let go of the pain and move forward.

Dietrich Bonhoeffer, pastor and martyr in Hitler's Germany pondered upon the importance of forgiveness, and while in prison he writes, *"Forgiveness will have to come or we shall be destroyed, but not yet. Not until the violence has become justice, lawlessness has become order, and war has become peace."* (Letters and Papers From Prison) Bonhoeffer knew that victims of violence and torture required a different process of forgiveness and that violence would have to be brought to justice before forgiveness could actually occur. In addition, safety is required before the healing power of forgiveness can take place.

No battered woman should be encouraged to forgive her abuser until the abuse has stopped and the abuser has made efforts to repair the damage which he did to her and any children involved in the family unit. If at that point she feel that she can forgive, this means that she can let go of the pain and move on with her life. Forgiveness does not necessarily mean that she returns to the relationship, nor that she renews her relationship with her abusive partner.

God calls his people to bring an end to violence and commands those who are violent to change...

"Bring an end to the violence of the wicked and make the righteous secure." Psalm 7:9

"Give up your violence and oppression and do what is just and right." Ezekiel 45:9

Forgiveness With Safety,
Patricia Riddle Gaddis, 2002

WARNING SIGNS IN A POTENTIAL OR FAILED MARRIAGE

- The couple meets or married shortly after a significant loss.
- The couple meets and marries in less than six months.
- The couple wishes to distance from one's family of origin.
- The couple has family backgrounds which are different (religion, education, social class, ethnicity, age).
- The couple comes from incompatible sibling constellations (both are babies of the family).
- The couple resides either extremely close to or a great distance from either family of origin.
- The couple marries before age 20.
- The couple marries after a relationship of less than six months or after more than three years of engagement.
- The couple's wedding occurs without family or friends present.
- The wife becomes pregnant before marriage or within the first year of marriage.
- The couple may have a poor relationship with siblings or parents.
- The couple may consider his or her childhood or adolescence an unhappy time.
- The couple's marital patterns in either extended family were unstable.

RED FLAGS TO LOOK FOR IN AN ABUSIVE PERSONALITY

Many women and men are interested in ways to spot a potential abuser, especially once they have been involved in an abusive relationship before. Below you will find a list of behaviors seen in abusers; the **Last four signs listed are abusive behaviors that are often overlooked as the beginning of physical abuse**. If a person displays several of the other behaviors, **say three or more**, this is a strong indicator for physical violence. The **more signs** a person has, the more likely the person is an abuser. In some cases, an abuser may have only a few behaviors that the man or woman can recognize, but they are very exaggerated (for example, will try to explain the behavior as a sign of love and concern); a woman may be flattered at first. As time goes on, the behaviors become more severe and serve to dominate and control the woman.

CONTROLLING BEHAVIOR. At first the batterer will say this behavior is due to his concern for his or her safety, her need to use her time well, or his or her need to make good decisions. He or she will get angry if their partner is "late" coming back from the store or an appointment; he or she will question her closely about where he or she went and whom he or she talked with. As the behavior progresses, he or she may not allow the woman to make personal decisions about the house, children, her clothing, or attending church. He or she may keep all the money or even make him or her ask permission to leave the house or room.

JEALOUSY. At the beginning of the relationship, the abuser will say jealousy is a sign of love. Jealousy has nothing to do with love. It is a sign of possessiveness and lack of trust. The abuser may question their partner about who he or she talks to, accuse him or her of flirting, having an affair, or being jealous of the time he or she spends with family, friends, or children. As the jealousy progresses, they may call him or her frequently during the day or drop by unexpectedly. They may refuse to let them work for fear he or she will meet someone else, or even begin behaviors such as checking his or her car mileage or asking friends to watch him or her.

QUICK INVOLVEMENT. A large number of abused men and women dated or knew their abuser for less than six months before they were engaged, married, or living together. He or she comes in like a tornado, claiming, *"You're the only one who understands"*, **or** *"The only one I've loved this much"*. He or she will pressure the man or woman to commit to the relationship in such a way that the man or woman may feel guilty or that he or she is *letting him or her down"* if he or she wants to slow down the involvement or break off the relationship.

UNREALISTIC EXPECTATIONS. Abusive people will expect their partner to meet all their needs. He or she expects a perfect husband or wife, mother, lover, and friend. The abuser will say things such as *"If you love me, I'm all you need and you'll all I need."* The abuser expects their partner to take care of everything for him or her emotionally and in the home.

⚑ ***ISOLATION.*** The abuser tries to cut her or her partner off from all resources and support. If he or she has friends of the opposite sex, she will be labeled a whore and he will be labeled a cheat. If he has male friends, he will be called a gay man and she will be called a lesbian. If he or she is close to family, he or she is tied to apron strings. He or she accuses people who are his or her support of causing problems. He or she may want to live in the country, without a phone, or refuse to let him or her drive the car, or he or she may try to keep her from working or going to school.

⚑ ***BLAMES OTHERS FOR PROBLEMS.*** If he or she is chronically unemployed, someone is always doing him or her wrong or out to get him or her. He or she may make mistakes and then blame his or her partner for upsetting him or her and keeping him from concentrating on the task at hand. He or she may blame his partner for anything that goes wrong in his or her life.

⚑ ***BLAMES OTHERS FOR FEELINGS.*** The abuser may tell his partner *"You make me mad," you're hurting me by not doing what I want you to do"* or *"I can't help being angry."* He or she is the one who makes the decision about what he or she thinks or feels, but he or she will use these feelings to manipulate his or her partner.

HYPERSENSITIVITY. An abuser is easily insulted, claiming his or her feelings are *"hurt"*, when in actually he or she is angry or taking the slightest setback as a personal attack. He or she will *"rant and rave"* about the injustice of things that have happened, things that are just a part of living (for example, being asked to work late, getting a traffic ticket, or being told about annoying behavior).

CRUELTY TO CHILDREN OR ANIMALS. Abusers may expect children to be capable of things beyond their abilities (punishes 19 month-old for wetting diaper). He or she may tease children until they cry. He or she may not want children to eat at the table or may expect them to stay in their rooms when he or she is home. He or she may punish animals brutally or be insensitive to their pain or suffering.

PLAYFUL USE OF FORCE IN SEX. An abuser may enjoy throwing the man or woman down or holding him or her down during sex. The man or woman may use a weapon to keep his or her partner under control. He or she may want to act out fantasies during sex where the woman is helpless. He or she is letting his or her partner know that the idea of rape is exciting. He or she may show little concern about whether the woman wants to have sex and uses sulking or anger to manipulate him or her into compliance. He or she may begin having sex with their partner while he or she is sleeping or demand sex while she is ill or tired.

🚩 *VERBAL ABUSE.* In addition to saying things that are intentionally meant to be cruel and hurtful, verbal abuse is also apparent in the abuser's degrading of his or her partner, cursing her, and belittling him or her accomplishments. The abuser tells his or her they are stupid and unable to function without him or her. The abuse may also wake his or her up to verbally abuse him or her or not let him or her go to sleep. Thus, disabling them from performing their job successfully.

🚩 *RIGID SEX ROLES.* The abuser expects his or her partner to serve them. He or she may say the man or woman must stay at home and obey in all things – even acts that are criminal in nature. The abuser sees women as inferior to men, responsible for menial tasks and unable to be a whole person without a relationship.

🚩 *DR. JEKYll/MR. HYDE.* The abuser keeps his or her partner confused by sudden changes in his or her mood. He or she may believe he or she has some sort of mental problem because one minute he or she is loving and the next he or she exploding. Explosiveness and moodiness are typical of men and women who beat their partners.

🚩 *PREVIOUS ABUSIVE RELATIONSHIPS.* The abuser may say he or she has hit men and women in the past, but blame them for the abuse (*"they made me do it"*). His or her relatives or ex-partners may warn him or her that he or she is abusive. An abuser will abuse any man or woman he or she is with if the relationship lasts long enough for the violence to be introduced.

🚩 **THREATS OF VIOLENCE.** Threats of physical violence meant to control the partners: *"I'll kill you"*, *"I'll break your neck"*, and *"you'd better watch yourself, or else"*. Most people do not threaten their partners. Abusers will try to excuse their threats by saying, *"Everyone talks like that"*.

🚩 **BREAKING OR STRIKING OBJECTS.** Breaking cherished possessions is used as punishment, but mostly to terrorize the man or woman into submission. The abuser may beat on the table with his or her fist, or throw things around or near the partner.

🚩 **ANY FORCE DURING AN ARGUMENT.** This may involve the abuser preventing the man or woman from leaving a room, by restraining, pushing, or shoving. He may hold his or her partner against the wall telling him or her *"You're going to listen to me!"*

Something to Think About!

How many of the red flags did you see in yourself or others?

1.
2.
3.

If you have to continue --- you're in danger.

WHAT IS CODEPENDENCY?

- My good feelings about who I am stem from being like you.

- My good feelings about who I am stem from receiving approval from you.

- Your struggles affect my serenity. My mental attention focuses on solving your problems or relieving your pain.

- My mental attention is focused on pleasing you.

- My mental attention is focused on protecting you.

- My mental attention is focused on manipulating you "to do it my way".

- My self-esteem is bolstered by relieving your pain.

- My own hobbies and interest are put aside. My time is spent sharing your interests and hobbies.

- Your clothing and personal appearance is dictated by my desires as I feel you are a reflection of me.

- Your behavior is dictated by my desires as I feel you are a reflection of me.

- I am not aware of how I feel. I am aware of how you feel. I am not aware of what I want. I ask you what you want. If I am not aware, I assume.

- The dreams I have for my future are linked to you.

- I use giving as a way of feeling safe in our relationship.

- My social circle diminishes as I involved myself with you – ISOLATION.

- I put my values aside in order to connect with you.

- I value your opinion and way of doing things more than my own.

- The quality of my life is in relation to the quality of yours.

HOW TO TALK WITH SOMEONE WHO IS BEING ABUSED

- Listen without judging.

- Five simple things to say:

    1. I am afraid for your safety and for the safety of your children.
    2. The violence will only get worse.
    3. You do not deserve to be abused.
    4. You have the right to live free of violence. You are not alone.
    5. There is a safe place that he/she can go.

- Ask questions like "How can I help you?" and "What do you want to do about the situation?"

- Do not say, "Get out." It is not a safe piece of advice.

- Emphasize that you are concerned. Let him or her know that you support his or her and that he or she is not responsible for what is happening.

- Let him or her know that you and the organization (civic and/or religious) believe that verbal, emotional, or physical abuse in a relationship is never acceptable. There are no excuses.

- Let him or her know that domestic violence is a crime and that he or she can seek protection from the courts.

- Emphasize that when he or she is ready, he or she can make a number of choices with the support.

- Allow him or her to make decisions for him or herself. Do not try to diagnose or treat the problem yourself. Offer to contact referral agencies for him or her.

- Provide him or her with information. Accept that a victim's opinion and solutions may change over time. When a victim gets new information about domestic violence, he or she may change his or her mind about leaving the batterer. Some victims leave and return to their partners several times. Let him or her know this is not a failure.

- Suggest that she find out a safety plan; let him or her know that there are counselors (through local and national hot-line numbers) that can help him or her do this.

- Ask if he or she wants or needs to get a restraining order. When there is a restraining or protection order, a safety plan is a necessity.

HOW WILL I KNOW IF HE OR SHE HAS CHANGED?

There are times in a relationship when we go back to our abuser (male or female) in hopes that they will change or that you can change them. Before you do, ask yourself the following questions to make sure that you feel safe and secure.

- Has he or she stopped being violent or threatening towards you and others?

- Does he or she still make you afraid when you are with them?

- Is he or she able to be angry without becoming verbally or physically abusive?

- Are you able to express anger towards him or her without being attacked?

- Is he or she able to hear and respect what you are saying although he or she may not agree with you?

- Can he or she negotiate with you without being accusatory or controlling?

- Can he or she respect your right to say no?

- Is he or she able to let you know what he or she is feeling most of the time?

- Is he or she able to express feelings other than anger?

- Does he or she still make you feel responsible for his or her anger and frustrations?

- Does he or she respect your right to be different and to make your own decisions?

- Do you feel respected and listened to when you speak?

- Can you go out, go to school, go to church, and get a job without his or her permission?

WHY DO MEN OR WOMEN STAY IN ABUSIVE RELATIONSHIPS?

"Because leaving is a process ... not an event!"

Love
He/she has strong feelings for her partner. A bond has been established particularly if children are involved.

Fear
- Greater physical danger to himself/herself. Their level of danger increases when they attempt to leave.
- Lack of information regarding alternatives.
- The unexpected or change.
- Children.
- Greater physical danger to them.
- Emotional damage to children.
- Losing custody of children.
- Economics.
- Financial dependence on spouse/partner.
- He/she can not afford an attorney.
- Lack of job skills or lack of education.
- Losing everything he/she has.
- Guilt, shame, and embarrassment
- Failed marriage or making bad decisions.
- Having to ask for public assistance or assistance from relatives.

Religion
- Cultural and religious constraints.
- Social isolation resulting in lack of support from family or friends.

Denial
- He/she may deny that they are in an abusive situation or he/she may not be aware that abusive behavior is wrong.

Low Self-Esteem
- He/she has begun to believe that he/she is worthless, stupid etc. (all the things the abuser has called him/her)
- Commitment to Marriage/Relationship.
- Believes in the sanctity of marriage.
- Believes that the husband/wife will change.
- Believes that staying is the right thing to do.
- Believes that husband/wife is not able to survive alone.

WHY WOMEN LEAVE MEN?

- She is hurting all the time because she feels alone and abandoned.

- Her husband or partner is no longer her friend.

- The only time he pays attention to her is when he wants sex.

- He is never there for me when I need him the most.

- When he hurts her feelings and doesn't apologize.

- He lives his life as if they weren't married or partners; he rarely considers me.

- They are like ships passing in the night, he goes his way and she goes her way.

- Her husband or partner has become a stranger to her. She doesn't know who he is anymore.

- He doesn't show any interest in me or what I do.

Note: Women as well as men are frustrated about this pulling apart. What is disturbing is that they are willing to risk their families by separating rather than confronting the issues. All of these variables are lead-ins for domestic violence.

WHAT TO EXPECT IF HE/SHE LEAVES A VIOLENT PARTNER

Having left the violence of his/her home or relationship does not mean that the problems are over. The person that has recently and frequently used and abused his/her may be read in several predictable ways. Knowing what he/she may do may improve his/her ability to cope with his demands and attempts to persuade and intimidate him/her. It may also better enable him/her to make his/her decisions without fear or guilt.

Attempt to locate him/her
- One of his/her first efforts may be to try to locate him/her by contacting friends and family members to whom he/she thinks he/she might have gone. Depending on his/her relationship with them, he/she will either attempt to gain their sympathy or threaten them. If they do not know where he/she is, only that he/she is safe and well, they cannot be coerced or frightened into giving information. If he/she uses the sympathy line, his/her story may be such a distortion of what really happened that they might want to persuade him/her to return to this poor misunderstood creature. Remember, he/she can be very charming and persuasive (Dr. Jekyll/Mr. Hyde) (that's how he/she got his/her in the first place). Be prepared for him/her to use this on others.

Apologies and promise
- If he/she does make contact with him/her, he/she will probably first try a great apology line. This will include: promises of better behavior, gifts, things for the children or home, or anything else that he/she thinks will make you believe him/her and might bring you back within his/her sphere of dominance. Remember, that many men/women who batter have indicated that their men/women are their possessions, to do with as they please. They intend to establish and

maintain control and will use apologies and promises to do so.

Threats and intimidation
- The next pattern of behavior is generally one of threats and attempts to intimidate. This often includes: threats to attack family members and friends, threats to kill her or have her killed. Threats to take away children or get custody or threats to kill himself. Remember that he/she alone is responsible for his/her actions and the results of those actions. Take necessary safety precautions and refuse to listen to any additional threats.

Using Your Children
- One of the main threats may be that he/she will not let him/her have custody of or see his/her children. Remember, in this case, the law is, for the most part, on her side. In most cases, mothers receive custody of their children. However, he/she may need a good attorney and it may be very difficult. But he/she is usually not as powerful as he/she thinks he/she is. Also, there are a number of community agencies that are available to help her deal with the problems (the male victim are not so fortunate to have agencies available to them) of being a single parent.

Counseling/Religion Approach
- He/she may suddenly become 'religious' and attend church activities in the most obvious manner. Even ministers often doubt these sudden conversions. Or, he/she may begin the rounds of counseling services trying to find a counselor that will call him/her and tell him/her that he/she should go back to him/her and help him/her sort out his/her problems. Unless a person is willing to continue counseling whether or not he/she comes back, he/she is probably not very sincere in seeking to resolve his/her own problems. Even if he/she is sincere, it takes months, even years to change behavior and thought patterns.

Other Common Approaches
- If none of the previous approaches have worked, he/she may try others, including: crying and begging (particularly in public situations were he/she might be embarrassed), harassment by phone calls, legal frustrations, showing up at or calling her work place or hanging around her family members.

- Remember that he/she has rights and there are laws to help him/her protect those rights. Encourage him/her to stand strong in his/her battle to end the cycle of abuse. He/she cannot control his/her behavior or attempts to intimidate him/her, but he/she can control how he/she responds to them.

THE JOURNEY THROUGH GRIEF:
THE MOURNER'S SIX RECONCILIATION NEEDS

The loss of a loved one or a failed relationship changes our lives forever. And the movement from the "before" to the "after" is almost a long, painful journey. If we are to heal, we cannot skirt the outside edges of our grief and pain. Instead, we must journey all the way through it, sometimes meandering or strolling through it, sometimes meandering the side roads, sometimes plowing directly into its raw center.

This journey also requires mourning. **Grief** is what you think and feel on the inside after losing someone you love. **Mourning** is the outward expression of those thoughts and feelings. To mourn is to be an active participant in our grief journeys. We all grieve when we lose someone we love, but if we are to heal, we must also mourn.

According to Alan D. Wolfelt, Ph.D., there are six "yield signs" you are likely to encounter on your journey through grief-that he calls "reconciliation needs of mourning." For a while your grief journey will be an intensely personal, unique experience. All mourners must yield to this set of basic human needs if they are to heal. Let's'take a brief look at what happens during **The Journey Through Grief.**

THE JOURNEY THROUGH GRIEF

Acknowledging the reality of the loss.

Embracing the pain of the loss.

Remembering the person you lost.

Developing a new self-identity.

Searching for meaning.

Receiving ongoing support from others.

⬇

Reconciling Your Grief

THE JOURNEY THROUGH GRIEF

Let's look at what happens through **THE JOURNEY OF GRIEF** process. Once again, keep in mind that both victim and batterer experience this process. What makes it more intensely difficult is that these individuals are mourning a person who is, for the most part, still alive.

YIELD SIGN #1. *Acknowledging the reality of the loss.* This first need of mourning involves gently confronting the reality that someone you care about may never physically come back into your life again.

Whether the loss was sudden or anticipated, acknowledging the full reality of the loss may occur over weeks and months. To survive, you may try to push away the reality of the loss at times. You may discover yourself replaying events surrounding the loss and confronting memories, both good and bad. This replay is a vital part of this need of mourning. It's as if each time you talk it out, the event is a little more real.

Remember, this first need of mourning, like the other five that follow, may intermittently require your attention for months and maybe years. Be patient and compassionate with yourself as you work on each of them.

YIELD SIGN #2. *Embracing the pain of the loss.*
This need of mourning requires us to embrace the pain of our loss-something we naturally don't want to do. It is easier to avoid, repress or deny the pain of grief than it is to confront it, yet it is in confronting our pain that we learn to reconcile ourselves to it.

You will probably discover that you need to "dose" yourself in embracing your pain. In other words, you cannot (nor should you try to) overload yourself with the hurt all at one time. Sometimes you may need to distract yourself from the pain of the loss, while at other times you will need to create a safe place to move toward it.

Unfortunately, our culture tends to encourage the denial of pain. If you openly express your feelings of grief, misinformed pastors, friends and family may advise you to "carry on" or "keep your chin up." If on the other- hand, you remain "strong" and "in control," you may be congratulated for coping with your grief. Actually, doing well with your grief means becoming well acquainted with your pain.

YIELD SIGN #3. *Remembering the person you lost.*
Precious memories, dreams reflecting the significance of the relationship and objects that link you to the person (such as photos, music, food, souvenirs etc.) are examples of some of the things and testimony to a different form of a continued relationship. This need of mourning involves allowing and encouraging yourself to pursue this relationship.

But some people may try to take your memories away. Trying to be helpful, they encourage you to take down all the photos of the person. They tell you to keep busy or even to move on. Remembering the past makes hoping for the future possible. Your future will become open to new experiences only to the extent that you embrace the past.

YIELD SIGN #4. *Developing a new self-identity.*
Part of your self-identity comes from the relationships you have with other people. When you lose someone with whom you have a relationship, your self-identity, or the way you see yourself naturally changes.

You may have gone from being a "wife" or "husband" to a "single parent." The way you define yourself and the way society defines you is changed.

A death or loss often requires you to take on new roles that had been filled by the person who is no longer there. After all, someone still has to take out the garbage, someone still has to shop for groceries and pay the bills. You confront your changed identity every time you do something that used to be done by the person who left. This can be very hard work and can leave you feeling very drained.

You may occasionally feel child-like as you struggle with your changing identity. You may feel a temporarily heightened dependence on others as well as feelings of helplessness, frustration, inadequacy and fear. Many people discover that as they work on this need, they ultimately discover some positive aspects of their changed self-identity. You may develop a renewed confidence in yourself. For example, you may develop a more caring, kind and sensitive part of yourself. You may develop an assertive part of your identity that empowers you to go on living even though you continue to feel a sense of loss.

YIELD SIGN #5. *Searching for meaning.*
When someone you love dies or is taken from you, you naturally question the meaning and purpose of life. You probably will question your philosophy of life and explore religious spiritual values as you work on this need. You may discover yourself searching for meaning in your continued living as you ask "How?" and "Why" questions. "How could God let this happen?" "Why did this happen

now, in this way?" The death or loss reminds you of your lack of control. It can leave you feeling powerless.

The person who died or left was a part of you. This death means you mourn a loss not only outside of yourself, but inside of yourself as well. At times, overwhelming sadness and loneliness may be your constant companions. You may feel that when this person left, part of you died with him or her. And now you are faced with finding some meaning in going on with your life even though you may often feel so empty. This loss also calls you to confront your own spiritually. You may doubt your faith and have spiritual conflicts and questions racing through your head and heart. This is normal and part of your journey toward renewed living.

YIELD SIGN #6. *Receiving ongoing support from others.* The quality and quantity of understanding and support you get during your grief journey will have a major influence on your capacity to heal. You cannot nor should you try to do this alone. Drawing on the experiences and encouragement of friends or professional counselors is not a weakness, but a healthy human need. And because mourning is a process that takes place over time, this support must be available months and even years after the loss of someone in your life.

Unfortunately, because our society places so much value on the ability to "carry on, "keep your chin up" and "keep busy," many mourners are abandoned shortly after the event or loss."It's over and done with" and "It's time to get on with your life" are the types of messages directed at mourners that still dominate. Obviously, these messages encourage you to deny or repress your grief rather than express it.

To be truly helpful, the people in your support system must appreciate the impact this loss has had on you. They must understand that in order to heal, you must be allowed, even encouraged to mourn long after the death of a loved one or relationship. And they must encourage you to see mourning not as an enemy to be vanquished, but as a necessity to be experienced as a result of having loved.

Reconciling your grief
You may have heard indeed or you may believe that your grief journey's end will come when you resolve, or recover from your grief. But your journey will never end. People do not "get over" grief.

Reconciliation is a term more appropriate for what occurs as the mourner works to integrate the new reality of moving forward in life without the physical presence of the person who is no longer there. With reconciliation comes a renewed sense of energy and confidence, an ability to fully acknowledge the reality of the loss and a capacity to become re-involved in the activities of living.

In reconciliation, the sharp, ever-present pain of grief gives rise to a renewed sense of meaning and purpose. Your feeling of loss will not completely disappear, yet they will soften, and the intense pains of grief will become less frequent. Hope for a continued life will emerge as you are able to make commitments to the future, realizing that the person who is no longer there had a tremendous impact on you and your life, yet knowing that your life can and will move forward.

STALKERS

Stalkers can usually be sorted into one of three major groupings:

- Simple Obsession
- Love Obsession
- Other

Simple Obsession Stalkers
- These stalkers have previously been involved in an intimate relationship with their victims. Often the victim has attempted to call off the relationship but the stalker simply refuses to accept it. These stalkers suffer from:
- personality disorders
- emotionally immaturity
- extremely jealous
- insecurity
- low self-esteem
- feels powerless without the relationship

While reconciliation is the goal, this stalker believes they must have a specific person back or they will not survive. The stalker of former spouses or intimate partners, are often domineering and abusive to their partners during the relationship and use this domination as a way to bolster their own low self-esteem. The control the abusers exert over their partners gives them a feeling of power they can not find elsewhere. They try to control every aspect of their partner's lives. Their worst fear is losing people over whom they have control.

When they realize this fear as the relationship finally does end, the stalker suddenly believes that his/her life is destroyed. Their total identity and feelings of self-worth are tied up in the power experienced through their domineering and abusive relationship. Without this control, they feel that they will have no self-worth and no identity. They will become nobodies and in desperation they begin stalking, trying to regain their partner and the basis of their power.

It is this total dependence on their partner for identity and feelings of self worth that makes these stalkers so very dangerous. They will often go to any length and stop at nothing to get their partner back. If they can not have the people over whom they can exert dominance and total control, their lives are truly not worth living.

- **Unfortunately, along with becoming suicidal, they also often want to kill the intimate partner who has left them.**

Stalking does not always begin with violence or trying to terrorize, it usually starts with "Can I just talk to you or meet with you one last time?" "If you just talk to me I'll leave you alone." According to experts, "He wants him/her back, and he/she won't come back." Everything escalates from there and sometimes he/she snaps and assaults or kills him/her. In his/her mind, he/she makes the decision, "If I can't have you, no one else will." When he says this, he/she is attempting to cover his/her fear that he/she will meet another man/woman and leave him/her. Far too often, the police find that these stalkers follow through on their threats. They kill the victim(s) and then many times committing suicide. For them, death is better than having to face humiliation of the stalking victim leaving them for someone else, and the humiliation of having to face their own powerlessness.

- **Love Obsession Stalkers**

These are individuals who become obsessed with or fixed on a person with whom they have had no intimate or close relationship. The victim may be a friend, a business acquaintance, a person they met only once, or even a complete stranger. Love obsession stalkers believe that a special, often mystical, relationship exists between them and their victims.

Any contact with the victim becomes a positive reinforcement of this relationship and any wavering (even the slightest) of the victim from an absolute "NO" is seen as an invitation to continue the pursuit.

These stalkers will often read sexual meanings into neutral responses from the victim. They are often loners with an emotional void in their lives. Any contact with the object of the infatuation, even negative, helps fill this void. Failed relationships are the rule among these individuals.

Many suffer from erotomania (sexual desire). They have the delusion that they are loved intensely by another person, usually a person of higher socioeconomic status than them or an unattainable public figure. They are totally convinced that the stalking victim loves them dearly and truly and would return their affection except for some external influence.

During questioning, police find that most love obsession stalkers have fantasized a complete relationship with the person they are stalking. When they attempt to act out this fantasy in real life, they expect the victim to return the affection. When no affection is returned, the stalker often reacts with threats and intimidation. When the threats and intimidation do not accomplish what they hoped, the stalker can often become violent and even deadly.

- **Other Stalkers**

Some stalkers harass their victim not out of love but out of hate. Occasionally, stalking becomes a method of revenge for some misdeed against the stalker, real or imagined. Stalking can also be used as means of protest. This is the smallest group, but this type of stalking, for revenge and protest, can be especially dangerous. There have been several killings by stalkers at abortion clinics, and mass murders around the country by employees who have been fired and then returned to stalk and eventually kill those who have fired them.

Common Traits of Stalkers

- **Stalkers will not take NO for an answer**

They refuse to believe that a victim is not interested in them or will not rekindle their relationship and often believe that the victim really does love them, but just does not know it and needs to be pushed into realizing it. As long as they continue pursuing their victim, the stalker can convince themselves they have not been completely rejected yet.

- **Stalkers display an obsessive personality**

They are not just interested in, but totally obsessed with the person they are pursuing. Their every waking thought centers on the victim and every plan the stalker has for the future involves the victim. Ask yourself this. Is the person totally involved in and completely overwhelmed with pursuing?

Someone who has no and never will have any interest in him or her?

Along with obsessive thinking, they also display other psychological or personality problems and disorders. They may suffer from erotomania, paranoia, schizophrenia, and delusional thinking. These stalkers have rigid personalities and maladaptive styles. These disorders in themselves are very stable and not treatable. There are drugs to treat certain specific mental disorders, but stalkers, when given the choice, seldom continue with their medication or treatment.

Stalkers are above advantage in intelligence and are usually smarter than the run of the mill person with mental problems.

They will go to great lengths to obtain information about their victims or to find victims who have secretly moved. They have been known to hack into computers, tap telephone lines, take jobs at public utilities that allow them access to the victims or information about the victims, and even to travel thousands of miles and spend thousands of dollars to gain information about or find their victims. Stalkers many times use their intelligence to throw others off their trail.

- **Most stalkers do not have any relationship outside the one they are trying to re-establish or the one they have imagined exists between them and their victim. Because they are usually loners, stalkers become desperate to obtain this relationship.**

- **Stalkers do not display the discomfort or anxiety that people should naturally feel in certain situations.** Normal individuals would be extremely embarrassed to be caught following other people, going through their trash looking for information about them, leaving obscene notes, and other inappropriate behavior displayed by stalkers. Stalkers, however, do not see this as inappropriate behavior, but only as a means to gain the person's love.

- **Stalkers often suffer from low self-esteem, and feel they must have a relationship with the victim in order to have any self-worth.**
  Preoccupations with other people almost always involve someone with weak social skills and low self-esteem.

- **Few stalkers can see how their actions are hurting others.**
  They display other sociopathic thinking in that they cannot learn from experience, and they do not believe society's rules apply to them. Most stalkers do not think they are really threatening, intimidating, or even

stalking someone else. They think they are simply trying to show the victims that they are the right one for them. To the victims of stalking, it is like a prolonged rape.

- **Stalkers, like rapists, want absolute control over their victims.**
  They do not regard what they are doing as a crime, or even wrong. To them it is true love, with the exception that the victim does not recognize it yet. With enough persistence, stalkers believe they will eventually convince the victims of their love.

- **Stalkers many times leave a mean streak and will become violent when frustrated.**
  How violent? Often deadly.

Top Mistakes That Stalking Victims Make

Not listening to your intuition. You need to keep your internal radar tuned to pick up signals that something might be wrong.

- Letting someone down easy, instead of saying a definitive NO if you are not interested in a relationship. Trying to be nice can lead to a potentially obsessive suitor to hear what he or she wants instead of the message that you are not interested.
- Ignoring the early warning signs that annoying attention might escalate into dangerous harassment and pursuit.
- Responding to a stalker in any way, shape, or form. That means not being agreeable to your stalkers demands even once he or she has introduced threats.
- Trying to reason or bargain with a stalker. Stalking is like a long rape. Your natural reactions almost automatically put you at a disadvantage.
- Expecting police to solve your problem and make it go away.
- Taking inadequate privacy and safety precautions.
- Neglecting to enlist the support of family, friends, neighbors, coworkers, therapist, and other victims. It may be tough to admit that you are being stalked, but it is not your fault.
- Ignoring emotional needs during and after a stalking.

MYTHS ABOUT LESBIAN AND GAY DOMESTIC VIOLENCE

- Only heterosexual women get battered. Men are never victims of domestic violence and women do not abuse.

- Domestic violence is more common in heterosexual relationships than it is in lesbian or gay male relationships.

- It isn't really violence when a same-sex couple fights. It is just a lover's quarrel and a fair fight between equals.

- It isn't really violence at all when gay men fight; it's just boys being boys.

- The batterer will always be butch, bigger and stronger. The victim will always be femme, smaller and weaker.

- People who are abusive under the influence of drugs or alcohol are not responsible for their actions.

- Gay men's domestic violence has increased as a result of alcoholism, drug abuse and the AIDS epidemic.

- Lesbian and gay domestic violence is sexual behavior, a version of sadomasochism. The victims actually like it.

- The law does not and will not protect victims of lesbian and gay men's domestic violence.

- Lesbian and gay male victims exaggerate the violence that happens to them. If it were really that bad, they could and would just leave.

- It is easier for lesbian or gay victims of domestic violence to leave the abuser than it is for heterosexual battered women.

- Domestic violence primarily occurs among gay men and lesbians, who hang out at bars, are poor or are people of color.

- Victims often provoke the violence done to them. They are getting what they deserve.

- Lesbian or gay male victims of domestic violence are codependent.

Reproduced from: National Lesbian and Gay Health Foundation Conference, July 1990

A Brief Safety Plan

"Write the vision make it plain on tablets so that a herald (angels or those who read it) may run with it."

Habakkuk 2:2
New International Version

"Whether you stay in an abusive relationship or plan to leave, you MUST consider your safety."

Gather all-important papers for yourself and your children. These include social security cards, birth certificates, financial records, immigration papers, passports, etc. Put them in a safe place where you can get to them in a hurry.

Try to set aside some extra cash, checkbook, savings account or credit cards. Be sure to hide any cash or financial records of your savings in a safe place.

Hide an extra set of car and house keys in a safe place or give to a friend or neighbor.

Pack a suitcase or bag containing essential clothing, toiletries and medications. Anything you would want if you must leave in a hurry for yourself and your children.

Plan ahead where you could go for safety in an emergency and how you would get there. If your plan includes other people, discuss it with them ahead of time. You may want to arrange a signal that will indicate to them that you need help. (**Begin to leave items at a family member or friends home**).

If danger is imminent, leave at once. Try to take your suitcase and other items, but do not risk your safety for them. Take your children if you can.

Talk with your children about safety if they are old enough to understand. Teach them how to call for help on 911 and where to go to be safe. You may want to set up a signal with them so that they will know when to call for help or leave.

If your phone has a redial function, be sure to clear it if you call a hotline or someone for help, so that your partner can't trace your calls. After you hang up from the call, pick up the phone again and press any number. If your phone has Caller ID, you can clear any number from it and there will be no record that the call was made to you.

Note: Please Be Careful – This is Very Serious !

Notes:

PERSONALIZED SAFETY PLAN

Planning to leave...

- If I decide to leave, I will _____. Practice how to get out safely. What doors, windows, elevators, stairwells or fire escapes would you use?

- I can keep my purse and car keys ready and put them _____ in order to leave quickly.

- I will leave money and an extra set of keys with _____ so I can leave quickly.

- I will keep copies of important documents or keys at _____.

- If I have to leave my home, I will go _____.

- If I cannot go to the above location, I can go _____.

- The Domestic Violence hotline number is _____. I can call it if I need shelter.

- If it is not safe to talk openly, I will use _____ as the code word/signal to my children that we are going to go, or to my family or friends that we are coming.

- I can leave extra clothes with _____.

I can use my judgment...

- When I expect my partner and I are going to argue, I will try to move to a space that is lowest risk, such as _____. (Try to avoid arguments in the bathroom, garage, kitchen, near weapons, or in rooms without an outside exit)

- I will use my judgment and intuition.

- If the situation is very serious, I can give my partner what he wants to try and calm him down. I have to protect myself until I/we are out of danger.

- I can also teach some of these strategies to some/all of my children, as appropriate.

- I will keep important numbers and change for phone calls with me at all times. I know that my partner can learn whom I have been talking to by looking at phone bills, so I can see if friends will let me use their phones and/or their phone credit cards.

- I will check with_____ and _____to see who would be able to let me stay with them or lend me money, if I need it.

- I can increase my independence by opening a bank account and getting credit cards in my own name. I can take classes or get job skills. I can get copies of all the important papers and documents I might need and keep them in a safe deposit box or with a trusted friend or relative.

- Other things I can do to increase my independence include: _____.

- I can rehearse my escape plan and, if appropriate, practice it with my children.

- If I have a joint bank account with my partner, I can make arrangements to ensure I will have access to money. I will go immediately to the bank to withdraw money.

I can get help...

- I can tell _____ about the violence and request that they call the police if they hear noises coming from my house.

- I can teach my children how to use the telephone to contact the police and the fire department. I will make sure they know our address.

- If I have a programmable phone, I can program emergency numbers and teach my children how to use the auto dial.

- I will use _____ as my code word with my children or my friends so they will call for help.

After I Leave...

- I can enhance the locks on my doors and windows.

- I can replace wooden doors with steel/metal doors.

- I can install security systems including additional locks, window bars, poles to wedge against doors, an electronic system, etc.

- I can purchase rope ladders to be used for escape from second floor windows.

- I can install smoke detectors and put fire extinguishers on each floor in my home.

- I will teach my children how to use the phone to make a collect call to me if they are concerned about their safety.

- I can tell people who take care of my children which people have permission to pick them up and make sure they know how to recognize those people.

- I will give the people who take care of my children copies of custody and protective orders, and emergency numbers.

At Work and in Public...

- I can inform security, my supervisor and/or the Employee Assistance Program about my situation. Phone numbers to have at work are _____ I can ask _____ to screen my calls at work or have my phone number changed.

- When leaving work, I can _____.

- When traveling to and from work, if there is trouble, I can _____.

- I can ask for a flexible schedule.

- I can ask for a parking space closer to the building.

- I can ask to move my workspace to a safer location.

- I can ask security to escort me to and from my car.

- I can change my patterns to avoid places where my partner might find me, such as _____ (stores, banks, laundromats).

- I can tell _____ and _____ that I am no longer with my partner and ask them to call the police if they believe my children or I are in danger.

- I can explore the option of communicating with my supervisor and human resources office.

With an Order of Protection... (Remember, this is not a sure proof document)

- I will keep my protection order _____, where I know it will be safe.

- I will give copies of my protection order to police departments in the community in which I live and those where I visit friends and family.

- I will give copies to my employer, my religious advisor, my closest friend, my children's school and day care center and _____.

- If my partner destroys my protection order or if I lose it, I can get another copy from the court that issued it.

- If my partner violates the order, I can call the police and report a violation, contact my attorney, call my advocate, and/or advise the court of the violation.

- I can call a domestic violence program if I have questions about how to enforce an order or if have problems getting it enforced.

Items to Take When Leaving...

- Identification for myself
- Children's birth certificates
- My birth certificate
- Social Security cards

- School/vaccination records
- Money, checkbook, bank books, cash cards, credit cards
- Medication/prescription cards.
- Keys - house, car office
- Driver's license/car registration.
- Insurance papers
- Public Assistance ID/Medicaid Cards.
- Passports, work permits
- Divorce or separation papers
- Lease, rental agreement or house deed
- Car/mortgage payment book
- Children's toys, security blankets, stuffed animals Sentimental items, photos

My Personalized Safety Plan

My Emotional Health...

- If I am feeling down, lonely, or confused, I can call_____ or the domestic violence hotline.

- I can take care of my physical health by getting a checkup with my doctor, gynecologist, and dentist. If I do not have a doctor, I will call the local clinic or to get one.

- If I have left my partner and am considering returning, I will call_____, or spend time with before I make a decision.

- I will remind myself daily of my best qualities. They are: _____.

- I can attend support groups, workshops, or classes at the local domestic violence program or _____ in order to build a support system, learn skills or get information.

- I will look at how and when I drink alcohol. If I am going to drink, I will do it in a place where people are committed to my safety.

- I can explore information available on the websites. Other things I can do to feel stronger are: _____.

THE SAMPLE PROTECTION ORDER

STATE OF NORTH CAROLINA	File No.
_____ County	In The General Court Of Justice District Court Division

Name Of Plaintiff

VERSUS

Name And Address Of Defendant

ORDER SETTING ASIDE DOMESTIC VIOLENCE PROTECTIVE ORDER

G.S. 1A-1; Rule 60(b)

Pursuant to the motion filed in this case and after proper notice, the Court held a hearing to determine whether the Domestic Violence Protective Order issued on *(state date)* _____ should be set aside.

FINDINGS

The Court finds: *(state facts found)*

CONCLUSIONS

Based on the facts found, the Court concludes that:

☐ It is no longer equitable that the domestic violence protective order should have future application.

☐ There is good reason justifying relief from the operation of the domestic violence protective order.

☐ There is no good reason justifying relief from the operation of the domestic violence protected order and there is no equitable reason that the order should not have future application.

ORDER

Therefore, the Court orders that:

☐ the Domestic Violence Protective Order entered on *(state date)* _____ be set aside.

☐ the motion to set aside the domestic violence protective order be denied.

Date	Name Of Judge (Type Or Print)	Signature Of Judge

AOC-CV-314, Side Two, Rev. 11/03
© 2003 Administrative Office of the Courts

STATE OF NORTH CAROLINA

_____ County

Name Of Plaintiff

VERSUS

Name And Address Of Defendant

File No.

In The General Court Of Justice
District Court Division

**ORDER RENEWING
DOMESTIC VIOLENCE
PROTECTIVE ORDER**

G.S. 50B-3(b)

Pursuant to G.S. 50B-3(b) and the motion filed in this case, the Court held a hearing to determine whether the previous Domestic Violence Protective Order should be renewed. The previous Domestic Violence Protective Order is attached and incorporated by reference.

FINDINGS

The Court finds:

1. The motion to renew ☐ was ☐ was not filed before the previous order expired.
2. (State facts that give or do not give good cause to renew the order - a new incident of domestic violence is not required.)

3. Other:

CONCLUSION

The Court concludes that
there ☐ is ☐ is not good cause to renew the protective order.
☐ Other:

ORDER

It is ORDERED that
☐ the Domestic Violence Protective Order entered on *(give date)* _____ and attached is renewed and valid until the date of expiration listed below.
☐ the motion is denied.
☐ Other:

Date

Signature Of Judge

Date Of Expiration Of This Order

Name Of Judge (Type Or Print)

CERTIFICATE OF SERVICE WHEN DEFENDANT NOT PRESENT AT HEARING

I certify that this Order has been served on the defendant named and at the address listed above by depositing a copy in a post-paid, properly addressed envelope in a post office or official depository under the exclusive care and custody of the United States Postal Service.

Date   *Signature*   ☐ Deputy CSC   ☐ Assistant CSC
☐ Clerk of Superior Court

NOTE TO CLERK: *A copy of this Order shall be mailed or given to each party, to your sheriff, and to the police department of the plaintiff's residence, if any.*

AOC-CV-314, Rev. 11/03
© 2003 Administrative Office of the Courts

(Over)

DOMESTIC VIOLENCE AND THE AFFECTS ON CHILDREN

The Impact of Domestic Violence on Children

Confusion and Children

- Domestic Violence is confusing to children in many of the same ways that it confuses men and women who are abused.
- Children are being hurt emotionally by watching their fathers and mother being abused.
- Children are learning that they can get their way through the use of power and control.

Impact of Abuse

- Emotionally
- Behaviorally
- Socially
- Physically

Key Issues for Children

Children feel:
- **Powerless** because they can't stop the violence.
- **Confused** because it doesn't make sense.
- **Angry** because it shouldn't be happening.
- **Guilty** because they think they have done something wrong.
- **Sad** because it's a loss.
- **Afraid** because they may be hurt, they may lose someone they love, others may find out.
- **Alone** because they think it's happening to them.

Key Needs of Children
- To be listened to and believed.
- To have a safe place to express their feelings.
- To be told that they are not alone.
- To be told that the violence is not their fault.
- To have support from family, friends, counselors, or all of these.
- To learn that conflict can be resolved without abuse or violence.
- To develop their own personal power.

EMOTIONAL REACTIONS OF CHILDREN TO DOMESTIC VIOLENCE

There are several general reactions that children from violent homes are likely to show. The same emotional reaction can be acted out differently according to the child's age. A brief description of these reactions is given below as a way of educating individuals with the feelings they might expect to hear about. A feeling, word or phrase that best explains the issues describes the general reactions.

- **Responsibility** – Children often feel they are to blame for the abuse. They might think, "If I had been a good boy or girl, Daddy and Mommy wouldn't hit each other."

- **Anxiety** – Children from violent homes live in a constant state of anxiety even when things are calm because they never know when the next fight will start.

- **Guilt** – Children often feel guilty about the abuse because they feel as though they should or could have done something to stop it. Children also experience guilt over the good feelings they have about the abuser.

- **Grief** – Children who are separated from the abuser are in the process of grieving over the loss of not living with that parent. Children may also grieve over losing the lifestyle and positive image of the abuser they had before the violence began.

- **Ambivalence** – The idea of not knowing how one feels or having two opposite emotions at the same time is very difficult for kids. When a child says, "I don't know how I will feel about it", they may not be hedging, but very definitely are confused about how to sort out the feelings, thoughts and events they are experiencing.

- **Fear of Abandonment** – Children who have been removed from one parent as a result of violent acts may have strong fears that the other parent will also leave them or die.

- **Need for Adult Attention** – As true for children going through any kind of crisis, children from violent home. If children don't receive the amount of attention they need, they are likely to act out or misbehave in order to get it. This need can be especially troublesome for mothers who are trying to deal with their own pain and decisions. As a routing is established and children begin to feel less anxious, the extreme need for adult attention lessens.

- **Transfer of Anxiety from Mother to Child** – Children are very sensitive to the facial reactions, body language and gestures of adults. Even if children can't understand adult words, they seem to be wizards at knowing how adults feel. Very often, children's anxiety and acting out decreases as soon as the mother begins to make decisions about her life.

WAYS TO HELP CHILDREN COPE WITH DOMESTIC VIOLENCE

Domestic Violence can seriously affect children, producing both short-term and long-term problems. Parents and other concerned adults can help reduce negative effects of domestic violence on their children by providing them with positive ways to vent their emotions and to express and understand their feelings.

- Tell the child that he or she is not the cause of the violence.

- Teach the child that he or she cannot control the violence.

- Support the child after the violence has occurred (sometimes the batterer may not allow you to comfort the children).

- Inform the child that he or she is not responsible for making the family happy.

- Encourage the child to talk about the violence.

- Have the child talk with a trained counselor about the domestic violence.

- Reassure the child that he or she is loved and is an important person.

- Accept the child's feelings or reactions related to domestic violence.

- Reassure the child that his or her feelings are okay.

- Encourage the child to participate in activities that will divert his or her attention from the domestic violence: playing a musical instrument, sports, games, reading, writing and listening to music.

- Motivate the child to participate in activities that will redirect his or her energy toward positive and creative outlets: dancing, running, jumping rope, playing sports.

- Teach the child age appropriate relaxation techniques.

- Have the child write poems, stories, letters, or keep a diary that describes his or her thoughts and feelings about domestic violence.

- Encourage the child to join social organizations to enhance his or her feelings of belonging and self-esteem.

- Reassure the child that he or she can choose not to be violent when he or she grows up.

- Share your feelings about domestic violence with the child.

WARNING SIGNS OF YOUTH SUICIDE

- *Suicide notes.* There are a very real sign of danger and should be taken seriously.

- *Threats.* Threats may be directed ("I want to die." "I am going to kill myself") or, unfortunately, indirect ("The world would be better without me," "Nobody will miss me anyway"). In adolescence, indirect clues could be offered through joking or through references in school assignments, particularly creative writing or art pieces. Young children and those who view the world in more concrete terms may not be able to express their feeling in words, but may provide indirect clues in the form of acting out, violent behavior, often accompanied by suicidal/homicidal threats.

- *Previous attempts.* Often the best predictor of future behavior is past behavior, which can indicate a coping style.

- *Depression.* Helplessness/Hopelessness. When symptoms of depression include pervasive thoughts of helplessness and hopelessness, a child or adolescent is conceivably at greater risk for suicide.

- *Masked depression.* Risk-taking behaviors can include acts of aggression, gunplay and alcohol/substance abuse.

- *Final arrangements.* This behavior may take many forms. In adolescents, it might be giving away prized possessions such as jewelry, clothing, journals or pictures.

- *Efforts to hurt oneself.* Self-mutilating behaviors occur among children as young as elementary school-age. Common self-destructive behaviors include running into traffic, jumping from heights, and scratching/cutting/marking the body.

- *Inability to concentrate or think rationally.* Such problems may be reflected in children's classroom behavior, homework habits, academic performance, household chores, even conversation.

- *Changes in physical habits and appearance.* Changes include inability to sleep or sleeping all the time, sudden weight gain or loss, disinterest in appearance, hygiene, etc.

- *Sudden changes in personality, friends, behaviors.* Parents, teachers, and peers are often the best observers of sudden changes in suicidal students. Changes can include withdrawing from normal relationships, increased absenteeism in school, loss of involvement in regular interests or activities, and social withdrawal and isolation.

- *Death and suicidal themes.* These might appear in classroom drawings, work samples, journals or homework.

- *Plan/method/access.* A suicidal child or adolescent may show an increased focus on guns and other weapons, increased access to guns, pills, etc., and/or may talk about or allude to a suicide plan. The greater the planning, the greater the potential.

National Association of School Psychologists, 2001

YOUTH SUICIDE: TIPS FOR PARENTS

- *Know the warning signs!*

- *Do not be afraid to talk to your child.* Talking to your children about suicide will not put thoughts into head. In fact, all available evidence indicates that talking to your child lowers the risk of suicide. The message is, "Suicide is not an option, help is available."

- *Suicide-proof your home.* Make the knives, pills and, above all, the firearms inaccessible.

- *Utilize school and community resources.* This can include your school psychologist, crisis intervention personnel, suicide prevention groups or hotlines, or private mental health professionals.

- *Take immediate action.* If your child indicates he or she is contemplating suicide, or if your gut instinct tells you they might hurt themselves, get help. *Do not leave your child alone.* Even if he or she denies "meaning it," stay with him or her. Reassure them. Seek professional help. If necessary, drive your child to the hospital's emergency room to ensure that he or she is in a safe environment until a psychiatric evaluation can be completed.

- *Listen to your child's friends.* They may give hints that they are worried about their friend, but be uncomfortable telling you directly. Be open. Ask questions.

National Association of School Psychologists, 2001

YOUTH SUICIDE:
TIPS FOR TEACHERS

- *Know the warning signs!*

- *Know the school's responsibilities.* Schools have been held liable in the courts for not warning the parents in a timely fashion or adequately supervising the suicidal student.

- *Encourage students to confide in you.* Let students know that you are there to help and that you care. Encourage them to come to you if they or someone they know is considering suicide.

- *Refer students immediately.* Do not "send" a student to the school psychologist or counselor. *Escort the child* yourself to a member of the school's crisis team. If a team has not been identified, notify the principal, psychologists, counselor, nurse or social worker. (And as soon as possible, request that your school organize a crisis team!)

- *Join the crisis team.* You have valuable information to contribute so that the school crisis team can make an accurate assessment of risk.

- *Advocate for the child.* Sometimes administrators may minimize risk factors and warning signs in a particular student. Advocate for the child until you are certain the child is safe.

National Association of School Psychologists, 2001

TIPS FOR PARENTS AND OR FRIENDS OF BATTERED MEN AND WOMAN

- Don't think that it is a private matter, not your business, or that he or she will be all right. They need support, guidance and information.

- Tell him or her what information you have that you believe or know that he or she is being hurt and controlled. Tell him or her that you are concerned for their safety.

- Tell him or her that they don't deserve to be treated badly and that no one deserves to be abused.

- Don't agree to keep confidence when your child/friends safety is at stake. If you feel he or she is in danger, don't hesitate to seek help, this means call 911.

- Let him or her know there are ways to keep them safe and together you, he or she will get the help they need. It is important for them to understand that they have options. Help them to devise a safety plan (Personalized Safety Plan).

- Don't say anything against the batterer. Don't say he or she doesn't deserve him or her, they are bad for you. Keep him or her out of the conversation as much as possible. Remember, he or she has strong feelings for them. Focus on him or her, their safety and your love and concern for them.

- If he or she is eighteen or older, let them know that you know they are an adult and he or she is the one who must decide on what action to take and when. Tell him or her that when he or she is ready, you will be there to help them get to a safe place.

- Be supportive of him or her, but not the abusive relationship. Do not loan them money, which will enable him or her to stay in the violent situation, even for children's clothes, doctor's bills, etc. Let him or her know you will support him or her as much as you can when he or she is not in the violent relationship.

- Learn about domestic violence, so that you will understand as much as possible about what he or she is experiencing and why she is confused.

- Encourage him or her to call their local **Domestic Violence 24-Hour Hotline** to speak with a counselor. Let them know that they can all anytime.

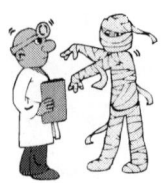

DOMESTIC VIOLENCE GUIDE FOR PHYSICIANS

Domestic violence is a pattern of assault and coercive behaviors including physical, sexual and psychological attacks that adults or adolescents use against their intimate partners. Without intervention, the violence usually escalates in both frequency and severity resulting in repeat visits to health care facilities. Listed below are some helpful tips when interacting with patients.

- **Talk to the patient alone in a safe, private environment.** When the patient is a female, it maybe helpful to have another female physician to interact with her. The victim at this point is not happy with men and may not be as open with a male physician.

- **Ask simple direct questions such as**: *Because violence is so common in many people's lives, I ask all my patients about it. Are you in a relationship with a person who physically hurts or threatens you?* Your patient may hesitate to answer this question. At their state of mind, they are looking for a way out. They see no real benefit in answering the question if you are asking them to return back to the abuse. *Did someone cause these injuries? Who?* If the batterer is in the treatment room or have accompanied them, the victim will not answer this question. They are fearful of their batterer. *Do you feel safe at home?* The patient will probably not answer this question since they may have to return to the abuse.

- **Look for other symptoms present by the patient.**
    - A history suggesting domestic violence: traumatic injury or sexual assault; suicide attempt; overdose; physical symptoms related to stress; vague complaints; problems or injuries during pregnancy; history inconsistent with injury; delay in seeking care or repeat visits.

    - Behavioral clues: evasive, reluctance to speak in front of partner; overly protective or controlling partner.

    - Physical clues: any physical injuries; unexplained multiple or old injuries.

- **Record the history of Domestic Violence.**
    - Past history of domestic violence and sexual assault.

    - History of abuse to any children.

    - History of abuse in family. This is particularly helpful in assessing the patient. This question should be asked just like, any history of heart, high blood pressure, etc. in your family.

- **Five things you can say to support the patient:**
  - I am concerned for you (and your children).
  - You are not alone.
  - You are not to blame.
  - There is help available.
  - You do not deserve to be treated this way.

- **Assess Safety.**
  - Are you afraid to go home?
  - Have there been threats of homicide or suicide?
  - Are there weapons in the home?
  - Can you stay with family or friends?
  - Do you need access to a shelter?
  - Do you want police intervention?

- **Make referrals.**
  - Involve the hospital social worker, if available.
  - Provide list of shelters, resources and hotline numbers.

- Document Findings.
  - Use the patient's own words regarding injury and abuse.
  - Legibly document all injuries; use a body map.
  - Take photographs of injuries.

***It should be noted that the patient maybe, for the most part, fearful. Please do not try to pressure them to do something that will put their safety at risk. The patient may take your referral information; however, they may not take the information home with them in fear that their abuser will find it.

Durham Crisis Response Center

NATIONAL DOMESTIC VIOLENCE HOTLINE
1-800-977-SAFE (7233)

WHAT IS ADVOCACY?

ADVOCACY IS...	ADVOCACY ISN'T...
Providing a man or woman a safe space within which he or she can be in crisis.	*Forgetting that the man or woman is in crisis.*
Listening.	*Telling a man or woman what he or she should be feeling.*
Asking a man or woman what he or she wants to do.	*Telling a man or woman what he or she must work on.*
Respecting his or her limits.	*Rescuing him or her and encouraging him or her to feel dependent on you.*
Providing resources and referral information.	*Thinking you can protect a man or woman.*
Asking if he or she needs help.	*Encouraging him or her to think of themselves only as a victim and not a victor.*
Encouraging him or her to help himself or her self and his or her children.	*Thinking you will be the influence that changes his or her life.*
Recognizing his or her inner strength and pointing it out to him or her.	*Pressing a man or woman to deal with issues he or she is not ready to confront – like leaving the abuse.*
Helping him or her draw on that strength.	*Getting frustrated because things are not moving as fast as you would like.*
Complimenting him or her for their hard work.	*Calling agencies for a man or woman when he or she has not asked for help.*
Calling agencies on a man's or woman's behalf when he or she requests your help.	*Not sharing with him or her what you feel about his or her situation.*
Being honest and nonjudgmental.	*Telling him or her how much worse you had it.*
Empathizing with him or her. Recognizing that each reacts differently to crisis.	*Thinking that his or her reactions are inappropriate.*
Focusing, clarifying, being honest, real, and present.	*Not paying attention.*
Having a support system for your self.	*Believing you are a super hero.*

The Love Bank

Inside all of us is a *Love Bank* with accounts in the names of everyone we know. These people are associated with our good feelings, "love units" are deposited into their accounts, and when they are associated with out bad feeling, love units are withdrawn. We are emotionally attracted to people with positive balances and repulsed by those with negative balances. This is the way our emotions encourage us to be with people who seem to treat us well, and avoid those who seem to hurt us. The emotional reactions we have toward people, whether its attraction or repulsion, is not a matter of choice. *Love Bank* balances cause them. Try "choosing" to be attracted to those you associate with some of your worst experiences – it's almost impossible. Or, try to feel repulsed by those associated with your best feelings. You do not decide whom you will like or dislike – it's their association with your feelings, whether they have made *Love Bank* deposits or withdrawals that determine your emotional reactions to them.

We like those positive *Love Bank* balances and dislike those with negative balances. But, if an account reaches a certain threshold, a very special emotional reaction is triggered – romantic love. We no longer simply like the person – we are in love. It's a feeling of incredible attraction to someone of the opposite sex.

The feeling of love is the way our emotions encourage us to spend more time with someone who takes especially good care of us – someone who is effective in making us very happy, and also knows how to avoid making us unhappy. We would certainly want to spend time with someone we simply liked, but by giving us the feeling we call love, our emotions give us added motivation. We find ourselves not only wanting to be with the person, but also craving that person. When we are together we feel fulfilled, and when apart we feel lonely and incomplete. So, the feeling of love is usually effective not only in drawing people together for significant amounts of time, but also in encouraging them to spend their entire lives together in marriage.

But our emotions give us more than the feeling of love. When they identify someone who makes us happy, they also motivate us to reciprocate by encouraging us to make that person happy. They do this that when you are in love, you seem instinctively affectionate, conversant, admiring and willing to make love? That's because your emotions want to keep that person around, so it gives you instincts to help you make that person happy which, if effective, triggers his or her feeling of love for you. The **"look of love"** not only communicates our feeling of love for someone, but also reflects our instinct to do whatever it takes to make that person happy.

When a man and woman are both in love, their emotions are encouraging them to make each other happy for life. In fact, the thought of spending life apart is usually frightening. It seems to them that they were made to be together for eternity. In almost every case, a man and woman marry because they are in love, and they are in love because their love bank balances are above the romantic love threshold. But, what goes up can usually come down, and love bank balances are no exception. As almost every married couple has discovered, the feeling of romantic love is much more fragile than originally thought. And, if *Love Bank* balances drop below the romantic threshold, a couple not only lose their feelings of passion for each other, but they lose their instinct to make each other happy. What was once effortless now becomes awkward, and even repulsive. Instead of the look of love, couples have the look of apathy. And without love, a husband and wife no longer want to spend their lives together. Instead, they start thinking of divorce, or at least living their lives apart from one another.

It should be obvious to you by now that the *Love Bank* is an extremely important concept in marriage. If you want your instincts and emotions to support your marriage, you must keep your *love bank* accounts over the romantic threshold. But, how can you keep your balances that high? And what can you do if they have already fallen below that threshold? This answer holds the key to saving marriages and relationships. Without love, spouses are very poorly motivated to remain married for life, but with the restoration of love and its accompanying instinct to spend life together, the threat of divorce and abuse is overcome. Marriages and relationships are saved when love is restored.

Couples must make as many *Love Bank* deposits as possible and avoid making withdrawals if they want a happy and fulfilling marriage and relationship. And to achieve this, behavior must change. A husband and wife must learn to do things that make each other happy, and learn to stop doing things that make each other unhappy.

Unknown

QUICK TIPS TO GIVE YOUR ATTITUDE AN EXTRA BOOST

The difference between a positive and negative attitude could be the difference between positive or negative grades or outlook on life. The tips below are quick and highly effective. Make use of them today and start getting results immediately.

- **Rise and Shine**. Getting up early and taking a walk in the morning is a great way to start the day. Fifteen or twenty minutes is plenty of time for a quick walk in the brisk morning air.

- **Tomorrow is a New Day**. When things aren't going the way you might like them to go, remember that as time passes, so do your troubles. At the time it may be hard to realize that things will get better, but rest assured they will.

- **Control**. The only one who can give you a good attitude is you. And the great news is, it can happen whenever you want it to. You could wake up tomorrow with a brand new outlook on life. Any why? Because your attitude is yours to control.

- **Circle of Friends**. You may be trying to stay positive, but if your friends or coworkers are negative, it may make for a losing battle. The company you keep impacts your attitude greatly. Seldom will you find a group of negative thinkers and one positive attitude together. Negativity can spread, so be sure to keep clear of noticeably negative situations.

- **Healthy Diet.** You have heard it a thousand times, and this will make it a thousand and one. A good diet is vital to maintaining energy, alertness, and a positive attitude. Without the necessary amount of fuel for your body, it cannot function properly. If you find yourself in a tired and negative mood, ask yourself, "Have I eaten yet today?"

- **Sleep.** Just as important as a healthy diet is the right amount of sleep. It seems obvious but many people don't get enough sleep at night. Without rest, the body and mind become irritable, fatigued, and they drag through the day. The same effects can result from oversleeping. Make sure you get the sleep you need each night.

- **Your Hobby to the Rescue.** It is important to have a hobby or activity that you can do when facing a problem or a long, hectic day. Sports, books, collecting, etc. are great ways to get away from the hustle and bustle and enjoy you.

- **Do Unto Others.** It's true what they say, you get what you give. When you focus on treating others positively and with respect, you will, in most cases, receive the same treatment. Change the focus from yourself to others and let the giving spirit be the reason for your improved view of the world.

- **The Bigger Picture.** When you think of the world as a whole, it may service to downplay the obstacles in your life that cause frustration or complication. You might have it bad, but the odds are that someone else has it worse. That in by itself is enough to make people thankful for what they have.

- **Try Something New.** If you feel like you're stuck and you need a way to break out, try something new. Picking a new instrument, trying out a new sport, or discovering a new talent may add some excitement and enjoyment to your life.

Written by: Jason Garcia

UNLOADING BAGGAGE

- **You have a destiny while you are here on earth.** Begin to map out your destination. The new directions you will begin to undertake will require goals and a plan of action. Your destiny is on God's mind. Read the following scriptures: Jeremiah 29:11 and 3John 1:2.

- **God's word goes beyond your human understanding.** As a victim of domestic violence, you may not understand why bad things happen to good people or why good girls like bad boys. But know this, what you have endured will pass if you be willing and obedient (mentor or spiritual advisor). Read the following scriptures: Isaiah 1:19 and Jeremiah 1:5.

- **God will come to your rescue.** When no one else was available to help me, while I transitioned out of domestic violence, I spent lots of time in the Word of God in my quiet place. He proved Himself to me that He will supply all of my needs and yours. Read the following scripture: Psalms 91:1-16.

- **Never be fearful.** When you walk in fear, it will hold you back from your destiny. When leaving your batterer, they will begin to stalk you. This fear will grip you to keep you from breaking free. Please. Don't look back. Read the following scriptures: Isaiah 46:9 and Isaiah 55:11.

He is a God of truth.
- Dare to believe that it will happen – never doubt.
- To be successful you have to deny something in life.
- Your destiny will cost you something – don't be afraid to launch out into the deep.
- You can not put a dollar amount on your destiny.
- Put yourself around successful people who can pour into your life.
- Be willing to face all opposition.
- You will never be the same.
- You will only be what you see yourself becoming.
- You will begin to have a new level of confidence.
- You will be able to help others who are going through.
- You will need a place and a people to help you unload the baggage and get to your destiny.

Suggested Readings: Numbers 23:19 and Isaiah 46:9.

God has given you the power. You may not feel like you have much strength to unload the baggage and move on, but you do. Once you begin to set the wheels in motion you will be surprise how much strength and stamina you have. *Suggested Reading: Luke 10:19.*

Unload Anything That Weighs You Down !

Pastor Brenda Timberlake-White

REDEFINING YOUR IMAGE:
Who do you see when you look in the mirror?

If you want to have a positive imagine, get rid of your enemies.
Zig Ziglar

Image is defined as a representation of the outward form of a person or thing. Something very like another in appearance.

If you ever get a true revelation of the way that God sees you and the way you see yourself, never again would you allow anyone to verbally or physically abuse you. God's opinion of you makes man's opinion irrelevant!

If you are not a church going individual, somewhere throughout the course of your life you may have heard that God created man in His own image. In that image He created male and female. He possesses your reins (seat of your feelings and passion). That He has covered you even in the belly of your mother's womb. You may not have considered or thought about this but, He is concerned about you. Remember that He created you and knows all needs and concerns.

You are fearfully and wonderfully made. He has strategically placed every hair follicle in place and designed all of our organs so it would bring life to our being. Have you ever notice that a newborn baby has toes and fingers that look perfectly manicured? He created us with perfection! For no other reason than that He loves you and I with an agape love. What does Agape mean? Unconditional!

Now that you have a better understanding of how He sees you, let me share with you how to maintain this knowledge:

- **Say only what the Word of God has to say about you.** Contrary to what others may think, you are beautiful in the eyes of Him. Man looks on the outward appearance, but He looks at your heart.

Know who you are in Him.
The only way to come to that knowledge is to study His Word daily! You know, the BIBLE.

Stay encouraged in the midst of trials.
You can't let that old man or woman rise back up with negative thinking or talking. When a trial comes your way, remember that death and life are in the power of your tongue. The words you speak have power.

Spend time with people that can see your full potential and will breathe life in you. If at this time in your life these people don't exist, then do like David did in 1 Samuel 30:6, he encouraged himself in the Lord.

Identify things/people that deplete your energy. Get rid of them! People who drain you of your energy will weaken your motivation.

Know when you should love someone from a distance. We are commissioned to love everyone, but we do not have to spend time with everyone in order to love them.

Take authority of the spirit of fear! Isaiah 41:10 says to "Fear thou not; for I am with thee: be not dismayed; for I am thy God: I will strengthen thee; yea, I will help thee; yea, I will uphold thee with the right hand of my righteousness."

Remember... fear will grip you and tell you that God's Word won't work for you.

No weapon that is formed against you shall prosper, because if God be for you, who in the world can be against you!

Statistics will tell you that if you were raised in a one-parent household, lived in the projects, become an unwed mother at the age of 17 and have a nick-name of "pothead" then you can forget having any kind of meaningful life. Well, I can tell you that neither statistics nor circumstances have a right to dictate your future.

Remember we read that God knew you in your mother's womb. He had a wonderful plan for your life before we were conceived. You choose if you want to break free or stay bound.

Although my teen years and early 20's were filled with partying, pot, speed and cocaine, I knew in my uttermost being that there was a bigger picture for my life. I wasn't raised in the church, but I remember praying every night that God would forgive for my sins, and to please be patient with me because one day I would serve Him.

Now why would I pray a prayer like that when I was having fun doing those things? It's because of the way that God created us.

He intentionally made us with a void in our hearts. If we're not taught this at an early age, then we go through life trying to fill that void with all of the wrong things.

Ever wonder why some people commit suicide when it appeared that they had everything to live for? (money, cars, homes & prestige) Well, they longed to fill a void that could only be filled with God.

I found out at the age of 22 that I was created in the image of the creator of this entire universe and that excited me. I also learned that He loved me in spite of the mess that I was in and wanted to set me free. He showed me that there was a bigger picture than what I was seeing and He wanted me to make a u-turn so that I could see that picture.

Each day as I spend more time in God's Word, I am seeing that bigger picture – that image of Him that He wants me to imitate. I'm still not perfect by any means. But, my new image is developing and manifesting itself everyday. And what I'm not - I can see myself becoming. Other people might not see the whole picture of me yet, but I do, and that's important.

When I look in the mirror I see the image of God. What do you see?

Mrs. Delphine Riley, Imagine Consultant

ARE YOU MASTERING MONEY
OR
IS MONEY MASTERING YOU?

Congratulations!

You have just stepped into the beginning of a new day. Your decision to read this book thus far is proof that the road of life has many detours in the area of finances. Economics play a strong role in closing the door to an abusive relationship or for someone you know. This section on mastering money is written to help you think about ways to save money, and to help you become financially independent. Many victims feel that they would not be able to make it on their own if they left their abuser. As a victim, whether male or female, you know that the control of the finances is in the hand of the abuser. For the victim, these are real concerns that need to be addressed. He or she may worry that, without a mate, they will not be able to support themselves or their children. To the pastor(s) and lay person(s), this will be a great resource of training for your organization to help aid the victim. Or, if you are just reading this book for insight on the epidemic of Domestic Violence, you will find this helpful as well. On a personal note, these principles work, I have put them into practice. Remember,

"If you want something you never had, you have to do something you never done."
Dr. Mike Murdock

Financially, when do we say we have had enough? It can be a habitual pattern of overeating, staying in an unhealthy relationship or excess spending. The commonality of all of these is that they all can be detrimental to you. So what should you do once you have been "fed up" with one of these categories? You begin to make a plan of escape.

This section of the book will discuss how you should plan for getting enough finances to be on your own, getting out of debt, and developing a budget. This is great stuff and it works (smile).

This is the only way that you can maintain consistent wealth. If you are just getting started, hopefully you will not have a debt issue. Perhaps these suggestions will provide you with helpful information to make quality decisions about debt and developing a budget. It does not matter where you are in the financial arena. It does not matter how much money you make or do not make. What matters is how much money you have left after your expenses that will make the difference.

Are you mastering your money or is your money mastering you? It is very easy to loose control with money. Think about it. If you go to the ATM machine, usually the minimum withdrawal is $20.00. Guess what, it does not take long before you have spent the $20.00 and are back at the ATM for another $20.00 plus. What are you doing with your hard-earned money? Or the little that he or she may let you have while you are being held hostage in your circumstances. Do not concentrate on what you have not done in the past with the money, it is gone. Use your "now" energy to establish a basis of building wealth today and begin to build a wealth for tomorrow.

It is your choice. Theory has it that you make over 2,000 choices per day. Some are so unrecognizable because you make them subconsciously. For instance, like which route to take to work. You are so accustomed to driving that route that you are on "automatic pilot". You may not notice the details of the route sometimes. Some choices you make are not as significant as others are. For example, the color of the pen you use. However, the choices you make with your money are very significant. Whether you purchase that soda from your job site vending machine for $1.00 versus buying that same soda by the case and spending about $.27 to $.35 and bringing it to work. The choice you make can make a difference (think about it). The amount saved by changing your spending habits can save you from $.73 to $.65 per soda. This may seem insignificant, however, if you purchase two to three sodas per day and you work forty weeks per year, you could have saved between $182.50 to $162.50 per year. If you add snacks like peanut butter crackers, chips, or candy bars from the vending machine, which could cost from $.60 to $.75, you have spent more money than you realized. Using the same analogy of fifty weeks per year times two snack purchases per day; your annual savings could be from $35.00 to $50.00. If you add that to your soda dollars you could have saved well over $200.00 per year. These savings may not seem much, however, that is just one area where you could save money. Some other areas that you can realize significant saving are phone services. You could eliminate all services that are unnecessary. Such examples are, call waiting, call forwarding, etc. Your cable or satellite services could be trimmed to basic rather than having the movie and other specialty channels. This could substantially save you from $50.00 to $100 monthly or $600.00 to $1,200.00 a year. Be very selective in your grocery and clothes shopping. Make sure the sales items are really sale items and have not been marked up to put them on sale. Also, verify that sales items such as furniture and cars have not been marked up to take advantage of special interest offers. If you think the deal is too good to be true, it probably is.

A large area where consumers may lose a lot of hard-earned dollars is through credit cards. Most of us have been lured into a false sense of security with these infamous cards. Read the fine print on offers! Credit card companies who offer 0% financing will typically raise the interest rate after the introductory period to from 7.9% to 13.9%. The introductory period is usually six months. If you are late making your monthly payment twice, the rate can increase 18% to 21%. Unless you read your statement, you would not even know it. Most of the clients serviced tell me they pay their bill every month, however, the balance does not go down. Please wise up to these tactics. It is recommended not carrying a balance for longer than ninety days. Make three equal payments for three consecutive months and charge another balance to pay off in three months. This will allow you to maintain excellent credit. You really only need one "universal" credit card. By "universal" I mean a credit card that can be used at any store. Another recommendation would be if you are a member of a credit union, to utilize their credit card services as their interest rate maybe much less than banks. Remember that interest on credit cards does not serve you, the consumer any good. You can not use it as a tax deduction. For example, clothing, a vacation trip, food, etc. However, the interest rate converts to finance charges for the credit card companies and does benefit them. While they are getting richer, you the consumer are getting poorer.

Let us look at car loans. Most every one needs a vehicle loan, right? Here is another item that is typically financed. Now, vehicles are pricey and are usually financed as much as seven years. If your interest rate is 10.50% bank financing, and the vehicle is financed for five years on a $21,000 loan, total finance charges would be $6,082.31 or comes to a total of $27,082.31. The car is depreciating on the day that you drive it off the lot. Again, the vehicle does not bring you any type of tax benefit. Let us look at the type of loan if it were financed through a credit union or bank. We find that the interest rate will be lower. If the interest rate is 4.75%, the total finance charge for the five-year term is $2,633.71 and the total cost would be $23,633.71. The difference between loan 1 and loan 2 is $3,448.60. This is a pretty significant savings you think. The vehicle will, of course, cost you much more with just the basic expenses (gas, taxes, maintenance, taxes, and insurance). As you can see that new car can be very costly. You can accelerate your car loan payments by paying in advance of the five-year term. You see there is not a tax deduction for auto loans per se, unless you get the vehicle financed via a home equity loan. You can consult your tax consultant regarding benefits to you.

You could always save money in advance of major purchases. In fact, your goal should be to purchase items on a cash basis only. Also, you should try to bargain shop and/or negotiate prices. After all, if you have saved the money in advance, you have more bargaining power. Try to stay away from finance companies that have high interest rate loans. Usually finance company loans decrease your credit score, regardless of whether you make payments on or before your due date. Other companies to avoid are rent-to-own companies, check cashing companies, payday lenders and gambling (e.g., lottery tickets). All of these will constantly and consistently drain your pocketbook while they are making big profits. Put a stop to it.

You may be wondering how you can purchase the things that you need and desire. The key is a BUDGET. The word budget can be somewhat restrictive so let us use the word SPENDING PLAN. You can determine where you want to direct your money. If you do not direct your money, your money will direct you. It is not a good feeling to receive your paycheck and the next week you have no money to tide you over.

First, determine what you are spending on a daily basis before trying to develop a budget. Track your spending. You can develop a spreadsheet or purchase a software program to track your spending habits for thirty to thirty-one days. Head your columns: rent/mortgage, car payment, gas, groceries, eating out, saving, etc. The first time I tracked my spending for the thirty-day period, I was surprised at the amount of money I spent on clothing and food, which included eating out. In most cases, you will make the changes to your spending categories when you see how much you actually spend in writing (we are moved by what we see). Once YOU have determined how you want your money spent, based on your current spending habits, now you are ready to BUDGET or make your SPENDING PLAN. One thing about preparing your budget/spending plan is that if you do not make it realistic, it will not work. Your budget/spending plan has to be re-evaluated regularly. You must account for everything that would include personal care needs (e.g., golfing, fishing, beauty salon, nails, etc.). Remember, the purpose of the budget/spending plan is for YOU to assign a mission for your money. Only YOU can determine how YOU want your money spent for a comfort level. Once you have done this I know that you will be happy and enjoy your life. Make wise decisions and be disciplined. Stop to count the cost for being financially independent. Take inventory of your household. Count the number of dresses, shoes, suits, electronic equipment, and other items. If you purposed not to purchase anything for six months to a year, you will be surprised the amount of money you could save. For some of you, it just might encourage you to loose those well-needed pounds and ----- ---slide into some of that beautiful attire that has been hanging in the back of the closet. You can develop these principles in anything you decide to do. The key is diligence and self-commitment.

In your budget/spending plan allow for savings. You owe yourself to be paid regardless of whether it is $5.00 per week or $100.00+ per week, start saving. With an unstable economy, you can not afford not to save. You should develop, if possible, several savings and investment accounts. Remember with discipline, you can do it. Have a short-term savings account for pleasurable items (e.g., vacation, new appliance). Have an emergency savings account that should account for total living expenses (grocery, utilities, rent/mortgage, car, insurance, etc.). Calculate how much these categories would be for one month and multiply that number by six or nine months. You can also begin to save for that next vehicle purchase. When you pay for a car in cash you have no monthly payments and most of all you have bargaining POWER.

Another form of savings is retirement. Depending upon the rate of return received on your investment, you could save significantly. A $50.00 investment at the age of 25 could yield you a half million dollars if invested well. Think about it, if you increase your investment by $50.00 per month or $100 per month, your investment could yield over $1 million. Remember, start now and be consistent. As you begin to move out of your present circumstances, start by saving where you can with that $1 or $5 and put it in a safe place. There may come a time when you may have to flee. Money will help you. If you are still in the home with your abuser, use wisdom and do not put yourself in jeopardy with trying to make all the above work for you. As you make the transition, I strongly encourage you to get out safely with the finances you have. Then, begin to use the above principles to help you become financially independent. It is a great feeling.

How do you build a foundation, one brick at a time? It takes time to build a home.

GO GET IT !

Isaiah 1:19 – <u>Insert Your Name Here</u>, if you only Let me help you, I will make you rich.
Living Bible

Written By: Mrs. Catherine Harris, Owner, Turning Point Financial Services

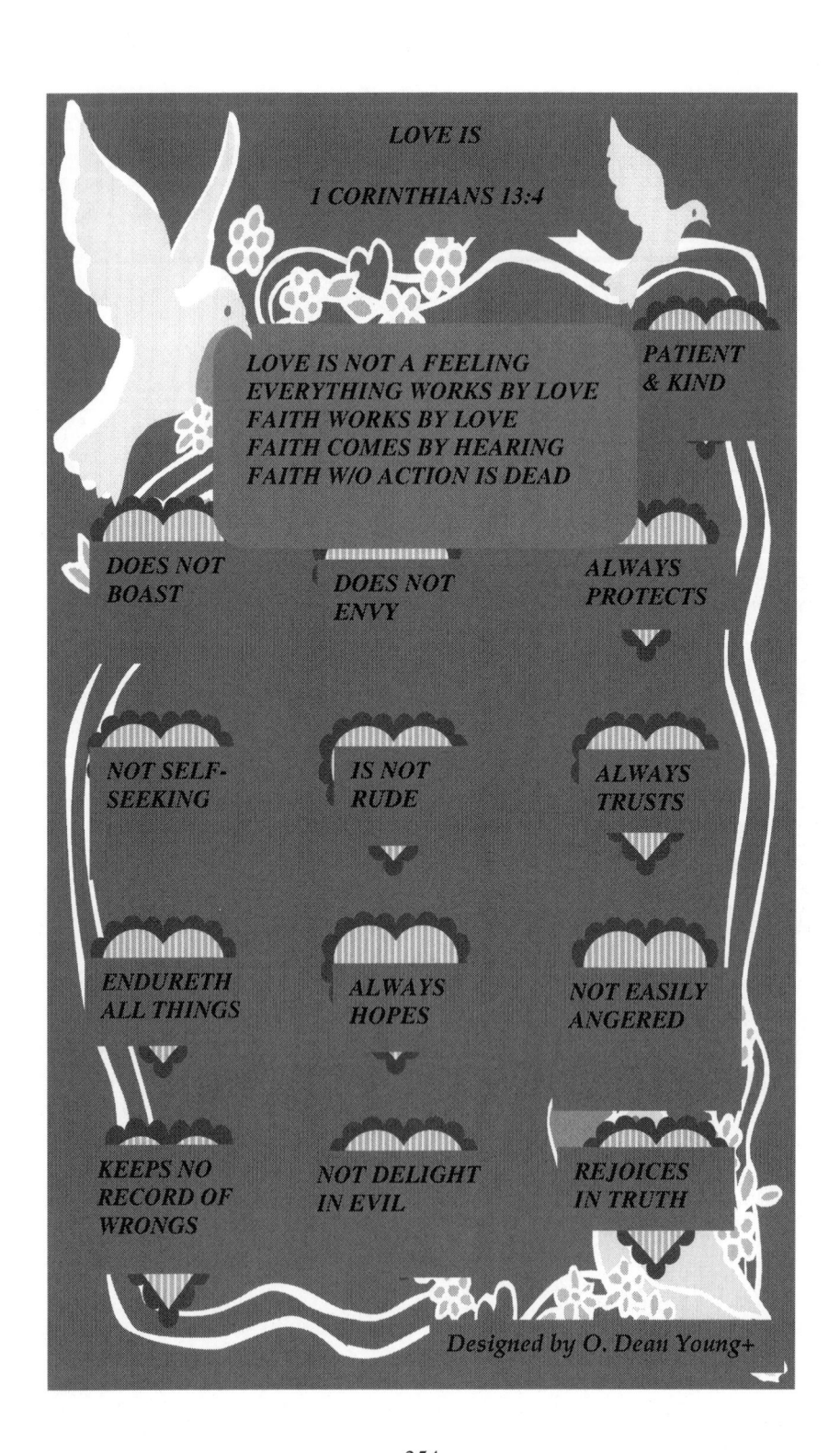

LOVE IS

1 CORINTHIANS 13:4

LOVE IS NOT A FEELING
EVERYTHING WORKS BY LOVE
FAITH WORKS BY LOVE
FAITH COMES BY HEARING
FAITH W/O ACTION IS DEAD

PATIENT & KIND

DOES NOT BOAST

DOES NOT ENVY

ALWAYS PROTECTS

NOT SELF-SEEKING

IS NOT RUDE

ALWAYS TRUSTS

ENDURETH ALL THINGS

ALWAYS HOPES

NOT EASILY ANGERED

KEEPS NO RECORD OF WRONGS

NOT DELIGHT IN EVIL

REJOICES IN TRUTH

Designed by O. Dean Young+

YOU ARE SPECIAL – READ DAILY!

- *I am Special.*
- *I will decide who will step into my space today.*
- *I have dreams and goals (write them out).*
- *I will always evaluate my environment.*
- *I am a good seed and will be careful in what kind of soil I plant in.*
- *I will not hang out with people who do not have a passion for my success.*
- *I will learn to eliminate the things that are not healthy for me.*
- *I will only attract what I value.*
- *I will regain my connection with myself and my spirit.*
- *I will learn to have order in my life for it gives me direction.*
- *I will work on one daily thing that will benefit me and me alone.*
- *I have been given an assignment here on earth that is why I am still alive.*
- *I will and I shall have a great life.*
- *I am Special.*

Cheryle E. Dawes

REFERENCES

Abused, Battered, Brokenhearted and Restored. Cheryle E. Dawes, Prophetic Pen Publishing, 2001. **Amazon.com**. ISBN 0970584040.

Full Esteem Ahead. Rob Solomon, Kincaid House Publishing, 1992. ISBN 0943793335.

Adam Where Are You? Jawanza Kunjufu, 1994. ISBN 0913543438.

What To Do When It Hurts So Bad? Ed Montgomery, Destiny Image Publishers, 1993. ISBN 1560431245.

Rebuilding When Your Relationship Ends. Bruce Fisher, 1981. ISBN 091516695.

Who Moved My Cheese? Spencer Johnson, 1999, Putnam Press. ISBN 0399144463.

The Angry Man: Why Does He Act That Way? David Stoop and Stephen Arterburn, 1991, Word Publishing. ISBN 0849907799.

The Language of Letting Go. Melody Beattie, MJF Books, 1990. ISBN 1567312381.

Taking Control of Your Life and Making it Matter. Melody Beattie, Harper Collins Publishers, 2002. ISBN 006008829X.

Codependent No More. Melody Beattie, Hazelden Foundation, 1987. ISBN 0894864025.

Abused Men: The Hidden Side of Domestic Violence. Philip W. Cook, Praeger Publishing, 1997. ISBN 0275958620.

Acts of Faith. Iyanla Vanzant, Simon and Schuster, 1993. ISBN 0671864165.

Unbroken Curses: Hidden Source of Trouble in the Christian's Life. Rebecca Brown and Daniel Yoder, Whitaker House, 1995. ISBN 0883683725.

Battered But Not Broken: Help for Abused Wives and Their Church Families. Patricia Riddle Gaddis, Judson Press, 1996.

Broken By You: Men's Role in Stopping Woman Abuse. Morton Patterson. United Church Publishing House, 1995.

The Dream Giver. Bruce Wilkerson. Multnomah Publishers, 2003. ISBN 159052201X.

The Principle of Fatherhood: Priority, Position and the Role of the Male. Dr. Myles Munroe. Pneuma Life Publishing, 2001. ISBN 1562291742.

ABOUT THE AUTHOR

She is a woman who loves God. She is a loving mother, motivational speaker, workshop leader, facilitator, and compassionate all with great sense of humor. She has served on various boards for domestic violence and presented at various medical institutions, workshops and seminars. She is a survivor of rape, the suicide of her oldest son and domestic violence. In all of these horrific experiences, she has pulled from her faith and commitment to serve others.

It has been said that from pain great things have been birthed. As the old folks would say, "the proof is in the pudding." The author has truly proved to herself, that no matter what the circumstances, life is good. She has pushed through her pain like a mother in labor. Through her pain she has given birth and stepped into the arena of authorship in helping to mend the heartaches of broken people. Her first book entitled, "Abused, Battered, Broken-hearted, and Restored", is her personal testimony of what life had dealt her within a seven-year span. The book is full of hope and encouragement for people to understand that no matter what hand life deals you, you can make it.

The author unequivocally believes that the key to restoration is the healing of oneself and education. She has for some years now been fortunate to sit under the mentorship and wisdom of great Christian and secular leaders. All of this has made her wiser and productive in life. She has learned that if you are hurting anywhere, you are hurting everywhere. She stresses that in order to be healed you MUST learn to forgive yourself and all people for all things they may have done to you. She has learned that in order to move on from the pain of domestic violence, (which left her disfigured in her face and beaten almost to death); she had to forgive her batterer.

From the experience of domestic, she had to truly learn how to let go and let God. Dr. Mike Murdock has said, "That what you are obsessed with or whatever pains you deeply is a strong indication of your assignment here on earth." Her assignment is to help hurting people learn how to get healed and move on, especially in the area of domestic violence. She is committed to helping the batterer get healed too. She realizes that no one wins in this situation (victim, batterer, children, etc.). She has committed herself to understanding why the batterer does what they do no matter what the gender. She is a seeker of wisdom and knowledge to teach herself and others how to embrace and forgive (Proverbs 4:7). She endeavors to boldly go where most people dare to in this area by continuing to write books, educate pastors, schools, community organization, family members and friends. Her style of presenting is insightful and relaxing. Her favorite saying, "**We Need Each Other**".

You can contact the author to order books at the following locations:

godmbtcfc@yahoo.com (Abused, Battered, Broken-Hearted, and Restored - Domestic Violence: Both Sides of the Coin, Video – Telling My Story)

www.FYOS.com (Abused, Battered, Broken-Hearted, and Restored)

www.trafford.com (Domestic Violence: Both Sides of the Coin)

www.amazonbooks.com (Abused, Battered, Broken-Hearted, and Restored - Domestic Violence: Both Sides of the Coin)

www.barnesandnoble.com (Domestic Violence: Both Sides of the Coin)

Or write or email for speaking engagements or workshops:

>Cheryle Dawes
>P.O. Box 51273
>Durham, NC 27713
>www.godmbtcfc@yahoo.com

ISBN 141202380-7

Printed in Great Britain
by Amazon